The Last
of the
Wild West
Cowgirls

The Last of the Wild West Cowgirls

Kay T~~~

A True Story

Kay Turnbaugh

First Edition 2009
Second Edition 2017

ISBN   0-9702532-2-2
          978-0-9702532-2-4

Cover photo courtesy *Buffalo Bill Museum and Grave, Lookout Mountain, Golden, Colorado*

For my husband Bill,
who helps me with unfailing patience,

and for my friend Lee,
who suggested I write a book about Goldie Griffith Cameron

Author's Notes

I finished *The Last of the Wild West Cowgirls* after four years of researching and writing, and on a warm fall day I visited Goldie's grave in Green Mountain Cemetery in Boulder, Colorado, the final resting place of many of Boulder County's most famous residents. The towering, stately trees glittered with autumn's fiery colors, and leaves crunched under my feet as I wound my way from the office up the hill to Goldie's headstone. After visiting her grave and wandering past some of the other headstones, I left the cemetery and climbed to a spot with views of the city of Boulder, the plains that flowed on and on, and, in the other direction, the mountains where I knew Nederland nestled next to its reservoir. As I looked back at the cemetery, I wondered if Goldie had picked this spot because it reminded her of Buffalo Bill's choice on Lookout Mountain. It seemed a fitting resting place for this feisty woman who never let the world tell her she couldn't do something.

Eighty years after Goldie was born, I moved to the small mountain town of Nederland, twenty miles west of Boulder. It was 1973, and that October the wind blew so hard I had trouble standing up straight when I walked to a neighbor's house at daybreak to catch a ride to Boulder for work. I lived at the western edge of the reservoir, at the end of the street where Goldie had lived before going to a nursing home. The wind would sometimes stop for a day or two, but usually it blew so fiercely it picked up snow and dirt from the streets in town and blew them through my little one-room log cabin and across the reservoir. When I moved in, I didn't know how to build a fire in a cookstove, but I learned quickly. I learned how to saw and chop my own wood because I liked being warm. I learned how handy a pee pot was if you didn't want to get up and wrestle the wind to get to the outhouse in the middle of the night. I learned that lettuce would freeze in the refrigerator which never bothered to run because the closet where it sat hardly ever got above freezing that whole winter. On Halloween night, two children died when their house burned down just up the street from me. I never heard the sirens over the wind.

When spring finally arrived, a friend and I put two inches of insulation in the attic and chinked up the holes between the logs. The next winter was much more bearable. I loved being able to walk for miles from my front door. Some days I walked to the old Tucker homestead on Caribou Road after work. On others I explored the area near Caribou Ranch, not knowing that all these haunts had been some of Goldie's too. I started making wine, nothing very good, but I met my future husband over a bottle of homemade potato wine. Maybe three hundred people lived in Nederland, and every house except mine had three or four dogs which together wandered town in packs. When I walked out my front door I scooped up handfuls of rocks from the driveway to throw at the dogs that charged me. I would have to guess that many of those dogs were descendants of some of Goldie's precious pets.

I never met Goldie. A year after she died, I started a newspaper in town. In the first issue in that October of 1977, I asked the town to name it, and Marguerite Shellhaas, one of Goldie's first friends in Nederland, won the contest with The Mountain-Ear. Hers was our first obituary. Over the years, I wrote several times about Goldie, but I didn't really know that much about her.

It turned out that she and I had a lot in common. She ran a still and made her own booze; I made my own wine. She was a female business owner for almost thirty years in Nederland, as was I, although our businesses differed quite a bit. She ran restaurants; I owned a newspaper. She loved telling stories; so do I. And now I've had the chance to tell hers.

Place names change over the years. For instance, the name Nederland Lake was gradually changed to Barker Reservoir, and Boulder Cañon (also Canon) became Boulder Canyon. In all cases, I tried to use the name that was being used at the time. At the time of the Wild Wests, they were just that. There was no need to add the word show because everyone knew what the wildly popular Wild Wests were.

When I began researching Goldie's life, I had much to learn about Wild Wests and cowgirling. I grew up in Colorado, but my childhood was spent in Colorado Springs, not on a ranch. I did go to a few rodeos, and I learned to ride a horse, but they were passing fancies, so in researching this book I had to learn about the sport of cowgirling. In Goldie's time, cowgirls weren't restricted to barrel racing. Between 1886 and 1911, thirty-eight cowgirls competed in rodeos and performed in Wild Wests. The cowgirls were as famous as today's football stars, and they usually competed in all the events. This is not to say that they were better athletes than their counterparts today, but they did have more opportunities to prove their prowess on a horse.

Goldie worked as an athlete even before she became a cowgirl. She started her career as a fencer, boxer, and wrestler. America's first female athletes were thought of as anomalies and freaks, but the cowgirls' enormous popularity helped bring female athletes into the norm.

I spent many hours at the Buffalo Bill Museum and Grave on Lookout Mountain pouring over their collection of scrapbooks and photos of Goldie. Their exhibits and films of the Buffalo Bill Wild Wests allowed me to ride alongside Goldie in my imagination. The

Goldie's wedding outfit was the centerpiece of an exhibit at the Colorado History Museum in Denver in 2008.

Kay Turnbaugh

Colorado History Museum produced an exhibit about cowgirls while I was writing this book, and it featured Goldie's wedding outfit and saddle. It was a thrill to walk through the doors to the exhibit and see a figure that could have been Goldie standing there. Goldie's grandson Mike completed the picture of Goldie with his many remembrances of "Grandma Goldie" in Nederland.

Goldie was a colorful character. Much of her story came from her own words. All the events are true. All the major characters, and all but a few of the minor characters, existed. When I put myself inside Goldie's mind, her thoughts came from what she had said in recorded oral interviews and to friends and relatives. All the dialogue is based on my research.

In a few instances, I couldn't verify the date of an event because, although those interviewed in the oral histories I listened to could clearly remember the event, they couldn't recall exactly when it happened, or because the dates remembered by different sources conflicted. In particular, when asked when she moved to Nederland, Goldie recalled several different years in the early 1920s. I spent many long afternoons at the library in Boulder looking through microfilm of old newspapers, trying to find some verification of which year. Although I found lots of news that I could use in telling Goldie's story, I couldn't figure out which year she moved to Nederland. I finally arrived at my best guess, and that's what I used.

I could tell as I talked to people in Nederland or listened to their oral history stories that they had discounted most of Goldie's stories as fabrications woven from many tellings into flights of fancy. I listened over and over to the two oral histories Goldie recorded before her death, and I faithfully took notes on her many exploits as she described them. I too thought, "How could one woman have done all that?" As I continued researching, I validated every one of her stories.

She left behind several scrapbooks and many file folders that she had filled scrupulously throughout the years with newspaper and magazine clippings about herself and her friends, including one well-worn, postcard-sized black book filled with photographs that she did not donate to a museum, presumably because its contents were "private." Her grandson kindly shared it with me, and in it I found the story of her tour with Lucille Mulhall's Girl Rangers and clues to her relationship with the Mulhalls, one of the most famous of the Wild West families. Her scrapbooks were treasure troves of information.

Goldie wasn't modest. She loved telling stories about her life. She was obstinate, opinionated, and fiery. She also was incredibly generous. She was the epitome of the cowboy-girl (their original name) who could ride the rodeo, hit the dust, brush herself off, and appear at a tea in town—all in the same afternoon. Although she could dress for tea and manage the etiquette of the "society" experience while expressing her strong opinions about politics and the state of the world, her speech never lost the coarseness of an uneducated, hard-working woman. A contemporary newspaper story referred to her as "a heller in skirts." She wasn't liked by everyone, and that bothered her some. She thought she'd lived a life worth sharing and had planned to write a book about it, but she never quite got to it. Fortunately, she left us with her stories.

CONTENTS

PROLOGUE

"The divorce records are over there."

I had interrupted the two young men—one was leaning over the other's shoulder as they looked at a computer screen.

"Okay." Only one other person was in the room, and she was taking notes from one of two obscenely huge books at a heavy wood table.

"And I'm wondering about this." I pulled out the copy I'd made that morning before I left Nederland for the long bus trip to Denver. It was a court receipt from 1916.

"Well, I don't know." The young man frowned at it. "Those numbers might not mean anything. I don't recognize them..." He shrugged his shoulders.

"Could you check?"

"This could take a long time," he warned. He looked at me as if he were hoping I'd go away, but I smiled. I had all day. He disappeared with my piece of paper, and I settled on a hard chair and started looking for divorce records. The microfilm scratched through my machine, and the woman with the big books occasionally turned a page—otherwise the room was silent.

Was it a half-hour? An hour? The young man slapped a slim packet on the counter and beckoned to me. The legal-size papers were folded into fourths and filed inside a heavy, brown paper jacket tied with a tiny red ribbon. It looked like no one had untied the ribbon since that day in March ninety years ago. Gingerly I picked it up and moved to the other big table.

With a small tug, my treasure opened. Inside was proof that the events I had been researching really happened. The people involved existed—they had given evidence to a policeman. I wanted to whoop for joy, but I stifled my shout with a gagging sound that made the woman look up from her big book for a second, and the young man who was still standing at the counter stared at me curiously.

I had a new respect for her tales. I'd been listening to her stories as other people could recall them and on two oral history tapes she'd recorded. I'd seen the newspaper stories—the ones in her scrapbooks and the ones I'd found through my research—but there was something so much more concrete about this little packet of court papers.

That day, sitting in the basement of a sterile government building in downtown Denver, Goldie Griffith Sterling Cameron came alive for me. She danced across my mind—a beautiful young cowgirl trying to make sense of what had happened to her life in Denver in 1916.

Part 1

〜 Bucking Broncos 〜
1893–1923

A promotional shot of Goldie, probably taken at the beginning of her career as a cowgirl with the 101 Wild West.

Buffalo Bill Museum and Grave, Lookout Mountain, Golden

ONE

A Kind of Nightmare

HE DIDN'T HAVE HIS SPURS ON, so he didn't jingle as he walked. He sounded like any other man—his boot heels drummed a hollow thump, thump, thump on the tatty pine floorboards. He shrugged his slim shoulders into a worn work jacket and grabbed his wide-brimmed hat and leather gloves. Goldie could tell by the way he squinted at her suspiciously over his shoulder before he stepped out the door that he knew she was up to some mischief.

She followed him outside into the frosty air.

She hadn't seen him since that horrible day in Texas. She'd been on her own the last couple of months, and she was broke—she was down to her last twelve cents—a dime and two pennies, three little coins that wouldn't last long. They hardly weighed anything, and when she rubbed her fingers across the outside of her coin purse, she couldn't even feel them. But then, if she went to jail, she wouldn't have to worry about her next meal, would she?

Her husband should have come back to Denver with her, especially after what she'd done for him before his trial. Instead, he'd disappeared. When she heard he was back in town, she was furious. She found out that he was staying with his friend A.W. Simuel. This morning, when she'd walked uninvited into Simuel's house, A.W. sneered at her. "What do you need her for, Harry? You don't need her. She ain't nothin'." Harry didn't defend her, and he and Simuel got ready to leave the house, as if she didn't even exist.

The smells of thousands of cattle and horses from the next-door stockyards permeated everything in this part of the city. Today the breeze was slight, and that was good because she was only a pretty good shot. Not having to adjust her aim for the wind would make it easier to hit her target. Looking at the clouds gathering overhead she thought it might even snow one more time tonight, but what did she care, she wouldn't be back in her drafty apartment—all she could afford since Harry had left her—she'd be in jail.

Harry and Simuel stopped before stepping from the yard into the street. A young boy in overalls led an old, dappled horse down the middle of the dirt street, the horse limping and the boy skipping. A Model T rattled around them, honking before it disappeared around the corner, and a dog barked once in response. Then twice for good measure.

The men glanced back at Goldie. She walked toward them and pulled the gun out of her muff. Simuel started to run, but he slipped on a lingering patch of ice. Harry began backing into the street, wanting to run like his friend, she could tell, but unwilling to take his eyes off her. Time stopped, and the three other men who happened to be out in the street were frozen with it. Only Goldie moved, inexorably, toward her husband.

The trigger felt alive under her finger. She wanted so desperately, so fiercely to kill him. She didn't know she would cry, but she was blinking back tears, and she aimed unsteadily at Harry's chest. She squinted at the buttons of his shirt, sucked in her breath, and aimed a bit lower. "After all you've done to me, it's the least I could do for you," she couldn't believe she could say it so coolly.

He was too calm, standing there, smiling at her like a naughty child. She hated him even more for it. "Goldie, darlin'," he drawled. Simuel had recovered from his fall and pulled at Harry's arm, trying to drag him away.

It was enough to stop her tears. "Don't darlin' me, you sidewinder. And Simuel, you piece of shit, I should kill you too." She waved the gun at the other man, and he jumped away from her husband. She took aim again at Harry and squeezed the trigger—just the way he'd taught her. She wanted him to suffer, and after she settled the gun so it was level again from the recoil she pulled the trigger a second time.

She wanted him dead.

The white cloud that had billowed from the gun with the first shot now totally enveloped her, and it grew impenetrable when she fired again. The last thing she could see was Harry walking away like nothing had happened. She was still aiming at him, and her arm was steady, so she fired again. The acrid smoke was unbearable—it made her eyes gush with more tears, and she started coughing. She could no longer see anything, no buttons, no Harry, not even the gun in her hand, although she could feel her wet cheeks begin to freeze in the cold March air.

She was pretty sure she hadn't done the job. If she'd shot him, she would have heard him fall and maybe cry out in pain. But there'd been no other sound since the shots which still bounced around in the opaque air. She tried waving the smoke away from her stinging eyes. That was it—the smoke—she should have guessed that the ammunition in her gun might have gone bad sitting in her trunk while she waited for Harry to come back.

Finally, she could see again. She couldn't make out either a corpse or a writhing body. Damn. He'd slipped away again. It was the story of their life together. Furious, she turned to go back to her apartment.

A rough hand grabbed her arm and ordered her to stay put until the police arrived. The thought of the police made her hopeful that she had killed him.

"Is he dead?" she asked anxiously, coughing and spitting up the words through the smoke still caught in her throat.

"No—no thanks to you," growled the deep male voice in her ear. Goldie heard other voices and squinted to see who it was through the haze. It was Harry and Simuel. With them were a tall bearded man in workman's clothes and a man she recognized from the stockyards. "Don't you want to talk to the police?" It was the bearded man, talking to Harry. Goldie saw Harry look her way, and she held her breath.

"No sir, I don't."

"But, mister, I think, I mean she just shot at you, don't you think…?"

The smoke had evaporated into the few trees, and Goldie could hear the mounted policeman galloping down the street towards the fracas. He probably heard the shots at the stockyards.

"Shit." Ladies in Denver in 1916 didn't say words like that, but it happened to be the perfect word to express her feelings. Besides, she was no lady. She tried to shake off the man who was gripping her arm. "Don't worry 'bout him, he's just a slippery ol' snake," she muttered, but the man wouldn't let go, in fact, his hold on her arm tightened, and he looked down at her with such distaste she almost felt like laughing. It had felt so good to aim the gun at her husband and fire. She was so tired of his tomfoolery. He was such a low-down, lyin', good-for-nothin'—she couldn't think of a word vile enough to describe him— and the sooner she got him out of her life the better. The only good thing in their three-year marriage was the wedding, but no matter how many times she pulled out her scrapbook to look at the newspaper stories of that grand day in Madison Square Garden it didn't change the rest.

Officer Art Wachter slid off the handsome bay with the white stripe that zigzagged from ear to nose. The officer dropped the reins and ran toward her. Lightning was trained to stand still when his reins were on the ground, and Goldie admired both the horse and the six-foot-tall man who stopped first to speak to Harry. She strained to hear what they were saying, but she couldn't make it out. She trusted Art to get it worked out.

As Art walked over to her he shook his head. "You'll have to come with me to the jail, Goldie. It looks like you've really done it this time—I'm going to have to charge you with assault to kill." Art sounded reluctant, but he added, "There's witnesses, and that's what they said happened."

Goldie just shook her head.

The man who had hold of her arm gave Art her gun, which he had twisted out of her hand, but he didn't want to let go of her. He obviously didn't know who she was, but that would change when the newspaper people came to interview her. *This time the whole world will know what a skunk you are, Harry, I can promise you that.*

"You can let go of her now," Wachter told the man. "She's not going anywhere, are you, Goldie?" Art had been friends with Harry and Goldie since their first week in Denver. "Goldie, Goldie, Goldie. Why'dya have to start shootin', at Harry, of all people? Can't you people just have regular arguments? I don't think I can help you out of this one."

"That's okay, Art. I'm ready to go to jail. I could'a spent the rest of my life in jail if I'd jus' killed 'im." Goldie sneaked a look at Harry and then turned so she couldn't see him.

Art caught her hate-filled look. "You and Harry have had your troubles, but that doesn't mean you should go and try and kill 'im. Harry swore to me he'd take care of you." Art bit his lip. "Maybe you should'a given him a little more time, what with what he's been through." The bull of an officer cussed softly under his breath as he opened the door of the police automobile that had arrived to back him up. Goldie climbed into the back seat.

She had been hoping she'd get to ride to jail on Art's magnificent horse. It would have made a grand exit from the scene, but the machine from the police department would have to do.

She took one last look at the horse quietly waiting for Art and the small crowd that had assembled to watch the action, making sure they were watching her. Art had asked Harry and the witnesses to wait for him, and they stood off to one side, talking among themselves.

Art leaned over and spoke to her through the open door of the automobile. "I'm sorry, Goldie, but we gotta take you to jail."

"Don't worry 'bout me, Art. It was worth it. I jus' wish I'da done the job." She said the last just loud enough for the small crowd to hear and was gratified to hear several gasps.

She meant what she'd told Art, even if it meant she'd never ride a horse in the arena again.

She'd been in jails before, but it was to visit, not to sit behind the bars. Yesterday she had decided that even the prospect of being in jail forever would be a small price to pay to get Harry out of her life. When she heard he was in Denver and hadn't lifted a finger to see her, she was livid—after everything she'd done for him—he should have come to see her, his wife. Overnight, her fury grew, and this morning she pulled the little gun from her show trunk, hid it in her muff, and, well, it was just too bad the ammunition had gone bad since the last time she'd used the gun, and up in smoke, instead of into Harry.

She was in the matron's quarters of the Denver jail, and she should have been crying, but instead she found herself almost giddy with relief. Thinking back on it, it was a stupid thing to do, but it sure had felt good. She knew it would be a big story in the newspapers—"Wife shoots at husband, but misses,"—and she talked to all the reporters—knowing that her best defense—if she ever got to court—was her story. It was time to tell the world what had really happened. The reporters loved the story—she made sure of that—even if it meant she had to invent a few picturesque details. All part of the entertainment business.

"Why'd you do it?" The young reporter for The Denver Post leaned toward her as he scribbled in his notebook.

That was the question, wasn't it? Three years of lies, that's what did it, she thought. It was the lies that turned her heart to stone and put her finger on the trigger.

The young man stopped scribbling and looked up. He seemed fascinated by her serene smile. She knew that he would believe what she told him. He was mesmerized as she recounted her wedding on horseback in Madison Square Garden. She didn't have to embellish that at all. It was grand—grander than grand. She was a cowgirl with the Buffalo Bill Wild West and Pawnee Bill Wild East—the Two Bills show—and Harry was a dashing, daredevil cowboy. Their wedding was part of the evening performance at the Garden. At the time, May of 1913, the audience of eight thousand was the biggest on record for a wedding.

OF COURSE, IT ALMOST DIDN'T HAPPEN. Now that she thought about it, it seemed that the whole year that ended in 13 was jinxed.

The day before her wedding she was a nervous wreck, or at least that's what the newspapers reported. She was the butt of numerous practical jokes by the other cowgirls, and the newspaper stories said she fainted before that night's performance, although she didn't remember fainting—feeling a little faint maybe—but not actually crashing. Unfortunately, that wasn't the worst of it.

During the show, she was riding as one of many escorts to two large prairie schooners circling the garden. That was one newspaper's version. Another paper reported that it was during a mock Indian battle. Another said it was during a Virginia Reel on Horseback which was part of the portion of the show known as A Holiday on the Ranch. She put all the stories in her scrapbook. All agreed that her horse bolted, probably from a blank cartridge she (or someone else) fired in the air too close to its ears. The horse careened to the Fourth Avenue side of the Garden, reared and tossed Goldie into a front row box.

A letter from a friend to Goldie when she was in jail: "March 14– 1916. Dear Mrs. Walters—I was in to see you this afternoon, but the Chief was out, and I could not get a permit. Am very sorry to learn of your trouble, and hope you will soon have things straightened out again. Have not forgotten the lift you gave me in Chicago, when I was down and out, and wish to say that if there is anything you need, and the Chief is willing, I will be glad to get for you. You can have the matron phone me at the office, and if I am not in, leave word to call you, or I can be reached at home after 6:30 p.m. York 615. Don't hesitate to ask, for I owe you more than you gave me. Yours Very Truly, J.G. Middleton."

Buffalo Bill Museum and Grave, Lookout Mountain, Golden, Colorado

No.

IN THE

DISTRICT COURT

THE PEOPLE OF THE STATE OF COLORADO

vs.

Goldie Sterling, alias

Goldie Smith,

INFORMATION FOR

Assault to Kill.

Filed this .... day of ....
A. D. 191...., by leave of Court, and bail
fixed at

MAR 20 1916

$2000.00

Judge.

A. B. HIRSCHFELD PRESS, DENVER

The top section of the packet of court documents from Goldie's arrest in March of 1916. Goldie and Harry were using their rodeo name of Smith at the time.

Some thought it was part of the show. But the bastion of sports news, The New York Herald, reported that "many men and women in the audience stood up, and some put their hands over their eyes in horror." The cries of alarm attracted ushers who sent for an ambulance to retrieve the unconscious bride-to-be. Some of the papers reported that her fiancé, Harry, sprang from his horse and carried her out of the arena.

The next thing she knew, she was flat on her back in an ambulance. Her head throbbed, and she wasn't sure she could move her right leg. "My wedding," she croaked through parched lips. The ambulance nurse shook her head and shushed her.

The Bellevue Hospital doctor examined her and pronounced that she would have to spend the night. They gave her something for the pain, and she drifted off to sleep thinking only about her aborted wedding. The doctors wouldn't let reporters into her room, but they were quoted as saying that Goldie was resting easily and they wouldn't know until the morning how seriously she had been injured.

She was in the hospital all the next day—the day she was supposed to be married. "What about my wedding?" she kept asking. "It won't be today," the doctor said. "Maybe next week. You must get some rest." Oh dear, she thought, Colonel Cody won't like that. He had told her how proud he was to host her wedding, and she knew he was counting on it to sell more tickets than usual. But she could hardly walk—every movement shot pain through her back, and her head still throbbed, so she reluctantly laid in bed. Several times she cried, and then the nurse would bring her something for the pain.

Many years later she would tell a reporter that it was a kind of nightmare.

The next day when Harry dropped by to see her he seemed too cheerful. He looked her up and down. "Let's see you move." Obligingly, she slowly and painfully bent each arm and leg for him. "I don't think you're so bad. Let's get you out of here. We got'a weddin' tonight." He kissed her on the cheek, and that was that.

The show went on.

The beads that had been strung into the fringe on her cherry red leather riding skirt tinkled and flashed in the arena lights as she mounted her horse with a helping hand from her maid of honor. The beaded steer's heads on her back and on her skirt were exquisite, but the outfit had felt heavy as she dressed, trying to avoid banging the beads into the worst of the bruises. Her bridal outfit was complete with her big-brimmed hat, scarf, tall boots, spurs, and gauntlets on her gloves that were beaded with her name. She flipped open the tin embedded in her bracelet and dabbed at some rouge. Holding her arm so she could see what she was doing in the tiny mirror, she patted her cheeks with the pink powder, and she was ready.

She was limping and a mass of bruises, but she could ride. On their cue, she and Harry rode to the middle of the arena to the thunderous cheers of those eight thousand fans. Buffalo Bill, the legend himself, gave the bride away. Pawnee Bill was the best man, and fellow cowgirl Eva Fisher was her maid of honor. The glass plate of the photo of the wedding would become one of Goldie's prized possessions. It showed the wedding party on horseback before the Reverend Robert Ryan of the Brooklyn Missionary Society, who stood in front of them because he didn't ride. Ribbons adorned the heads of Harry's and Goldie's horses, and Harry's fancy woolly chaps draped over his boots. Buffalo Bill was hidden from sight, only part of a stirrup showed in that famous photo, a trick of fate that incensed the aging promoter who was direly in need of any publicity at that point in his career.

Looking back, she wasn't sure she was ready to get married. She was nineteen, certainly old enough, but in some ways she was too trusting and too naïve, even though she had been raised in show business.

A page in one of Goldie's scrapbooks.

The Sterling family

⤝ TWO ⤞

A Decided Novelty

SHE DIDN'T TELL THE YOUNG REPORTER, but she figured it was really, ultimately, Charley's fault—if she hadn't fallen for him, she wouldn't be a cowgirl, and she wouldn't have married Harry. She was seventeen when she first met Charley. He was twenty-one.

She'd been sneaking out beyond the tents to the corrals where the Wild West horses were kept after her shows with the Lady Athletes in Knoxville. She'd always loved animals, and she felt a strong attraction to the show horses. She talked to whichever horse would come to her and scratched behind its ears. A voice behind her made her jump.

"Like horses?" It was him, Charley. Her knees wobbled, and her heart felt like it might stop, but at least she didn't fall over. She stopped stroking the horse's nose and stared at him. He was as good looking up close as he was riding by on his horse during the frequent parades staged by his father's show. Curly hair popped out here and there from under his big hat and framed a boyishly handsome face and deep-set, serious eyes. He obviously liked dressing the part of one of the best-known cowboys in the

Goldie fell for the young, handsome Charley Mulhall, posing here for a publicity photo for the Mulhall Wild West Show.

Reprinted from Lucille Mulhall: Her Family, Her Life, Her Times
by Kathryn Stansbury

nation. He wore a bright green, over-sized silk neckerchief tied loosely, tall boots with tall heels, and one of the biggest hats Goldie had ever seen. From head to toe, Charley Mulhall was a bronco rider in his father's Wild West show. She thought he was *the most handsome* man she'd ever laid eyes on.

"Always did like 'em." She nodded at the horse who was giving up on her and moving away. "What's his name?"

"That one's Bill Oliver, my sister's horse."

"Who's Bill Oliver?"

"Bill Oliver is the president of the Exposition."

She thought about it a few seconds. "Does he have other names when you're somewhere's else?"

Charley laughed. "Sure does."

An old show business trick was to find a way to relate to the local crowd. Sometimes performers changed their hometowns or their names to this end, so why not their horse's name?

"You're over at that Blanche Whitney show."

She blushed. He knew who she was. "I'm Goldie Griffith." She extended her hand and thought to herself that her mother might not approve of introducing herself to this handsome young man, but, really, he already knew who she was.

"Pleasure. Charley Mulhall." He gave her hand a tiny squeeze. "I seen your show. You girls're pretty tough." Goldie blushed again. *He'd been to her show.* He didn't seem to notice her red face. "Wanna see the broncs I ride?"

A young woman who Goldie recognized immediately appeared behind Charley's shoulder. "Oh, darling brother, are you pestering this young lady with your outlandish stories?" She put the emphasis on the word pestering, brushed his cheek playfully, and winked at Goldie.

"He's not bothering at all," Goldie assured her earnestly.

"Miss Goldie Griffith, my sister, the esteemed Lucille, who will never leave me alone, even for a minute." Charley's tone was teasing.

A publicity photograph of Goldie for the
Blanche Whitney Lady Athletes at the Appla-
chian Exposition in 1910.

Buffalo Bill Museum and Grave,
Lookout Mountain, Golden, Colorado

(Next page) This photo may have been taken in Chicago
before Blanche Whitney's troupe left for the Appalachian
Exposition, where the price of admission was raised from 10
cents to 25 cents and where Goldie met Charley Mulhall.
Goldie is the fourth girl from the right.

The Sterling family

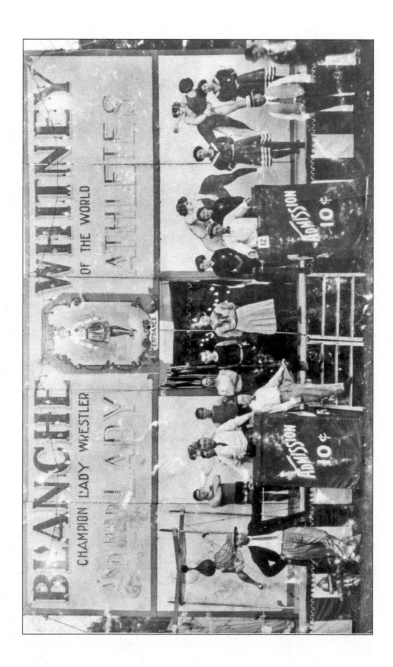

A publicity photo for Blanche Whitney's Lady Athletes shows Goldie Griffith, right, wrestling another woman.

Buffalo Bill Museum and Grave, Lookout Mountain, Golden, Colorado

"Nice to meet you, Miss Goldie Griffith." Lucille smiled and offered her hand. Goldie was honored to take it. Lucille was famous, not only in America, but in Europe too. And she wasn't finished teasing her brother. She winked again at Goldie. "Watch out for my brother. He fancies himself a ladies' man, although he's really nuttin' but a cowpoke from Oklahoma."

"Watch out, sis. You're an Okie too."

"So I am. I just came to warn you. The Colonel is lookin' for you. He'd better not find you here." With that, she sidled off, waving good-bye over her shoulder.

Charley sighed. "Guess I gotta go. Maybe you'd like to meet my other sisters, Mildred and Georgia? Come see a show? I got'a extry ticket."

Goldie nodded, hardly believing her ears. He separated a ticket from several that he pulled out of his shirt pocket and handed it to her. "So long, Miss Goldie." As he turned to leave her alone in the corral he said, "Come soon, I'll be watchin' for you."

Goldie couldn't believe her good luck—he was so fine-look-ing. She stuck the ticket in the waistband of her skirt so she wouldn't lose it. She'd have to run to make lunch on time. If she was too late, Miss Whitney would be mad. If Miss Whitney got mad, there was the chance she would telegraph Goldie's mother. And that might mean that Goldie would have to go home. She was wearing the Blanche Whitney outfit, the one they were supposed to wear out to promote the show. Her short skirt came to just below her knees, and her tights showed off her legs below the skirt's blue stripes. Her scarf, which she had carefully tied over her shoulders, flopped around as she ran through the crowd in the Midway Jungle to the big tent that housed the Blanche Whitney Lady Athletes.

This was her home for a whole month. She was one of the Blanche Whitney Lady Athletes. The newspaper clipping that she had stuck in her scrapbook called them *a decided novelty*. It was the same way the press had treated Blanche Whitney in Chicago where a police censor was "agin'" wrestling exhibitions in which women took part, reported the newspaper, *at least when he got orders from headquarters*. The paper went on to report that *He stopped an exciting contest between Miss Cora Livingstone, 'champion woman wrestler of the world,' and Miss Lou Harris.*

Miss Whitney, reported The Chicago Daily Tribune a short time later, *bears a striking resemblance to Miss Livingstone, whose title she appears to have usurped.* As Blanche Whitney, the female wrestler was meeting all comers at the American Theater in defiance of the police censor. Reported the newspaper, *Her opponent is Miss Belle Myers. The way they yesterday mauled and pulled each other around the dirty mat used in the exhibition was marvelous, considering that they go through the same performance once an hour from noon until close on to midnight every day.*

When June's heat wave started suffocating Chicago, Blanche moved out to the amusement park in the White City next to the lake. Reporter Richard Henry Little visited the park and was shown around by the assistant manager on a day when the temperature hovered around 90.

After a long, hard winter, he wrote, *the ballyhoos, whose voices have long been silent, were upraised in a gladsome chorus. The girls at the ticket booths were chattering like a lot of song birds in the tree tops, and the band poured forth paeans of joyous melody.* The manager hummed a few bars of "Angel Eyes" and led Little to where a woman was giving wrestling exhibitions.

The 'robust' woman [Blanche Whitney] told Little: *"I have four classes of society women. They come out here and I wrestle with them and teach them the half-nelson and the hammerlock and the rest of the game."*

Blanche told the reporter about the benefits for women to learn to wrestle. *"If a husband is cross and disagreeable, just put him on his back as fast as he can get up. This clinging vine stuff is all right, but believe me, the woman is a winner who can look her husband straight in the eye and say, 'What about the coin for that new dress? Do you come across like a little man or do I throw you down and sit on you while you think it over?'* Men are just big bullies,"* Blanche pontificated. *"When women are able to take care of themselves it will be a different world."*

Little reported the manager exclaimed, *"My, my! Are you a suffragette?"*

"I am not," said the lady wrestler.

"You ought to join. They would make you a walking delegate. When woman gets her rights I'm for you for chief of police."

Blanche's next engagement was the Appalachian Exposition, and she decided to take a troupe. She didn't have to look far to find athletic girls who were willing to join her show—performers like chorus girl Goldie Griffith who, in spite of the heat, did four turns a day in a vaudeville show in the White City amusement park. When Goldie suggested to her mother that she wanted to join Blanche's show, it was a tough sell. But finally Allie relented, and at the beginning of

November her daughter left Chicago on the train with the rest of the troupe.

It was a small show compared to the Zack Mulhall Wild West, but it was where Goldie would work for the month she was in Chilhowee Park, three and a half miles north of Knoxville. The whole Appalachian Exposition of 1910 covered about 100 acres, and the gleaming white main exhibition hall was a voluminous 80,000 square feet behind its massive columns and formidable stairs. Goldie hardly ever went there. Mostly she liked to visit the Livestock Building or the Women's Hall. There was a lot to see and do on the vast fair grounds, but now Goldie knew there was only one place she'd be visiting, and that was the corral behind the Mulhall Wild West where she could see the horses and where she might run into Charley.

Just the day before, Mary Church Terrell had given a speech about "equal rights" for Negro women. Blanche's girls were still talking about it at lunch when a breathless Goldie slipped into her seat, although none of them had heard it in person because they were, of course, performing. They compared what they heard Mary Church Terrell had said to their experiences in Chicago. While in Chicago, before they came to Knoxville, the girls had met Jack Johnson, the heavyweight boxing champion. In the mornings the Whitney girls worked out in Connell's gymnasium. Among the men who worked out in the afternoons at the same gym were Fatty Nelson and Jack Johnson.

Johnson was the first black athlete to break the color barrier in sports, long before Jackie Robinson stepped on the major league baseball field in 1947. Almost 40 years earlier, in 1908, Johnson, one of the most powerful counter-punchers ever, knocked out Tommy Burns in Australia to become world champion, but he wasn't given the title until 1910, the year Goldie met him, when he beat Jim Jeffries in Reno in a fight that ignited race riots. Johnson was famous for more than fighting. He was a flamboyant character who had his own jazz band, owned a Chicago nightclub, acted on stage, drove flashy yellow sports cars, and reputedly walked his pet leopard while sipping champagne. He loved white women and married three of them. In spite of the flash, the son of a former slave knew what it was like to make-do. When he saw the troupe of pretty white girls working out in the gym, he offered them use of his apartment since the men all had their own private rooms for changing clothes and cleaning up after their workouts, but there were no facilities for women because, of course, women didn't go to gyms.

The girls' workouts for wrestling were mostly just learning how to get out of a hold—quickly. They practiced whipping their heads around, throwing their shoulders back and fighting off an opponent's half-Nelson. They practiced tricks for defeating all the holds, including the hammerlocks, scissors, and hip locks. Workouts for the fencing and boxing were more strenuous, and Blanche made them work hard. The Whitney girls appreciated the use of Johnson's apartment after their sweaty workouts, and Goldie had a great admiration for the massive boxer.

⌇ THREE ⌇

Ladies' Champion of the World

SHE HAD TALKED MISS WHITNEY into letting her go to the afternoon Wild West show. Usually everyone in Miss Whitney's small troupe had to work at every performance. The company ran a show every hour from one in the afternoon to eleven at night, but once in a while Blanche would allow one of them to skip a performance or two.

"Hurry up, Babe," Bessie hissed. "You need to be dressed in five minutes." Babe Griffith was Goldie's first stage name.

"Guess what—I'm gonna go to the Mulhall show today," Goldie whispered back as she pulled off her dress and squirmed into her leotard and tights. She and Bessie were 'wrassling' in the first show today. The five girls took turns exhibiting the different sports. Goldie pinned her long hair up and back and she was ready. Although women wrestlers were at the height of their popularity in 1910, to say that what Goldie was doing was a novelty was quite an understatement.

Young ladies in 1910 did not go to gyms and work out. They did not go on stage. They did not wrestle, for heaven's sake. Boxing, another contact sport, was just as bad. In fact, American girls knew little to nothing of the benefits of exercise for health. They learned how to make mayonnaise, how to serve tea. Doctors advised women to refrain from vigorous physical activity or risk destroying their reproductive capabilities. Most women who participated in sports were considered unfeminine and often faced social isolation. Attitudes in the West were not as restrictive as on the East Coast, but what Goldie was doing was not in the mainstream of any part of the country.

What she was doing may have seemed anomalous to much of America at the time, but for her it was normal. Goldie grew up in show business. She was born on the last day of September 1893 in her grandfather's house in Kinmundy, Illinois, in Marion County. Her father, John Griffith, had a medicine show, and he and his wife stopped traveling just long enough for Allie to give birth. Goldie later told a newspaper reporter she was named after the gold rush and had a cousin named Silver.

Goldie's earliest memories were of dancing and singing with her mother to draw customers to the wagon, which was always parked off the road a good bit to allow for a crowd. The two of them would set up by the road, and Goldie danced and performed acrobatic tricks. She also helped her father mix up the liniment and put it in the bottles that they sold for a dollar. The "cure-all" was made of syrup, water and a bit of peppermint flavoring. "We told them they could rub it anywhere on their bodies or just drink it," she laughed during an interview years later. "Oh yes, father was a little crooked."

When she was seventeen, Goldie became a professional athlete, making her own money, and her mother allowed her to travel by herself. Goldie claimed she was always a tomboy, so for her it was logical to move on from acrobat and dancer to chorus girl to wrestler. She started wrestling as a 142-pound welterweight who challenged any girl to catch-as-catch-can wrestling and would take on any 160-pound man. Sometimes the girls would grab a man who had come to see the show to wrestle with them. If the man couldn't throw the girl in fifteen seconds, the girl won. With other girls, they had to go the full round.

Although the bill advertised the lady athletes, Blanche's show also included strongmen Bartell and Elson, acrobat Harry Morrison, and advance man Mr. Lousshy. Admission to their show at the Appalachian Exposition was twenty-five cents.

Goldie and Bessie peeked around the curtain as they waited offstage for their entrance. The house was about two-thirds full, not bad for the middle of the week.

"Babe, you're gonna get in trouble, chasin' after a man like that."

"I weren't chasin'. He's the one who gave me a ticket."

"You know what I mean."

WITH A FLICK OF HER DAINTILY GLOVED HAND, the rope began swinging in a growing arc that reached far in front of her and then over her head. The Mulhall Wild West announcer called out her tricks through his long megaphone. She stepped in and out of a flying loop, swirled a big circle out over the first few rows of the grandstand, balanced a whirling loop on her arm and then her leg, and kicked a loop so that it fell neatly over her pony's neck. Facing her, Sam Garrett was performing a mirror image of her act, but Goldie couldn't take her eyes off Lucille. She seemed so slight, but she was obviously a master at moving the heavy rope. A fringed sash was tied around her waist, and her heavy divided skirt swung around her ankles. Her neckerchief draped gracefully over her dark, pleated shirtwaist blouse. Lucille's long blond hair was pinned back with a wide bow that was fastened at the nape of her neck, and her serene expression under the wide-brimmed hat seemed real to Goldie.

For one of her tricks Lucille roped six horses running abreast. Charley was riding the inside horse that came closest to his sister. As soon as the gigantic loop settled over all six horses and riders, Lucille let go of it, and raised her arms in acknowledgement of the crowd's approval. Goldie's applause was ecstatic.

Goldie had seen a Wild West before—the best and biggest Wild West—Buffalo Bill's show—with her parents when she was little. The Mulhall show, even though it was smaller, was better than anything she'd hoped for. Charley, of course, was the best part, but everything else was pretty spectacular too.

Charley and his sister Lucille led the Grand Entry on their prancing white horses. Following them was their father Zack in front of the cowboy band, and then came sisters Georgia and Mildred. Mildred was about Goldie's age.

Goldie watched all the riders with new-found interest. The Nation Race pitted cowboys, cowgirls, and Indians in a daredevil contest twice around the arena. The Pony Express skit involved the rider changing horses each eighth mile and demonstrated the rider's agility in jumping from horse to horse.

A swaying stagecoach thundered away from outlaws in a cloud of dust in the Deadwood Stage Coach Robbery act. The announcer told them that the old coach belonged to the U.S. government and had been made available to Zack Mulhall with former President Roosevelt's help after the Mulhalls' coach was badly damaged in an accident in Kansas City. The hold-up in the Mulhalls' show was a realistic portrayal of an attack on the Overland stagecoach on the Deadwood Trail by the notorious white outlaw, the Apache Kid.

Lucille showed the tricks her trained horse, Governor, could do. The big sorrel horse picked up the wooden handle of a dinner bell with his mouth and swung his head back and forth to make the bell ring. At another command, he played lame and hobbled around. He also danced to music, reared on his hind legs and walked, and played dead. Lucille had even trained him to walk on his knees on a special mat. At the end, Governor bowed to the audience by falling to his front knees. Goldie watched with avid interest, and cheers rose from the audience.

The Sioux and Cheyenne Indians danced in native regalia. The Indians were recruited from the reservations, and curious audiences flocked to see the "wild" and "heathen savages." The

Lucille Mulhall throws her arms in the air to stop the clock after roping a steer in a Wild West competition. In 1900, the New York World described the cow-girl: *Little Miss Mulhall, who weighs only ninety pounds, can break a bronc, lasso and brand a steer and shoot a coyote at 500 yards. She can also play Cho-pin, quote Browning, and make mayonnaise.* When Lucille broke her leg in San Antonio, her adoring fans built a special stand at the show for her wheelchair. Later that evening her box at the opera house was filled with roses.

Oklahoma Historical Society Photograph Collection,
Courtesy Oklahoma Historical Society [16588]

Indian Boy race exhibited reckless bareback riding by the young sons of the Indians with the troupe. The Fight over the Water Hole enacted Frederick Remington's painting of the same name. Just as the cowboys found the water hole, they were attacked by the Indians who were trailing them. A battle fol-lowed, with the cowboys winning—of course.

Lucille, who was introduced to the admiring crowd as the Ladies' Champion Roper of the World, single-mindedly chased down a wild steer, her divided skirt and long hair flying. She threw the rope she had been twirling over her head and landed it neatly around the steer's head. She had changed horses, and this horse, Sam, stopped instantly, pulling the rope taut. Lucille leaped to the ground in a cloud of dust, running toward the thrashing steer. She whipped a small piece of rope out of the pocket in her skirt and tied two of the beast's ankles together. As she jumped up she threw her arms in the air in a triumphant salute to the crowd. Everyone stood, whistling and applauding enthusiastically. The announcer told them that in rodeos around the country she regularly beat out cowboys who couldn't handle a thousand-pound steer as quickly as the diminutive Lucille could.

A fake Mexican bullfight was staged since real bullfighting was illegal. And Henry Grammar wrestled with a 'Mexican' steer. The Chase For A Bride provided comedy as one of the cowgirls was chased by all of the cowboys. When one overtook her, she was lifted from her saddle to his while their horses were running at full speed. Goldie could feel herself riding behind that virile cowboy on his pony, circling the arena to the sound of stomping and cheering fans.

⤙ FOUR ⤚

In the Tanbark

GOLDIE'S FAVORITE ACT WAS THE BUCKING BRONCOS, where Charley Mulhall and other cowboys rode the violent horses. When the announcer called out Charley's name, listing his accomplishments as a former professional jockey and now a bulldogger, roper and bronc rider, Goldie stood and clapped hard. Lucille appeared, trotting her horse into the middle of the arena, where a couple of cowboys were holding a riderless horse. As Charley walked toward them, Lucille rode close the horse, bent over and covered its eyes with her arms. She seemed to be biting the horse's ear. Once Charley had a hand on the reins and a foot in the stirrup, Lucille let go, Charley swung onto his back, and the big gray horse arched his back and leaped high in a furious attempt to unseat the cowboy. Charley hung onto the wild-eyed bronc, who kicked and twisted and turned as hard as he could, and when Charley slid off the gray pony's bucking back, he got a rousing ovation from the crowd. The hairs on the back of Goldie's neck stood up. She got applause for her acts, but nothing like that.

The whole company spilled into the arena for the final act, a re-enactment of a dark page in western history, the Mountain Meadows Massacre.* As the last cowboy and Indian took their bows before the approving crowd, Goldie sprinted for the corral, pushing her way through the seats before the people around her started to pack up and leave. She was hoping to run into Charley before he disappeared into his tent. She wasn't disappointed. It was as if he knew she would come looking for him.

"It was fantastic," she enthused breathlessly. Charley grinned at the compliment and shook her hand vigorously.

"Wanna go for a ride?" He was reading her mind.

"Sure."

Charley led the way. "But this is the horse you rode in the show," Goldie protested. He seemed pleased that she recognized the horse. A stern-looking, well-dressed older man with a big hat and a big mustache strode their way, firmly planting the heels of his boots into the tanbark with every step. Goldie recognized him as Colonel Zack Mulhall.

"Hello, sir," she smiled at him.

"Hello, young woman." Zack looked pointedly at his son.

"Sir, this is Miss Goldie Griffith. With the Blanche Whitney Show. I told you about them."

"Yes, yes. Pleased to make your acquaintance." He tipped his hat. Goldie felt honored to be in the presence of a man who knew former president Roosevelt and owned a massive ranch in Oklahoma.

---

*About 120 men, women, and children were killed in the Mountain Meadows Massacre. The emigrants from Arkansas were traveling to California and stopped to rest and regroup at Mountain Meadows in Utah Territory. The local Mormon militia attacked the emigrants on September 11, 1857. The emigrants fought back, and the attack turned into a siege. The attackers had hoped to blame the attack on Native Americans, but the emigrants fought back, and when the militia realized that the emigrants knew their attackers were Mormons, not Native Americans, Col. William H. Dame, head of the Iron Country Brigade of the Utah militia, ordered their execution. The militiamen induced the emigrants to surrender and then executed everyone except for seventeen children under the age of eight. Only one of the local militia leaders, John D. Lee, was tried, and after two trials, he was convicted and executed by a firing squad at the site of the massacre.

"She'd like to try one of our horses. Would that be all right, sir?" Charley asked his father.

The older man stroked his chin. "Guess I don't see any harm in it. But, son, you thinkin' of takin' Soldier out again?"

"Yes, sir. And Buckwheat for Goldie. We won't be long."

The Colonel looked at Goldie, and she felt as if she had been assayed and evaluated, the way the old man would size up a cow or a horse. He turned back to his son with a severe look.

"Better not be long. You got work to do."

"Yes, sir." The older man turned on his heel and marched back the way he had come.

Goldie followed Charley to the corral where he showed her how to saddle the big oatmeal-colored horse he called Buckwheat. He handed her the reins, and Buckwheat nuzzled her neck. "I think he likes you. That's a good sign. You can always do a lot more on a horse that likes you." Goldie was pleased with the compliment.

"Do you need help gettin' in the saddle?" Goldie shook her head. Fortunately, she had on her Whitney outfit with the tights, or she wouldn't have been able to go on this impromptu ride. Her long skirt would have been too cumbersome to mount the horse. Good thing she had ridden once in a while in Forest Park in Chicago and knew how to get into the saddle by herself.

Charley swung a leg easily over Soldier's rump and settled lightly in the saddle, and the horses started walking toward the arena. As they came closer, Goldie could feel Buckwheat tense with energy.

The ponies entered the arena prancing sideways, stepping high. Goldie gasped with pleasure. She had never been on such a lively horse before. The horses she had ridden in Chicago had plodded through their day, never putting more energy into their trip around the park with each new rider than they had to. This was different. Goldie felt herself tense, but when she looked at Charley, he nodded approvingly, and she relaxed. She could do this.

"You sit that saddle like you were born in it," Charley grinned at her, and he reached over and slapped Buckwheat on the rump at the same time he spurred Soldier. His horse took off like a comet, streaking toward the other side of the arena. But Buckwheat didn't follow. Apparently, Buckwheat didn't like being slapped on the rump. The big horse's front legs rose up until they were even with Goldie's nose. She felt herself slipping, and then the empty seats spun around her as she gripped the saddle with every muscle in her thighs. She exhaled a gasp of relief when Buckwheat returned to the ground, but then he took a few steps and reared again with a fierceness that took her new-found breath away. She almost slid off the side of the saddle, but just as abruptly she was bounced back in. She had seen Lucille ride her rearing horse with one hand in the air, but she held on as tight as she could with both hands. When Buckwheat came back down to earth, he gathered his rear legs beneath him and shot off toward the other horse and rider. Charley had turned around and was tearing back across the arena toward her, but at that moment she felt herself slipping off the saddle.

"Kick free, kick free," he shouted.

Goldie opened one eye. The other one was pinned shut. Her body reverberated. She was looking at a pair of cowboy boots and a lot of bark. Had she passed out? She didn't think so. She thought maybe she had just lost her wind. Considering that wild ride, she thought she felt okay. Something hard poked at her shoulder. She turned just in time to receive a sloppy horse kiss from Buckwheat. His big eyes seemed worried, and he exhaled moist warm air noisily into her ear. Slowly, she sat up, and the big horse backed away from her. The cowboy boots were attached to legs, and a gloved hand appeared in front of her face. Willing herself up, Goldie grabbed onto the hand for a pull. Finally she could look up, and she saw Buckwheat and Soldier standing calmly a few feet away. In front of her stood Charley. Her legs felt a little wobbly, but she wasn't going to let

Charley know that. Charley was looking concerned, so she smiled, and she saw relief flood his face.

The bark that covered the dirt arena to help with dust control kept falling out of her clothes and hair, and she brushed at her face, hoping she didn't look too bad.

"Don't be forgettin' the time, Charles. You have work to do," Colonel Zack appeared at the edge of the arena and shouted at his son.

Charley winked at her. He turned and called out, "Yes, sir. I'll be right along."

Goldie assessed the damage. Her behind would be sore for a few days where it had smacked the swell on the back of the saddle. Fortunately, her dress wasn't ripped, but it was pretty dirty. She'd have to wash it out and hope that she could iron it dry in time for the next show.

"Hey, now, that was durn good. You'd make a good bronc rider." Charley was still grinning.

"But I fell off. That's not what you're supposed to do."

Charley tipped his hat towards her. "But you stayed with 'im when it was important, and you kicked free, that's just as good." Goldie thought he was just trying to make her feel better, but then he added when he saw her skepticism, "Yep, you'd make a good cowgirl. That was as good a first ride as any I ever seen."

She picked bark off her dress and her tights and wondered how many bruises she'd have. She now understood why Charley and the other cowboys stood in that funny way, like a wooden store mannequin with one stiff leg cocked out in front of the other. It was probably because of all the falls from the bucking horses he rode every day, twice a day.

"You should take—"

An angry shout from the corral interrupted them. They swung their heads in unison. It was Colonel Zack. He sounded enraged. Charley ran, and Goldie followed. By the time they got there, all they could see was the dust left in the wake of the Colonel's horse galloping toward town.

"What now?" Charley asked the hands who were standing around, smirking.

One of the cowboys took off his hat and scratched his head. "Them Injuns again. Two of 'em got arrested."

"It was just beads," offered another of the men, drawing circles in the dirt with the toe of his boot.

"Just beads?"

"Yep, in a dime store. In town."

That was all the cowboys were going to say, and all but one of them drifted off. Goldie recognized the last cowboy. He was Tom Mix, one of the stars of the Mulhall's show. "And who is this, Charley?" Mix teased as he waggled a finger at Goldie.

"This here is Miss Goldie Griffith, Tom, and don't you get any ideas. Goldie, this is Tom Mix. Maybe you've seen one of his flickers?"

Goldie shook her head. "No? Disappointed, Tom?" Goldie could tell that Charley was teasing Tom right back, but she couldn't help feeling let down when the gallant-looking cowboy swaggered away without saying goodbye even though Charley told her, "Don't mind him."

Later, Goldie heard that Zack paid the fine and got the Indians out of jail, but she heard that from the girls she worked with, not from any of the Mulhalls. Gossiping with the girls, she heard other rumors about Zack's temper. One was that he hit Tom Mix over the head with a two-by-four in a disagreement about Lucille. Before Mix became a famous movie star he was a hired hand on the Mulhall ranch, and Charley and Lucille grew up alongside him and the other cowboys. When Zack decided to take his talented children on the road with a Wild West show, he also took Mix, and it didn't seem too surprising to Goldie that a cowboy with as few manners as Mix would get in a scrape over the beautiful Lucille. Apparently the Colonel had forgiven him, because just as Mix was finishing his second motion picture, the Colonel tracked him down and asked if he would star in his Wild West show at the

Appalachian Exposition. Tom had three free weeks before his next picture, and he and his wife Olive agreed to Zack's proposition. When former President Theodore Roosevelt attended the Mulhall show at the Appalachian Exposition, Mix kept up a constant light banter with the former president, who was sitting in a special box seat on the reviewing stand with Colonel Zack.

After hearing all that, Goldie wondered if Colonel Zack had really hit Mix with the two-by-four. But most people believed the two-by-four incident probably did happen because Colonel Zack Mulhall had already shot three men in 1904 in a disagreement over the horses on the pike at the St. Louis Fair. Goldie tried asking Charley about the rumors, but he ignored her. The Mulhalls stuck by each other, and she could tell the family was dominated by Colonel Zack. After hearing Zack's explosion in the corral, she guessed that the threat of Colonel Zack's wrath was enough to keep anyone quiet, and sometimes she imagined the severe old man pulling out his gun, aiming at the men who had disagreed with him, and firing at them.

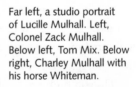

Far left, a studio portrait of Lucille Mulhall. Left, Colonel Zack Mulhall. Below left, Tom Mix. Below right, Charley Mulhall with his horse Whiteman.

The Sterling family and Kay Turnbaugh

"If you want, I could talk to the Colonel, see if you could join the show," Charley told her that day after she rode Buckwheat. She thought it a little odd that Charley called his father 'the Colonel,' but Colonel was what a lot of important men were called, and it had nothing to do with the military.

"Oh I can't do that." Her mother would kill her if she ran off to be in a Wild West, and she was still under contract with Blanche Whitney. But she thought there might be a future in learning how to ride, in more ways than one.

"How did you learn how to ride?"

Charley laughed. "I think I always knew. You know, when you grow up on a ranch." Almost all the cowboys and cowgirls in the Wild West shows learned to ride growing up on ranches in the West.

"How 'bout the broncs? When did you learn to ride them?"

"I guess that kind of came natural. My big sis and I played a lot of games on the ranch, and the hands thought it would be funny to put us on some buckers." What Charley didn't tell her was that he didn't come to his father's ranch until he was 10 years old, and at first was so scared of the boisterous cowboys and the new life he hid under his bed. His sister Lucille, who practiced her roping and riding almost all day every day, eventually taught him to rope and ride the bucking horses. "So we figured out how to ride 'em and how to take care of 'em. The Mulhall buckers are pretty special."

"Do you train 'em to buck?"

"Kinda," Charley squinted at her to see if she really was interested. Her rapt attention satisfied him, so he continued. "Well, first you have to find the right horse. Then you gotta wait until they're four or five years old. They need to be full-grown and strong as they're gonna get before you get on 'em the first time. Then you gotta make 'em feel like they're always the winner. You never, ever pull their head up. If you do that, they stop buckin' and then they're not worth much. You slide off 'em while they're still buckin' up a storm, and they think they did a good job—they got rid of you. You see?"

"Sure. Are they really worth a lot?"

"Almost more than any other horse, includin' race horses."

As Charley walked her back to the midway, she asked him, "Can you teach me how to ride?" At least that way she'd be able to see him for the next two weeks. Charley grinned at her and said it would be his pleasure.

They agreed on a schedule. She would come to the corral every day before her afternoon shows. They would have an hour before he had to get ready for his show.

The next two weeks slid by way too fast.

Before the Exposition closed, Goldie and Charley vowed to write to each other, even though Goldie had her doubts she would ever hear from him since she would be traveling with Blanche's show.

After the Exposition closed, Goldie traveled on with Blanche's show, and she worked at the some of the best theaters on the vaudeville circuit, including the Fox Theater in San Francisco on Market Street where she was billed as the first woman wrestler on the West Coast.

The entire Mulhall family returned to their ranch in Oklahoma after the Exposition. It turned out that the Appalachian Exposition was the last show ever for the Mulhall Wild West. The small show couldn't compete with the two really big ones—the Miller Brothers' 101 and the Buffalo Bill Wild West which by then had joined with the Pawnee Bill Wild East to become the Two Bills show.

Charley and Lucille didn't last long on the ranch. They had the spotlight in their eyes and the thrill of applause in their veins. Lucille was the most famous pioneer cowgirl, the best known woman in western entertainment other than Annie Oakley who was an incredible sharpshooter but who didn't ride or rope. Watching fifteen-year-old Lucille perform in 1900,

Theodore Roosevelt suggested to his friend Zack Mulhall that he exhibit his talented daughter to the entire country, and after that she was continually on the road with her father, brother, and sisters, charming crowds from New York to California. She could no more turn off that life than she could turn off the Salt River.

Following their failed return to normal ranch life, Charley and Lucille continued to cash in on Lucille's fame and perform on their own, and, when she could, Goldie looked at The Billboard for news of the Mulhalls.

She was daydreaming more and more about Charley Mulhall. She knew she was stuck on him. In her dreams she was riding bucking broncos. With one hand in the air.

⁓ FIVE ⁓

The Grandest Ranch in the World

A BUCKBOARD RATTLED TO A STOP next to the platform, and a grimacing, bowlegged cowhand jumped to the ground, little puffs of dust exploding around his high-topped, fancy-stitched boots. Beyond the buckboard the shimmering yellow-green grasses stretched forever. Behind her the train shivered in its own heat.

The cowboy coughed and wiped his mouth with his bandana. "You the folks goin' on out to the ranch today?" He peered down at Goldie from under his wide-brimmed hat with an appreciative leer. Then he glanced at the two men standing beside her, immediately deducing that they weren't traveling together. He turned back to Goldie.

"Yessir. Goldie Griffith," Goldie introduced herself. The cowboy grabbed her hand and gave it a rough shake.

"Jim. Yours?" he pointed to her trunk. She nodded. Another cowhand had appeared at Jim's side, and the two of them grabbed the trunk and slung it in a graceful arc into the back of the wagon alongside several other boxes and a canvas bag.

"George Taylor, from Philadelphia."

"Yessir. Good to meet you." Jim shook George's hand. "That's mine." George pointed to his large case. The two men tossed it into the buckboard.

"I'm Peter. Peter Graham." Peter tentatively extended his hand, looking uneasily at the well worn, dirt-encrusted glove that Jim shook it with. He lifted his own case into the wagon. Peter didn't say where he was from, but Goldie already knew. He was from Baltimore. She and the two men had chatted on the long train ride, and Goldie knew how fascinated both were with ranch life and with the Millers. And they were so excited to be on their way to the renowned 101 Ranch that when they found out that she going to work there as a cowgirl, they bombarded her with questions—too many questions. Always the entertainer, Goldie made up answers when she didn't know, or if necessary, she just changed the subject and started talking about wrestling. Of course, she didn't know the answers most of the time, since she had never been in Oklahoma, never been on a ranch, never met the Miller brothers, and never been a cowgirl before.

The Millers catered to Easterners who flocked to their 101 ranch to visit, work, or play at being a ranch hand for a few weeks. The official season for the Riverside Camp was May 1 to November 1, but visitors poured into the ranch pretty much year round. Peter and George were traveling west to learn about the frontier and themselves, and, as everyone knew, the 101 was the place to go.

The 101 Ranch was owned by the Miller family, the three sons of George W. Miller senior, who put together 110,000 acres in the Ponca Indian country of north-central Oklahoma. The granddaddy of all ranches was a working ranch and a tourist destination. Thousands of cattle roamed the ranch lands, and the 101 holdings included oil wells, trains, schools and churches, a telephone system, and a fabulously well-stocked store where ranch hands could pay with their "101" folding scrip and coins.

When the brothers took the ranch on the road as the 101 Wild West show, they took with them a thousand performers—cowgirls, cowboys, Indians, Russian cossacks, circus performers, clowns, and musicians. Many people thought the 101 name came from the ranch's acreage, but it really came from the time George W. Miller spent in San Antonio in the 1880s, trying to persuade his hands not to spend the night drinking and gambling before they started driving the longhorns north to their grazing lands. One of the favored saloons was named 101 East Second Street. According to one story, it took Miller and half the town's police to get his crew out of the wrecked saloon and back out to where the cattle were bedded down. Miller paid the proprietor of 101 East Second Street for the damages, but he figured his men would never forget their hangovers if he branded the cattle with "101." Those cowboys had to look at the brand every day during the long drive north, and Miller figured it would be a long, long time before they'd want to see that honky-tonk signboard again.

The man sent by the ranch to retrieve the guests from the railroad station moved past Goldie and her two fellow passengers and asked another ten people the same questions, and he and his partner threw all their luggage onto the wagon. Then his partner walked away toward the cattle pens, and Jim hopped up onto the driver's seat and clucked the horses into action.

Goldie, Peter and George exchanged glances, but before they could form their questions, a grand stagecoach pulled by a team of sweating horses rattled into the station. Excited chatter exploded around Goldie as the driver whoa'ed the team to a stop in front of them.

The short, wiry driver jumped down and helped six of them into the coach. Everyone else clambered up to the top, including Goldie, who didn't think she could sit inside another compartment even if they were only five miles from their destination. As soon as everyone was settled, they were off, bouncing through their own dust cloud.

MILLER BROS. 101 RANCH, THE HOME (

Headquarters Miller Bros., 101 Ranch, Bliss, Oklahoma

A panorama of the 101 Ranch. The White House is at the far right.

She could already feel the grit in her teeth and hair. She squinted into the sun as they jounced away from the train station, the warehouses, and the shipping pens for the cattle. They were driving into nothing—just rolling flatness for as far as she could see, but the excitement among the ranch's visitors was electric.

The day before, March 9, had been unseasonably warm—89 degrees—but today the temperature hovered in the more normal mid-50s. She hadn't been cold standing on the platform, but riding on top of the stagecoach Goldie could feel little blasts of cold air seep under her coat. She pulled the collar up around her neck.

As their heads bobbed from side to side, trying to take in the vastness of the prairie grasses rolling away in endless waves, Peter asked, "When will we get to the ranch?"

"You're on it." One of the other passengers, who had spent a month on the ranch last summer, waved his hand in a big circle. "The depot and all this is part of the ranch."

Goldie sucked in her breath. That was incredible. To own so much. And it went on and on. Chasing the endless telephone

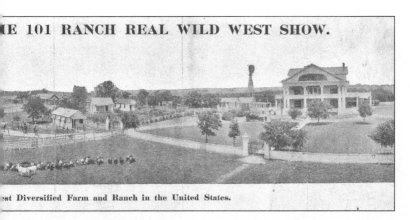

E 101 RANCH REAL WILD WEST SHOW.

st Diversified Farm and Ranch in the United States.

Cazrina Conlan Collection, Courtesy of the Oklahoma Historical Society [6519]

and electric poles, they passed herds of cattle and horses, mules and hogs, and some abandoned oil rigs. Then there were the oil rigs that were pumping up the black gold. After what seemed like an eternity of clinging to the rail against the uncomfortable rocking and bouncing, she gave up even trying to follow the men's eager conversations. She closed her eyes against the dust and the weariness of days of travel.

She bobbed awake just as the driver bellowed, "Be seein' the White House pretty soon." He didn't have to explain. The Millers' big house, the ever-bustling headquarters of the ranch, was famous, and, sure enough, a tall house was taking shape in the distance.

"That's the Salt River. Some of the orchards are over there." Again the other passenger, who had taken this journey before, waved ahead of them, and his fellow passengers looked eagerly past the big white house. "Wheat is over there. Cotton fields are beyond that." They craned their necks.

Other shapes began to take form out of the dust, and some of the men around her began whooping and waving their arms in anticipation. Silos, energy plants, restaurant, store, bunk-

The 101 Ranch White House.

Photo by Vincent Dillon, Cracraft Collection,
Courtesy of the Oklahoma Historical Society [19276.28]

houses and cookhouses for the hired hands, stables, machine shop, tanning factory, creamery, and meat packing plant. Of course, Goldie didn't know what all the buildings were, not yet. And then they could see a grass lawn bordered by a fancy wrought-iron fence and flowers bobbing in the breeze. Jim pulled the buckboard under the porte cochere and stopped beside a Model T automobile.

The weary travelers immediately began climbing out of and off the coach, slapping and shaking the dust from their clothes. The three-story White House loomed overhead, its steel-reinforced concrete walls as pale as the bleached animal bones they'd seen from the coach. Behind massive columns, shade beckoned from the deep porches. A woman, who was introduced to everyone as Mrs. Miller, stood nearby to greet them. The paying guests were escorted up the wide staircase and inside the house, which was kept cool in summer's shimmering heat and warm in winter's blizzards by its fancy hot and cold ventilation system. They would be staying on the third floor, a single room with enough four-poster beds for 100 guests. After a day or two some of them might go out to one of the ranch's camps that had been established to help work the cattle.

Goldie stood aside as all this took place until Jim reappeared with another woman. "This here's Miss Goldie," he said as he nodded from the woman to Goldie. "And, this is Mrs. Tantlinger, chief of the cowgirls." Unlike the woman who had greeted the eager Easterners, this woman was dressed like a working cowhand in a man's shirt, a heavy, divided skirt and sturdy, high-topped boots. Although most of her clothes could have belonged to a man, she looked so proper and feminine in them that Goldie immediately addressed her as "ma'am." The older woman— Goldie guessed maybe ten years older than her seventeen— squinted at her from under the wide brim of her hat.

"Shall we walk? Jim can take your things over to the bunk-house." The buckboard, now with only Goldie's trunk on board, rattled past them. A bird sitting on a fence post sang a series of melodic whistles that sounded like they rippled through a flute. Goldie was transfixed, watching the bright yellow-breasted bird.

"Those meadowlarks are pretty territorial, aren't they?"

Goldie hadn't known what kind of bird it was, and she'd never heard anything like it. "Thatsa real preddy bird."

Mrs. Tantlinger looked at her closely. "Haven't you been out on the prairie before?" Mrs. Tantlinger didn't talk like most of the other cowgirls or cowboys Goldie had met so far. She sounded schooled.

"No, I'm from Chicago." Too late, Goldie realized she could be putting her new job in jeopardy with her words. She tried to amend what she'd said. "That's where my mother lives, Chicago."

The dark V on the meadowlark's breast shone like polished stone in the late afternoon sun, and he took up his song again as soon as the two women had passed.

"And how long have you been riding?" Mrs. Tantlinger asked. Goldie hesitated. Should she tell her?

"I see." Mrs. Tantlinger's tone was teasing. Goldie didn't have to confess—this self-assured woman, who she would later learn was a school teacher before she became a cowgirl, had already guessed that she had exaggerated a little in her letter to the Miller brothers. Well, it didn't matter, Goldie thought, Mrs. Tantlinger would find out that she could do the job. She'd never been afraid of trying anything, and she was a fast learner.

Since she'd met Charley Mulhall, she'd known she had to go West and become a cowgirl. Every time she read in the newspaper about the fabulous opportunities available for gold seekers in Cripple Creek, Colorado, she knew it was the place for her. Just a couple of months ago she'd seen the ad in Billboard magazine that cowboys, cowgirls, and ranch hands were needed at the Miller brothers' 101 Ranch in Oklahoma. Everyone wanted to work with either the 101 or the greatest show ever, Buffalo Bill's Wild West. She laboriously composed a letter in her best handwriting telling the Miller brothers that she had ridden a horse quite often in Forest Park. Well, three or four times, but she had to get the job, so she exaggerated a little. She enclosed a picture of herself, and she knew she was pretty good-looking. The telegram that arrived five weeks later said they had an opening for a cowgirl. She was so excited she couldn't sleep that night. She was going to be a cowgirl, just like Charley Mulhall had said she could. Maybe she'd get to see Charley once in a while. And, then there was the most exciting possibility—this could be her ticket to fame. She knew she could be as big a star as Lucille Mulhall.

But even the stars, as Goldie was soon to find out, take their knocks.

The next few weeks at the Millers' ranch were a whirlwind of instruction, falls and bruises. She learned to saddle and groom her horse. At first the cowboys took her with them when they rode out to round up cattle or to do some maintenance in one of the fields. After a few days of that they switched her to working on a horse with the cattle in the pens, doing some of the smaller, easier jobs, which the cowboys assured her would be useful later as a performer in an arena. The smells of fresh horse dung mixed with hay and dust and soft, worn leather soaked with sweat didn't seem foreign any more.

Besides learning how to ride, she needed a costume for the show. She bought a big hat, a man's shirt, and a silk scarf at the store on the ranch. She could roll the shirt's sleeves up above her elbows, and, with the scarf draped loosely around her neck, she thought she looked pretty good.

Until she could make her own divided skirt, Mrs. Tantlinger loaned her one of hers. Inez, one of the other cowgirls, showed her how to stitch extra leather to the tops of her shoes, and Rose loaned her a pattern for a divided skirt and said Goldie could borrow her sewing machine to stitch it together. Back she went to the store to purchase six sheepskins with her ranch "bucks." She had to sew at night because they worked and practiced for the upcoming show season from before sunup to sundown.

Her new divided riding skirt came to her ankles, and as the ground continued to thaw with March's warming temperatures it turned to mud—especially deep, it seemed, in the arenas and corrals. When she jumped off her pony, she sank ankle-deep into the slime that would only reluctantly give up its hold on her boots with a sickening squish-slurp-suck. The bottom of her skirt was constantly muddy and wet, flapping around her ankles and making it difficult to walk. She borrowed Rose's sewing machine again and shortened the skirt that she had labored over a week earlier.

She purchased a pair of brown elk hide gloves with the Indian symbol for good fortune on the gauntlet that were made at the ranch's tannery. These were for parades. For working, she bought another pair of plainer gloves. She also bought two pairs of cotton gloves to wear inside the leather ones. And then there were the spurs. She chose a pair with diminutive rowels with a scalloped edge that she could button over her boots.

Edith took her and one of the other new girls down to the Salt River one day where she taught them how to run their horses in a straight line and start hanging off to one side of the saddle. Pretty soon they were dangling part-way out of the saddle, sliding one leg under the horse's belly, holding onto the saddle with one hand, reaching with the other outstretched hand towards the ground. The horses didn't run as fast in the sand alongside the river, and when the girls fell, the bounce wasn't as hard as it would be in the arena. Edith taught them how to fall away from their horses and roll so they didn't get caught under the flying hooves and minimized the chances of breaking a bone.

Next they practiced in the arena. When they could almost touch the ground with their outstretched hand, Edith filled handkerchiefs with sand and let them practice picking them up. The first time it took Goldie four or five passes before she could grab the white square of cloth, but by the end of the day she was getting better. Although she had taken only a couple of little falls the day before, she took a whopper that day in the arena, rolling up spitting bark, and the bruises were starting to show when she crawled into bed that night.

The following day was the one Goldie had anticipated ever since she'd ridden with Charley at the Appalachian Exposition. As she dressed that morning she considered every piece of clothing, how it would look to someone in the stands, how it would function in the arena. She had sewn shoelaces into the hems of her divided skirt so she could tie the legs up and make bloomers. The other girls told her it would be safer, and today she was ready to try it, even though she was scared she might be killed if something went wrong.

Colonel Joe Miller was back from his travels, and he had declared this day to be the one when he would decide who would ride the bucking broncos in the show. It seemed to Goldie that the show was getting bigger and bigger every day. Elephants paraded through the arena, followed by the cowboy band, practicing their steps and songs. Cowboys and their 'high school' horses practiced their tricks. Princess Wenona rehearsed her sharpshooting from the back of a horse, flawlessly hitting the glass balls that her assistant tossed in the air. Vern Tantlinger, Edith's husband, rode his bicycle and shot at glass balls thrown in the air for him. Cowboys twirled their ropes into intricate patterns, tricks Goldie had yet to learn. The high-schooled horses that had been trained to do tricks were given pats and sometimes even treats for good performances. And, often, all this would be happening at the same time in the same arena. But this morning only one thing was scheduled for the arena. Today was the day for the bucking broncos and their would-be riders to show their stuff to the Colonel.

She took extra care pinning her hair tightly. She pulled her not-big-enough hat over the soft curls that framed her decidedly round face. She could look almost cherubic, but the sweetness in her smile was overpowered by its confidence, and the twinkle in her eyes told the world to "watch out, here I come." She cocked her head to one side—she wasn't looking at a sweet cherub in the mirror—not today. Today she was a cowgirl.

She had to admit there was another reason she felt excited. Harry would probably be there in the arena. The day before when she had taken that nasty fall, he'd been the one to pick her up, and he'd been nicer about it than most of the cowboys were. Most of them liked touching the girls—another incentive to get good fast and stay out of the dirt so you didn't need any help. Harry seemed to Goldie to be different—he offered his hand to her instead of pulling her upright without asking. He'd introduced himself, and they had walked and talked for a few minutes until Goldie was walking straight and answering questions to Harry's approval. She'd found out that he was from Mexia, Texas, and had worked just about everywhere.

The bucking horses, placid until weight was on their backs, were herded into a corral next to the arena. Some shows put the women on the less temperamental horses. But Colonel Joe expected his girls to handle even the meanest and toughest horses as well as the cowboys. The women rode first for the Colonel. They lined up along the arena fence. One by one they took their turns holding onto the thrashing horses with the colorful names. Neither of the Parry sisters slid off until after the whistle. Martha and Sophie also stayed on, but Edie wasn't so lucky. Goldie was watching so intently she didn't realize someone was at her side until she turned into Harry. He walked with her and steadied her horse while she slipped from her horse onto the saddle of the bucker. She didn't want to know the name of the horse she was going to ride, but Harry told her anyway. "Twister." Oh boy.

"Tickle 'is feet," Harry encouraged her as he turned to run the other way with her horse. The two cowhands who were holding an old shirt around Twister's eyes pulled it off and dashed out of the way. Goldie gripped as hard as she could with her thighs and willed herself to stay on the monster's back. Before she could even look up, Twister tried several tricks reminiscent of his name, and then he tried to smash her off against the fence. When that didn't work, he threw up his hind legs in frustration. Goldie had been hanging on as tight as she could with both hands, but as she was thrown up from the saddle she found she had one hand in the air, and it actually helped her balance. From that moment on, she knew she could do this, she could ride these broncos as well as anyone else.

She didn't recall hearing the whistle, but she found herself sliding off Twister's back and rolling into the tanbark. Her fellow cowboys and cowgirls applauded and shouted cheers.

After the adrenaline left her system, she felt more battered and bruised than the day before. That night, she had blood in her pee, but the other girls told her not to worry about it, it was normal after you rode a particularly tough bronc like Twister. When she closed her eyes, she could still hear Colonel Joe saying, *"You're coming with the show. Get ready for New Jersey."* When she smiled, he continued, *"and keep practicin'. You're not ready yet."* Yes sir, she told him, thrilled to be going on the road again.

Joe C. Miller & "Ben Hur"

Goldie's boss when she rode with the 101 was Colonel Joe Miller, photographed here with his horse Ben Hur.

Photo by Vincent Dillon, Cracraft Collection,
Courtesy of the Oklahoma Historical Society [19276.39]

She was so tired and sore she wasn't sure she could get into bed, and she was certain she probably wouldn't be able to sleep after everything that had happened that day. She was an official cowgirl—a bronco rider—and she might have a boyfriend. She rubbed her thumb on the leather of the bridle Harry had given her after Colonel Joe said she was going to leave with the show. "You'll be needin' somethin' like this," he'd told her, and he handed her the most beautiful bridle she'd ever seen. It had half-domes, conchos, he called them, set in a horseshoe shape on the stamped silver. The leather was so soft she didn't want to put it down so she could sleep. It was beautiful. Touching it, she could feel Harry's hand on her elbow, guiding her out of the arena after her triumphant ride.

⚘ SIX ⚘

A Doozy of a Season

EDWARD ARLINGTON, THE MILLERS' PARTNER and business manager, had booked a doozy of a season for 1912, and the entire trainload of entertainers, support staff, animals, and equipment loaded up in Bliss, Oklahoma, around the first of April.

Goldie had traveled with shows before, but the 101 was massive, like moving a city across the country. The first section of their train carried the performers and the cook house, the second section had everything else. The long string of cars hauled over a thousand people, including Indians and Cossacks, six hundred stock, including elephants, camels, horses, buffalo, long-horned steers, oxen, mules and horses, and all their associated equipment and supplies. Every car on the Millers' train was painted yellow, except the very last one. Inside that last, white, car were Madame Marantette's trained horses: Chief Geronimo, Sun Flower, and Saint Patrick, a jumper that had cleared six feet, four inches.

All sorts of supplies and cafeteria-style meals were available in the Privilege car, which also was the site of much gambling and drinking. Goldie shared a stateroom with Inez, a fellow cowgirl. The single girls had a Pullman sleeper, and the single cowboys had another, with the married couples in their sleeper in between. Edith Tantlinger was the head cowgirl, and her husband Vern was in charge of the cowboys. The single performers all knew that Edith and Vern could hear even the most padded, softest footfall, but that didn't stop them from trying to move between the single girls car and the single boys car.

Their first stop that season was Passaic, New Jersey, to meet the performers who had spent the winter there. From Passaic, the train rattled on to Boston, where Goldie performed in her first show as a cowgirl. Of course, they had put on practice shows while still in Oklahoma, drawing crowds to the ranch to ensure the horses got used to the sounds associated with arena performances. They even practiced parading on ranch roads with as many people as they could find to clap and cheer, making sure the horses and the performers could handle whatever might happen, like a child suddenly screaming or an automobile horn honking, which had sent several horses and riders skittering across the ranch compound.

But when they arrived in Boston, it was the real thing. People lined the parade route through Boston Commons starting in the early morning, and as Goldie mounted her horse, she could feel the tingle of nerves along her spine. She had been dreaming about this for a long time. At that moment she was glad she hadn't followed the gold rush to Cripple Creek in Colorado—this was far better. Around her, cowgirls were chattering about their new costumes and their boyfriends, and then they began picking out people in the crowd and making up stories about them. Goldie giggled with them when Lulu Parr, one of the renowned cowgirls who had joined up for a few shows, joshed that a man in a bowler hat with his arms crossed was really a spy from Ringling, and his wife had hired the man standing behind him to spy on her husband. A contingent of Boston policemen marched past, formally starting the parade, followed by the first cowboy band. A set of cowboys, dressed as ranchmen, followed, prodding their horses to raucousness. The long procession of Indians, with war paint and feathers, marched by. Then another band, and as the show wagons rumbled past, Goldie's horse got more restless, wanting to move. The cowgirls had been bunched together, trying to stay out of the way of the others, and now they rode to where they too would start on the parade route, following the last of the wagons.

Smiling, Goldie let out a whoop, and spurred her horse into the middle of the cowgirls. It was their job to charm the crowd, and although she was new to cowgirling, she wasn't new to show business or to the job of pleasing an audience. The cowgirls, dressed in their arena finest, rode back and forth, greeting the crowd with smiles and whoops. The high-schooled horses would occasionally stop and take a bow, much to the delight of those lining the street. Goldie's horse pranced and two-stepped sideways, showing off his tricks. Following the cowgirls was Bill Pickett, the Dusky Demon, on his horse Spradley. Pickett, the son of two former slaves, had pretty much invented the rodeo event of steer wrestling, or bulldogging. When Spradley got alongside a longhorn steer, Pickett jumped off and dropped the steer's head to the ground, twisting the head toward the sky and biting the steer's upper lip to get control of it. As he marched past, the crowd roared with recognition and anticipation. After Pickett were the Mexicans, the Cossacks, buffalo, more cowgirls and cowboys, and, finally, at the end, the calliope, piping music loud enough to be heard in the middle of Boston Harbor.

By the time the calliope slid under the arch that was the entry to the arena tent, Goldie was already in place for the first act. For the first of several times during the performance, she re-applied her lip rouge and powdered her face so she wouldn't shine in the lights. The crowd expectantly waiting under the huge arena tent fell silent as the last notes from the cowboy musicians faded. Into the suspense rode Joe Miller, a

Everyone pitches in to help unload the 101 Wild West train cars in the early morning in Camden, Maine, around 1908. As soon as the train arrived in the next town, the organized chaos of unloading and setting up a show was started all over again.

Photographer unknown. Tad S. Mizwa Collection, Dickinson Research Center, National Cowboy & Western Heritage Museum, Oklahoma City, Oklahoma

magnificent figure on his stallion. He stopped in the middle of the arena and, as his horse rose on its two hind legs, the Colonel raised his large white hat to thunderous applause. He introduced the show and then turned it over to the director.

Twenty acts and an hour and a half later, Goldie wearily dismounted. Her first show was a crowd-pleaser. They had stood and clapped and stomped, whooped and whistled after the band played the last song. It was five o'clock, time to get her horse walked and watered and turned over to the hands at the corral behind the arena. Time for her to wash the arena dust out of her eyes and get something to eat before the 8:30 show. Telling her pony what a good job he'd done, she pulled off her hat and ran her fingers through her sweat-streaked hair. Everything Mr. Joe had taught her and told them about the show had come true. It all seemed surreal at the moment, but now she was a cowgirl—a real cowgirl. She was so tired she let her horse lead her over to one of the horse tents, where she tied him next to the water trough before unsaddling him. She would ride another horse in the evening performance.

They were in Boston for a week. They had sixteen performances in Philadelphia, Baltimore, Trenton, New Brunswick, Newark, Brooklyn, and New England, then they went back to Pennsylvania and on to Michigan, Wisconsin, and Illinois. Somehow it seemed that their front man was thinking in tandem with the bookers for Ringling Brothers, Forepaugh-Sells and Barnum & Bailey, because they always seemed to be playing within a week of each other, which made it harder to attract crowds than had been the case in previous seasons. Slowly the Miller Brothers' 101 Wild West made its zig-zagging way west, and now they were in New Mexico.

Every day except Sunday they worked. Sundays were for rest, laundry, and maybe a parade. This Sunday, she did her laundry and lit her gas iron. It seemed like Harry always knew when she did that and would turn up with his hang-dog look, holding a couple of shirts. Did he love her, or did he just like having her around to help with his shirts? Usually, Goldie didn't think too much about it. Of course, she pressed them for him, because then he always asked her to go to dinner with him. Their ritual had become ingrained during those first few months on the road.

When she'd finished her chores and taken a bucket bath, she pulled her town clothes out of her trunk and changed. She put a few coins in the fringed purse that the other cowgirls had made for her out of soft sheepskin dyed turquoise. They painted her name, a sun, and the Indian symbol for good luck on it. It was one of her most prized possessions. Harry was wearing the same clothes he always did, which were the same clothes he wore in the arena but without his woolly chaps: jeans, step-heel boots, jingling spurs, work shirt and tie, and a wide-brimmed tall hat with a crease peculiar to cowboys from Texas. You could tell where a cowboy hailed from by the crease in his hat. On the rare occasion that Harry took his hat off, a shock of hair fell across his forehead in spite of the Pomade he used to keep it in place.

They left the show grounds and ambled into town as dusk rolled out of the flaming sky. Rarely did cowboys walk anywhere, but this town was close enough that it wasn't a reflection on their macho to walk, at least for most of them. There were a few horses tied up in front of the café when they arrived, and Goldie patted them, scratching an ear here and there, but she didn't tarry long—the smell of fried steak wafting out the open door pulled her inside after Harry. Everyone was tired and hungry, although no cowboy or cowgirl would ever admit to being tired. Harry sipped from a flask he pulled from his back pocket. It had been a long day, a long week, a long few months, rattling from town to town on the train, setting up the show, riding in a parade and doing publicity, practicing new tricks, and putting on two or three shows a day, which, for Goldie, always included trying to stay on top of a couple of bucking broncos and then doing a few rope tricks and some trick riding, hanging off her horse where a single instant's distraction could drop her under those thundering hooves. Then they'd clean up, go out to eat if they were near enough a town, sleep a few hours, pack up, and do it all over again. It was a routine Goldie had gotten used to, but it was an exhausting one.

When she first arrived at the ranch in Oklahoma, Goldie wasn't sure she would ever fit in with the people she met, almost all of whom had grown up on ranches in the West. They were self-sufficient, hardened to life in ways Goldie couldn't imagine. But after the first few weeks on the road she felt more like she belonged. She'd grown up performing on the road, and once they were on the road she could relax and be herself.

When she and Harry walked into the café in New Mexico, other performers from the show called hello from across the

room. It felt like she'd always been a cowgirl, even though it had
only been a few months.

Harry was pretty much still her favorite among the cowboys,
even though she hadn't seen him recently. When the 101 train
neared Texas, Harry disappeared. The other cowboys just shook
their heads and said something like "on the q-dado" when she
asked about him. They wouldn't explain what that meant. Vern
Tantlinger told her not to worry, he'd be back. She figured
Colonel Joe had sent him off somewhere on a job, maybe to
Mexico. One day he just showed up again, smiling crookedly as
she pulled her horse up next to him. She might have noticed
him earlier except that she was concentrating on her timing. She
had to start galloping her horse across the arena at the exact
same time as the girl on the other side of the arena. As they
passed each other in the center, they both swooped down from
their saddles and picked up a handkerchief from the ground.
Then they waved the white cloth triumphantly over their heads
as other performers took over the center of attention.

"Looks like you've been stayin' outta the tanbark, Goldie."

"I didn't know you were back."

Harry grinned again. "I'm the lucky penny that'll always
turn up in your purse."

She couldn't help smiling, but when she turned back to him,
Harry had vanished. Vern Tantlinger was slinging his boomer-
ang halfway across the arena to spirited applause, and it was
time for Goldie to dismount and climb on top of the old stagecoach for the next act.

A young Goldie in Chicago.

Buffalo Bill Museum and Grave,
Lookout Mountain, Golden, Colorado

⤠ SEVEN ⤟

A-Wooin'

THE FOUR OF THEM SAT A BOOTH.

Harry poured some whiskey into Melvin's coffee cup. "How about you gals?" Lillie held up a sideways finger, and Harry poured a finger's worth into her cup. Goldie shook her head.

"Sure?"

"Aw, she's just a kid—leave her alone—right, button?" Mel poked her in the ribs, and Goldie squealed.

"I'm no kid," Goldie pouted.

"Hey, Melvin." A cowboy had swaggered over to their table, one thumb hooked in a belt loop. He tipped his hat at the two women. "Lillie, Goldie, Harry." Lillie blushed. Goldie looked at him sideways, wondering if there was going to be trouble. Whenever two men were after the same woman, like Melvin and Oscar were with Lillie Francis, it seemed like there was sure to be trouble.

"Oscar." Mel tipped his head ever so slightly. The two stared at each other. Lillie started fidgeting with her cup. "Look, Oscar, I'm out with Mel here tonight. You go back and sit down." Her tone was firm, although her face was still red. Oscar swayed a little. He'd already had too much to drink. He licked his lips and blinked. Harry slipped out of his chair and pointedly looked at the open door of the café. Cowboys would never interfere with a private argument, and Harry was almost across that line.

Oscar wasn't going to get sidetracked. "Miss Francis, I just want you to know that I want you to marry me." Goldie gasped. Lillie gasped. Melvin, who had been quiet so far, stood up and took a threatening step toward Oscar. Goldie could feel her coffee in her throat. Lillie pushed her chair back and started to get up, but Mel pushed her back into her chair.

Other cowboys scrambled to their feet, scraping chairs loudly across the bare floor, and the café's short, stocky owner came out of the kitchen, flapping his apron at them. "Arguments outside. Outside," he was almost shrieking in his desire to avoid a chair-breaking fight in his restaurant. "God-damned show people—you're trouble, all of you, trouble." He began muttering unintelligibly as his face exploded in red patches. He fluttered his apron and took small steps toward Oscar and Harry. Mel had managed to step away from the table, in spite of Lillie holding onto him. Three of the other cowboys got to the table before the café owner and stood between him and the two feuding cowboys. Oscar leaned into Melvin and jabbed him in the chest just as Lillie shot out of her chair and fiercely held onto Mel's arm, squirming around until she was in front of him. Oscar turned on his heel and lurched out the door. Lillie turned Melvin's head down toward her and gave him a kiss. It broke the trance that had held the café breathless.

Melvin and Lillie slid back into their chairs. "See, we're not all trouble, are we, Goldie?" Lillie smiled disarmingly at Melvin, but Goldie was worried about Harry—Oscar had seemed in a murderous mood, and Harry had followed him outside. Goldie was torn between following and staying, but Lillie grabbed her sleeve and nodded at her to stay in her seat. Everyone else sat back down as if nothing at all had happened.

"Let's decide what we're going to eat, shall we? We can order for Harry." Lillie had taken charge, and although Mel was still edgy, he stayed, and so did Goldie.

A cowboy slumped into the seat next to Goldie. He nodded at Lillie and Melvin under the brim of his hat and casually put his arm around the back of Goldie's chair where it could touch her shoulders. Instinctively, she hunched forward in her seat, not wanting Harry to come back and get the wrong idea.

"You need someone else to escort you home, Miss Goldie?"

"No thanks, Slim. Harry will back in a few minutes." Goldie wished that Jane, Slim's girlfriend, hadn't left the show, and she wondered if Slim felt sorry for what he'd done to her.

"Don't appear to me like he's comin' back t'all." Goldie didn't like the way Slim leaned toward her as he said this, but before she could say something tart to him, Mel stared hard at him, and said, "Slim."

Melvin's voice had a tone of finality, like a last warning.

The door to the café opened, and Slim pulled his arm back to his side, uncoiling from Harry's seat.

"Offer's open, any time," he looked meaningfully at Goldie and began his retreat as Harry stomped across the restaurant toward the table, spurs jingling and flask disappearing into his back pocket. He sat down hard on the chair next to Goldie and squeezed her knee under the table. She tried to see around him, but she couldn't tell if Oscar had come back in the café or not.

No one said anything for a few minutes. Cowboys often didn't say anything, and sometimes Goldie felt like she was wringing water out of a rock to get Harry to talk. But then he broke the silence. "Aren't we a couple of lucky ones?" Harry's grin slowly grew, erasing his usual stern expression. He ran his fingers through his sandy hair, smoothing it away from his forehead. "We got the two best-looking gals in the state sittin' right here. Bottoms up." He and Mel drained their cups. Nothing more was said about the incident. Ever.

They all had the special—chicken fried steak, mashed potatoes and gravy, and peas—except Harry. "You can always tell a Texas boy—he doesn't give a damn about his taste buds," Mel snickered when Harry gave the woman his order.

The kid who brought their meals to the table couldn't have been more than ten years old. He proudly carried Harry's bowl of chili in both hands and dropped it in front of the cowboy, looking at him with wide admiring eyes.

"Bet you'd like to be a cowboy," Harry teased him. Finally, Goldie felt at ease again. Harry's intense blue eyes were bright with mischief, and he was grinning again.

"Yes sir, mister." The kid licked his lips and stared at Harry.

"What's your name?" Goldie asked.

"Frank, ma'am."

"I'm Goldie, and this here is Harry, Lillie, and this is Melvin. We're glad to meet you." Frank nodded his head gravely at each of them as Goldie introduced them.

"How come you wanna be a cowboy?" Melvin asked as he swallowed a heap of mashed potatoes.

"I like horses, sir, and I wanna see places."

"Well, you could do that—probably more'n you'd ever care to see," Mel said dryly.

"How old're you?"

"I'm old enough."

"I bet you are," Harry told him sincerely. "You like horses, huh?"

"Yessir, I like 'em a whole lot," the boy answered with a grin.

"Maybe he should come with us, we got us lotsa horses, don't we?" Harry asked the group.

"No he shouldn't. He should stay here with his ma and pa. They need him," Lillie said firmly. Someone yelled from the kitchen, and the boy scuttled away, running between the tables.

"You shouldn't go encouragin' 'im to run away from home. Shame on you," Lillie shook her head at Harry.

Hiram, the 12-year old son o
C J Sterling, left home Tuesday
with some horse traders. He was
heard of in Corsicana, but when
Mr Sterling went up after him yesterday the little fellow could not
be found Any information con-
cerning the boy will be gladly received by his parents

This notice about Harry, whose given name was
Hiram, appeared in the Mexia [Texas] Evening
Ledger on October 26, 1899.

"Why not? Everyone's gotta leave home—some sooner'n others."

"You ran away?"

"Yep, and I kept doin' it 'til it stuck."

"How old were you the first time?"

" 'bout twelve. I wanted to go with the horse trader who came by ever' few months. Seemed like the thing to do, so I done it."

Goldie couldn't help thinking that when Harry ran away he was much younger than she had been. The other three were looking at her—it was her turn.

"Ma had the cops come get me from the show I was in. She worries about me a lot. Too much." Goldie didn't tell them the whole story. When she was 16, her mother called the police and said that her daughter had disappeared and she feared for her safety. She said she had allowed Goldie to join a traveling whoopla show company, and a friend of the family had prom-ised to take care of the girl. Allie had traced the whoopla show to Wheaton but failed to find any trace of her daughter or the show, so she called the police and the newspaper, which ran a story about Goldie's disappearance and her picture. A few days later the newspaper reported that the police had found Goldie in Libertyville and brought her back to her mother in Chicago.

Goldie realized as she thought about it that it was natural her ma would worry about her more than most—she was an only child, and her pa had passed on. When she was small, the three of them trekked across Illinois and Missouri in their wagon, and Allie taught her to read and write. Goldie never stepped inside a school or sat at a school desk, but she did learn lots of tricks of the show business trade from her mother in their dressing room. About the time other youngsters were starting first grade, six-year-old Goldie began dancing in a vaudeville show in St. Louis with her mother, who was performing as Mrs. Klein and Her Dancing Dog. Often her mother's show was booked into a 'wine room' or a beer joint. Later Goldie would explain: "The women had to stay in the back of the old beer joints where they had tables where they could sit and drink with their husbands or somebody else's husband." Allie managed to book herself and her daughter in other small joints in Illinois and Missouri, often as entertainment between acts in a melodrama. In one of the mother-daughter acts, Goldie was dressed up as Jimmy, a raggedy news boy. "You are the real thing, Jimmy," she sang.

John Griffith died when Goldie was fifteen, but even before that Allie and Goldie often traveled alone for work. Outside St. Louis, Allie went to the booking agent looking for work as Madame Russell and her Trained Dogs, and Goldie would find some little singing, dancing or athletic part. After John's death, the two survived, but often they were broke and hungry. Since she'd signed on with the 101, Goldie had sent some of every paycheck home to her mother to help out with her expenses. As exciting as it was riding broncs with a Wild West, it also was the steadiest work Goldie had been able to find, and she realized as angry as she'd been with Allie for sending the cops to retrieve her from the whoopla show, she'd long since forgiven her.

They all turned to look at Lillie. "How 'bout you, Lil, why'd you leave your folks?"

"I wanted to rodeo. Then I liked it so much I never went back." They all turned to look at Melvin. He sheepishly threw his hands up in the air. "Hey, I never had no home to run from." For some unknown reason, maybe just because they all needed to vent the evening's tension, the four of them found his announcement hilarious.

Show people dominated the tables, and jokes, tall tales, and laughter ran through the room. The balmy night air washed through the packed café every time someone opened the front door. Chairs scraped across the wood floor as the weary performers and crew pulled them from table to table, socializing and sharing drinks from the flasks that seemed to be everywhere.

"How's them beans?" Mel asked Harry.

"Good fire in 'em."

"I'da thought you'd been away from Texas so long you didn't care no more for that fire in yur stomick." Mel's cheeks were beginning to glow from the liquor, and his words were starting to slur together.

"My stomick gets restless without frijoles."

"Mine gits restless with 'em."

"Mine gits restless listenin' to you two jaw," Lillie pronounced, putting an end to the chili talk. After their pie and spiked coffee Lillie gave Mel another peck on the cheek, and they all got up to leave.

As they walked back to the show grounds and to the train which was home, Harry and Mel dropped behind so Harry could pull out his flask one last time. The men's voices faded, and Goldie and Lillie found themselves alone. Goldie felt thoroughly relaxed and exhaled a deep, bottomless sigh.

Lillie squeezed her arm. "Homesick?"

"A little now and then."

"Miss your ma?"

"Ah," Goldie paused, thinking. "I never thought I'd miss her, but it's been a long time."

"Yeah, I know, and it always hits you at weird times. They can be hell to live with, and then, boom, you want to see her." They walked a few steps in silence.

"Was your ma in show business?"

"She is. I don't know, I guess she always thought I'd do things different, but show business is what I know best, and I'm good at it." Goldie found explaining her mother to someone else difficult.

Lillie spoke to a spot just over Goldie's left shoulder. "Well, I bet she can't argue with the money you make. My ma sure can't. I bet we make more money than almost any other girl in the country. And we do what we want."

"And we're outa-doors—I'd die if I had to be in a house all the time," Goldie added, thinking about how much she liked working with the horses.

"I know what you mean. And no frilly dresses or sittin' round a table makin' nice to some ol' biddy who doesn't know what she's talkin' about. Or learnin' how to make mayonnaise. Do you know how to make mayonnaise?"

"No," Goldie answered. "I don't. But I read that Lucille Mulhall knows how. She went to a fancy school."

"Well, I guess we went to the school of hard knocks. You know, my ma taught me how to ride, right after I learnt how to walk. You had to know how to ride, couldn't do your chores if you didn't. There never was nothin' she could say when I signed up for the rodeo, 'cause it was her fault anyway. And I thank her every day for what she done for me."

"I think I was always meant to be a cowgirl, even if I wasn't born on a ranch like you, Lillie."

"Hey, it don't matter where you're born. Not out here. Out here, all that matters is that you're a born rider, Goldie. You just gotta watch out for Harry."

"Waddya mean?" Goldie asked her friend, even though she knew what Lillie meant. Just talking about him, Goldie was touched by the little twinge of daring that she felt when Harry grinned at her. She liked flirting with the danger he radiated, and she wasn't afraid of him or any of the cowboys. Being around Harry made her feel grown-up.

"I just mean you're young, and some of the cowboys would like to take advantage, if you know what I mean. You don't want to settle down too soon."

"Why not? I wanna have a husband."

"Hmmm." Lillie stopped walking and turned toward her young friend. "Not all of 'em are honorable, that's all I'm sayin'."

Goldie was silent, thinking about Jane. What Lillie said was true. If all the cowboys were honorable, Jane wouldn't have had to leave the show to get an abortion.

"Lillie?"

"Yes, hon?"

"Are you talking about Jane?"

Lillie was still for a long time. Then she said, "Edith says that Jane is coming back next week."

Goldie didn't look at her friend. She couldn't. "How's she doin'?"

"She's okay. I guess she musta sent Edith a telegram because Edith said she should be ridin' agin by the time she joins up with us. Edith wasn't sure where—but this week for sure."

Goldie didn't know how to ask the other woman what she wanted to know. How did Jane know where to go, what to do? Why did she decide to have an abortion? The other girls said that Jane had to go back to Chicago for the abortion because they didn't know a doctor in New Mexico. It must have been awful to leave the show and friends behind and go through something like that by herself. Goldie shivered. Lillie may have sensed her questions. She threw an arm over Goldie's shoulders and squeezed hard.

"If ever there's anything you want to know, ask Edith." Goldie looked at the ground, nonplussed, and shrugged out from under her friend's arm, but Lillie wanted to make sure Goldie understood, so she reiterated: "Edith knows everything."

Goldie didn't want to talk about Jane or Edith any more. It was good to know that Edith would be able to help, but she knew she would never be in that situation. She wanted to change the subject, so she asked, "When are ya gonna decide between Mel and Oscar? I think you're drivin' 'em nuts."

"That's not a bad thing, is it?"

Goldie laughed. "Which one do you love?"

"Oh, that's the problem. I think I love both of 'em. Probably just 'cause they're causin' such a ruckus. It's awfully romantic, don't you think, to have two men who want to marry me?"

"Romantic, maybe, but don't you think it's dangerous? Are you sure you don't know which one you want to marry?" Goldie found it incomprehensible that her friend didn't prefer one man over the other.

"No, Goldie, I honestly don't know. I think I'd be happy with either one of 'em. Maybe I just haven't met my true love yet. But then how many of us ever do? I mean, meet our true love? From what I hear you've got two boyfriends yourself."

"Oh, you mean—"

"Yep, exactly. I think that Charley Mulhall would be a better catch for you than Harry Walters. Harry's a dangerous character, you know."

"What do you—" Goldie couldn't finish her question because Harry and Melvin caught up with them.

"You gals in a hurry to get back for somethin'?" Melvin gave Lillie a wicked wink. Lillie blushed again, but when Mel reached for her hand she didn't resist.

Harry poked his friend in the shoulder. "Me and Goldie, we'll be weavin' along now—you two don't need us to horn in."

As the other couple disappeared into the dark road behind them, Harry put his hand around the back of Goldie's waist. A lone coyote yipped soulfully, and he was joined by the anxious, ear-piercing cries of six or seven more, drowning out their crunching footsteps. Harry leaned down to kiss her, and she let him, but then she pulled away. *I am never, ever going to have an abortion,* she promised herself. Playfully, she tugged at Harry's shirt sleeve, and gave him another small kiss before starting to walk more quickly down the road toward the yellow train.

I guess that kiss makes him my official boyfriend, she mused as she climbed into her bunk. She wondered briefly about Lillie's comment about Harry being dangerous, but the Wild West show life was hectic, and other events intervened before Goldie would have a chance to think about Harry again.

Three days later, Charley Mulhall and his sister Louise visited the 101 show, and it was two more days before Goldie realized that Harry had disappeared—again. The Mulhalls performed with the show while they were there. The Wild West fans stood in awe when Charley climbed onto the back of a bucking bronco that tossed him in the air and sometimes plunked him into the tanbark. Lucille performed her rope tricks with the 101 men—six of them—twirling and jumping in and out of their ropes, and tossing the swinging loops over 'unsuspecting' riders who happened by. Lucille also showed off her mastery at roping calves, jumping to her feet and flinging her arms above her head as she finished. She was probably the best calf roper in the world, man or woman.

After New Mexico, they finished their shows in Texas, and when the train crossed into Oklahoma the Mulhalls left for their ranch. The 101 performers were all looking forward to the season finale on October 21 in El Reno, Oklahoma. But when they got there, Joe Miller told them the season had been extended, so the long yellow train backtracked to Texas, then turned west to play New Mexico and Arizona again before heading to California.

Lulu Parr posed for a publicity photograph in one of her famously fashionable outfits.

Buffalo Bill Museum and Grave,
Lookout Mountain, Golden, Colorado

Lulu Parr re-joined the troupe, and Goldie loved watching her. A self-made fashion-plate, she wore a cape with contrasting inlaid leather patterns, intricately beaded vests, gauntlets, and arm bands. Her leather skirt matched the cape with more inlaid leather. The next day she was even flashier with the two rows of fringe that hung from colorful beads that encircled her skirt, and her high-top, lace-up boots and hatband that were beaded to match. Goldie thought she had never seen someone so dashing.

On November 8 they arrived in Barstow and finally played their last performances of the season in towns south and east of

Los Angeles. By the time they took down the tents and packed up the last show in Pomona, they had been on the road seven and a half months and had traveled 14,097 miles through twenty-five states.

Just before that very last show of the season the train rumbled down the spur track at the rear of the Sunset Avenue barns, and an overloaded flatcar tipped over and destroyed two wagons. Despite the accident, the crew rallied, and the parade through Venice, just outside the burgeoning metropolis of Los Angeles, already home to 320,000 people, started on time. Called the "Coney Island of the West," Venice's Midway-Plaisance, where the 101 show staged its parade, wound its way along a swimming lagoon. The cowboys and cowgirls riding their prancing horses were just one more spectacle for the crowds wandering through the many new attractions that had recently popped up in Venice, including the Aquarium, the Scenic Railroad ride that carved its way through mountainous terrain, and a Rapids Ride where boats floated through a serpentine canal with the surrounding walls depicting scenes from an Irish castle, the Panama Canal, and the western frontier.

After that final performance of 1912, Joe Miller decided not to take the show back to Oklahoma but to winter in California. Finally, the 101 Wild West was de-rigged and packed up for the winter, and everyone, animals included, found lodging for the next few months in Venice.

The 101's show stock and equipment were quartered on the grounds of the Los Angeles Gun Club. Goldie and her friends, including Harry, who had re-joined the show with no explanation, found rooms at the St. Marks Hotel in Venice. The hotel was in the city's St. Mark's Plaza, a replica of sorts of Venice's Piazza San Marco.

Life slowed down as December arrived, and the 101 crew relaxed, taking in the many amusement rides, exhibits, sideshow freaks, and honky-tonk attractions. Using huge megaphones, barkers enticed the wandering crowds into the tent shows as pickpockets and scam artists tried to separate visitors from their cash in other ways. Or the cowgirls and cowboys walked the almost quarter-mile-long Million Dollar pier with its dance hall, two carousels, the Crooked House fun house, the Grand Electric Railroad, the Starland Vaudeville Theater, and a Panama Canal model exhibit. Many of the cowgirls and cowboys had friends with the Al G. Barnes Wild Animal Circus which also was wintering in Venice, and the performers from both shows spent a lot of time together partying and exploring the town.

At the end of the month, Santa Claus arrived in Venice in a sleigh pulled by four Shetland ponies and passed out presents to masses of children. The palm trees lining the streets were hung with ribbons and streamers, and Goldie and Harry joined their friends in a mass amble to the pier where about a hundred Indians from the 101 had set up camp for a feast of barbecued ox. Four cooks and a team of assistants had spent twenty-four hours preparing the meal and were astonished that the crowd devoured everything in less than an hour.

On New Year's Day, Goldie and Harry were two of the performers who rode with the 101's band to Pasadena for the Tournament of Roses and a big parade called the Rose Parade, which seemed like it would be a good bit of fun. But what really inspired them to go was the chariot race and the possibility that Oscar and Melvin were going to hold their own race afterwards to decide once and for all which one would marry Lillie.

The chariot race didn't have a chance when the crowd learned about the cowboy race. It too was Roman style, and the cowboys stood on the bare backs of their ponies, a trick Goldie was still learning. Oscar was a better bronc rider, and Mel was the more accomplished Roman rider. Harry bet on Mel, and Goldie took a small bet on Oscar.

The night before when everyone had had too much to drink in celebration of the last hours of 1912 Goldie asked Lillie if she really was going to go through with this crazy idea of letting a race decide who she should marry. Lillie just grinned at her, and said, "I think I love both of 'em, and I cain't decide, and I cain't let them keep fightin' over me."

"Maybe if you can't decide, you don't really love either one?" Goldie suggested with a wink.

"Nope, I don't think that's it at all. I never could decide anythin' big. But I want to be married. You know, have kids and live a regular life." Lillie took another drink. In ten minutes a new year would be upon them, and they were shouting to hear each other over the partying crowd. "We'll just see who wins. I'll be happy no matter what!" Goldie wasn't sure she believed her friend who was slurring her words and holding onto Goldie's shoulder to stay upright. Eventually, the cowgirls dragged Lillie off to bed—it was, after all, the last night she'd sleep alone.

The next morning cowboys and cowgirls nursed their hangovers with coffee and pulled their big-brimmed hats low to shade their bloodshot eyes from the bright sunshine. The cowboy band had set up, and they played a few numbers before the race. Oscar and Mel appeared and jumped onto their horses to wild applause from the stands. After two laps around the tournament field accompanied by the frenzied yelling of the spectators in the overflowing stands, Oscar Rixon and his team pulled ahead. He steered his horse to the grandstand and shouted to Lillie, "I've got you, kid!" He bolted into the stands, crashed through the still-cheering fans who clapped him on the back and vehemently shook his hand as he barged past them, gathered the blushing cowgirl in his arms, and carried her back through the crowd to the arena where he planted her on a spare pony he had brought along.

They disappeared in a cloud of dust, and they were married the next day in Venice. Goldie cried at the wedding and laughed and celebrated with her friends at the party afterwards.It finally broke up as the cowboys and cowgirls took aim at the clouds with their six-shooters in a final salute to the couple who already were on their way back to the 101 Ranch in Oklahoma for a honeymoon.

Goldie donned a pair of woolly chaps and posed for a series of studio shots when she was working for the flickers in southern California. She saved the glass plate negatives in a Sancho Panza cigar box in her show trunk alongside her scrapbooks, newspaper clippings, and other mementos.

Kay Turnbaugh

⤖ EIGHT ⤖

Claustrophobic as a Branding Chute

HER HEAD ITCHED UNDER THE SCRATCHY FABRIC of the bonnet, and the heavy shirt they had given her to wear was stuck to her skin in the bright, piercing heat. The too-long and far too-full skirt kept getting caught on her spurs during the four-mile ride from the hotel. She wished she had on her wide-brimmed hat, and her comfortable split riding skirt, but they were told last night that today they would be immigrants. They were up with the sun and dressed in the day's costumes at the hotel before riding single-file up the coast to where the newest one-reeler was being filmed.

Some days she would get to do some trick riding as a double or as an extra. But not usually. Today she would probably be in the background of the scenes, walking in the dust behind a wagon, or some such thing. She missed riding all day—even when it was on a pony trying to relieve itself of her company.

They just had time to dismount and take care of the horses when Jim announced costume changes. No immigrants, today they would be Indians. Most all the girls walked meekly to the changing tent, but Goldie felt more like grumbling. The tent was already hot and stuffy, and the greasy dark makeup they had to put everywhere that wasn't covered by a costume made her feel ridiculous and out of sorts.

"Coulda tol' us last night," she growled as she and Gillian walked out of the big tent. Goldie didn't mind working long hours. She didn't mind putting her body on the line for a trick or a stunt. But she did mind standing around, and she didn't much like having to change clothes all the time for what she saw as someone else's whim. As soon as she stepped into the sun, she had to powder the makeup. They all had to powder their faces every fifteen minutes or so, much more often than when they were riding in the arena, to keep the heavy makeup from streaking in the heat. Goldie wasn't so sure that this was what she'd signed on for, but, for now, it was what she was doing because of the deal Colonel Joe Miller had made with the Bison Moving Picture Company. Colonel Joe told them last week that they had to decide by the end of the next week if they wanted to stay in Los Angeles or go back on the road with the Wild West.

The newly costumed cowgirls-as-Indians started walking toward the cameras.

"They probably didn't know last night," Gillian tried to make the best of their circumstances.

"Well, then, they could'a tol' us this morning, before we rode all the way out here dressed wrong." Goldie's usual smile and good nature were nowhere in sight today.

"Hey, I don't mind. I think it's a hoot bein' in the movies," Gillian called over her shoulder as she ran toward the man who was frantically beckoning to her.

"Did I hear someone call my name?" a devilishly charming cowboy fell in step with Goldie. "Now, my horse, which as I'm sure y'all are familiar, is also named Goldie, and she tol' me that another Goldie was thinkin' about leavin' the movin' picture business so's she can go on the road agin?" Hoot Gibson turned

Hoot Gibson, center, worked for Universal in the 1920s. He starred in many of the fledgling movie industry's westerns.

John Zeransky Collection, Dickinson Research Center, National Cowboy & Western Heritage Museum, Oklahoma City, Oklahoma

the end of the statement into a question. Goldie couldn't help grinning back at Hoot, he always made you smile. He'd been a stuntman the year before, and now he was already a headliner in some of the flickers, but he was still a nice guy, unlike some of the other headliners, and he just oozed charm when he was around the girls.

"Well, I'm still thinkin' on it. I'm not sure I like this movie falderol."

Hoot looked at her with mock astonishment. Goldie cocked her head and pursed her painted lips. "I never did like actin' anyway," she said. Hoot shook his head in mock disbelief. "And, anyway, I'd rather be ridin' than changin' clothes all day long."

"Oh, I agree all right. Nothin' like ridin' all day long and then packin' up and movin' on, just so's you can unpack, set up a show, go paradin', and ride all day long agin'. That is, when you're not spittin' up bark and dirt, or sleepin' on the hard ground. Yep, I'd say them are *joyful* times, to be sure." Goldie thought that for Hoot the flickers might be a better deal than they had been for her. His boyish charm seemed perfectly natural on the screen. And, he got to ride more than she did. He'd made his way in the fledgling movie business by being a dependable stuntman who wasn't afraid of dangerous falls and jumps, and he was a fantastic rider who could double for anyone.

One of the town girls sidled up to the charismatic cowboy. "Hey, Mr. Hoot," she batted her eyelashes at him, "where'd you git that name, anyway?"

"What, don't I look like a ol' hoot owl?"

Goldie had started walking away, but she laughed at the girl's question and stopped to look Hoot up an down, dramatically. "Not particularly," the girl squeaked.

"Ah ha. You're pretty smart," Hoot gave the girl a small smile and winked at Goldie.

"It had somethin' to do with the drugstore that I worked deliveries for, honey," Hoot answered the girl's question sincerely. "Bet you can guess its name." The girl shook her head, so Hoot told her. "Owl Drugs." The girl nodded sagely, still not understanding the connection, and smiled prettily at him before she ran off.

"Hey, Art and I are thinkin' 'bout headin' out to Oregon for that Pendleton rodeo show." Art Acord was Hoot's best pal, and, before hiring on with the Bison, Hoot and Art worked on a Tom Mix one-reeler called *Pride of the Range,* one of the few flickers Goldie had actually seen in a theater. When she saw it, she thought it was obvious Tom Mix was going to be famous. A good day of movie-making for Hoot and Art was when they got to beat each other up. They'd follow that up with a trip to the bar. "You and Harry thinkin' 'bout headin' up there? They got a good purse."

"Dunno—guess we hadn't thought on it."

"Harry still pullin' guard duty?"

"Yep, been doin' it ever' day for a week now." Usually the 101's toughest cowhands were assigned the duty of keeping anyone who wasn't supposed to be there out of the film set. While Goldie walked behind a prairie schooner or sat in front of a tipi, Harry was riding the fence or guarding the gate to the spread near the entrance to Santa Ynez Canyon.

The Bison Moving Picture Company, like all independent filmmakers of the time, was looking for ways to escape harassment from the Patents Trust. A few years earlier, Thomas Edison had organized several film producers into a larger company that recognized Edison as the inventor of the motion picture and agreed to produce films only with his permission. The companies turned their patent claims over to Edison and paid him a royalty fee for the right to produce and distribute films in the United States. Filmmakers who ignored the Motion Picture Patents Company risked harsh penalties, including criminal prosecution and imprisonment. Several filmmakers who didn't join were forced out of business. Others hid out in Cuba, Florida, Louisiana, Texas, New Mexico, and California.

The Bison Moving Picture Company moved to California, hoping to elude the detectives from the Patents Company. If they caught you working, they'd shoot the camera, and cameras were next to impossible to come by. The company found the hills around Los Angeles an ideal place to hide and film at the same time, and an attractive part of their deal with Joe Miller was the armed cowboys from the 101 who could provide security for the young film company. The Millers' cousin, Will Brooks, was put in charge and immediately had fences erected around the twenty-thousand acres of rolling hills covered with oak, chaparral, sage and poppies near Santa Monica. He had posters put up forbidding entrance. Then he scheduled armed cowboys to patrol the fence line.

For its twenty-five-hundred dollars a week, the Bison Moving Picture Company got about seventy-five cowboys,

Tom Mix & 'Duke' go after the Bad Men. Chicago, IL, 1920s ca.

Published by Exhibit Supply Company. John Zeranksy Collection,
Dickinson Research Center, National Cowboy & Western
Heritage Museum, Oklahoma City, Oklahoma

(Next page) Spectators watch a Western being filmed in Santa Ynez Canyon.

Woolaroc Museum, Bartlesville, Oklahoma

twenty-five cowgirls, and twenty-four oxen, some bison and lots of horses, as well as prairie schooners and stagecoaches.

The contract also included thirty-five Oglala Sioux and their squaws from the Pine Ridge Reservation in South Dakota with an interpreter. Using real Indians, instead of white actors or extras dressed like Indians, set the Bison flickers apart from their competition, but the film company also exploited its relationship with the placid Indians to boost ticket sales by advertising that the "dangerous" Indians could hardly be kept from scalping other members of the cast and crew.

None of the Indians was ever given a starring role in the flickers, even though Luther Standing Bear offered to provide script ideas and even volunteered to serve as a language coach for the other Sioux actors. Most of the Indians didn't like the way they were portrayed in the films, but for those who loved riding and performing in front of a camera, working on the flickers was a far better life than the poverty of the reservation. To supplement his income from the film business, Standing Bear also operated an archery concession on the Venice Pier.

When the deal was struck with the Bison Moving Picture Company, the film company adopted a new name in honor of its new partner: the Bison 101. At first Goldie thought it was exciting. Every few days they shot another two-reeler. And Goldie met all the stars: Hoot Gibson, Art Acord, Tex Cooper, Charles Inslee, Princess Mona Darkfeather, and Frank Montgomery, but, truth be told, Goldie was getting bored. She'd been in dozens of the wildly popular flickers, but the work was just as exhausting as being on the road, and she missed the audience, the applause which always made the hair on the back of her neck prickle, and the physical rush of a live performance.

They worked the same long hours as when they were on the road with the show, no matter what the job, from before sunrise until long after the sun had crept back under the horizon. But at least when they were on the road, they were always moving, always doing something. For Goldie, being in the flickers involved too much of doing nothing but waiting on other people.

Hours later, she was still thinking about whether to stay in California and stake her future on the moving pictures, which were taking the country by storm, or to return to the road when the director called through his megaphone for the stuntmen to assemble. It had been another long day and dark for a couple of hours, but that didn't stop production. As long as the prop men could line up cars and big sheets of reflectors to send the light from their headlights to where the cameras needed it, the filming continued. No matter that everyone—actors, stuntmen, extras, ponies, and drivers—was bone tired.

Goldie was standing near a tipi, waiting for the director to tell them what to do next. She thought about what Hoot had said earlier. "They were gonna drive the horses off a cliff today, but the boys said no, so after a bunch of negotiatin', now they're just gonna all fall off their ponies in a pile and then roll down the cliff." Hoot's sly grin didn't reveal if he was kidding or not, but knowing how little respect the movie people had for the stock or the people working for them, Goldie had decided it probably wasn't a joke.

"With the horses?" Goldie knew it would be a dangerous stunt, and even more dangerous if the men were rolling down a hill with horses possibly rolling over them.

Her reverie was shattered by the real-time scream of a horse that been seriously injured. She didn't want to see what had happened because it was surely bad, but when everyone else ran towards the sound, she did too. Many good horses were killed during the filming of the early westerns, before the Humane Society got powerful enough to stop the use of the stationary and flying W's, where a horse was stopped dead by a wire configured around his legs which when pulled by the rider would cause him to instantly fall and drop the cowboy on his back into the dust. The cowboys hated the use of the W and had tried to stop it, but so far film directors hadn't heard them.

The stunts were just as hard on the cowboys who would spend a very long day falling off their horses onto already aching shoulders and sore spines. Accidents and broken bones were common, even though the cowboys were some of the world's best riders who were skilled in sliding out of the stirrups and throwing themselves clear of their ponies. Safety was not on anyone's mind—directors were only interested in cowboys—and cowgirls—who were willing to put their lives and bodies on the line for the sake of a serial.

Goldie offered a little prayer for whoever was involved, and when she heard the shot she knew a horse had been put out of its misery. She saw an automobile's headlights bumping toward the scene, and the prop men moved the reflectors that had been bouncing the light from the headlights onto the treacherous hillside where the cowboys had been racing their ponies in a tight pack. She knew the automobile was going to be hauling a man to the hospital instead of a camera around the dark hills. Someone would be passing the hat soon enough to cover the man's hospital bills, or, if he was lucky enough to have the movie company pay his hospital bill, the collection would help cover other bills he wouldn't be able to pay while he was recovering. Thank goodness she always carried a few coins with her.

And thankfully Harry was riding the fence line where he was out of harm's way.

～ NINE ～

Reaching for the Stars

FRESH HORSES AND RIDERS HAD ARRIVED from the ranch in Oklahoma. Goldie said good-bye to her friends who had decided to remain in Los Angeles with the flickers. She and her fellow wanderers boarded the train for Bakersfield.

For fourteen days before they actually got on the road, they had performed in more than a dozen southern California cities. The only time the show stood still was to play three days straight at Praeger Park in Los Angeles. The Olympic Games Committee got a percentage of the advance ticket sales and had a ticket wagon on the showgrounds. The show hosted some of the athletes who were going to the Olympic games in Stockholm, Sweden, showing their skills in a few track and field contests. Before they left southern California, Jack Hoxie, a future Hollywood star, joined the show.

It was an unusual season in that all the shows were west of Ohio with no appearances in any of the larger metropolitan areas. Less than a month later, when the Titanic sank on April 15, the show had played all over northern California and

Nevada. Crowds jammed the grandstands in Idaho, Utah, Montana, and Washington. Then they traveled to British Columbia and Victoria, back to the United States, and then back to Canada. During the late summer and fall the show traveled to the Dakotas, Minnesota, Iowa, Nebraska, Wisconsin, Illinois, Indiana, Ohio, Kentucky, Missouri, Kansas, Oklahoma, Louisiana, Texas, Kansas, back to Oklahoma, and Arkansas.

In Texas, Harry vanished from the show, and Goldie didn't see him the rest of the season. In Wisconsin, the train struck a spread rail and five cars were demolished. Five valuable arena horses and five team horses were killed, and thirty horses were injured. Joe Miller contacted the Chicago Union Stockyards, and a few hours later horses from the stockyards were on their way. Although the show went on, the accident was hard on everyone, especially Colonel Joe, who always mourned the loss of any of his stock.

Large crowds came to see the Indians, the Mexican vaqueros, and the Imperial Russian Cossacks. *The 101 Ranch Wild West has more railroad cars, more wagons, more seats, more horses, more buffaloes and long-horned steers, more cowboys, more cowgirls, more Indians, more Mexicans...* declared the show's program. It referred to the *equine outlaws* and to the *bucking bronchos [sic] who hate mankind and were demons incarnate, a menace to life and limb.* The cowboys and cowgirls were *keen-eyed and clean-hearted...grown brown and strong on the tremendous stretches of Oklahoma range-land owned by the Miller Brothers.* The Indians were referred to as *pure blooded people of the wild old days.*

On the ranch and on the road, the curious crowds were encouraged to walk through the Indian camps thick with smoke from the cooking fires. Although they were some of the show's biggest stars, the Indians were paid far less than the other performers, which some people said was exploitation, and critics questioned the motives of the Wild West showmen—the Millers, Pawnee Bill, and Buffalo Bill. Others pointed out that the Millers provided their medical care, cattle for slaughter, water and feed for their ponies. When they went on the road with a 101 show, the Indians brought their own canvas lodges and basic clothing, and the Millers provided their headdresses and moccasins. Each Indian man appearing with the Millers' Wild West received five dollars in cash each week. The women received four dollars.

Every day, the "blood-thirsty redskins," many of whom were now Goldie's friends, attacked settlers or stagecoaches and were slaughtered by the cowboys and cowgirls. Were the shows just reinforcing the negative stereotypes and racial myths of Indians as "wild" and "heathen savages?" Goldie never knew which side to take. She counted many of the Sioux who traveled with the show as her friends. The Indians themselves hardly ever complained, and other than the few critics who were quoted occasionally in the newspapers, no one in the shows or their audiences questioned how much the Indians were paid or the way they were portrayed. The fact was that the Indians from Oklahoma, especially the Poncas, seemed to love the dancing, riding, whooping, and performing for themselves and others. And the crowds came in throngs to marvel at the 'authentic' Indians, a part of American history and culture that few had ever seen before.

Another hit with audiences was the addition of horse polo, played with balls about six feet in diameter. The cowboys and cowgirls ran their horses, with buffers on their chests, into the balls. Then the cowboys added auto polo to their repertoire, leaving their horses tied outside the arena while they competed from speeding automobiles.

Finally the season came to a close. Eleven days after Woodrow Wilson was elected president, the 101 played its last performance of the tour at the Arkansas State Fair. Everyone was whipped after 421 performances and 17,280 miles through twenty-two states and three Canadian provinces.

The 101 train made its final stop in its hometown of Bliss. The weary performers and crew unpacked one last time, sorting equipment for storage or repair. Goldie saddled her horse and rode from the station to the massive 101 headquarters. She was ready to sleep for a week.

Many of the cowgirls headed home to see their families, but not Goldie. She decided to stay and work on the ranch. One of her jobs that off-season was picking cotton. Most of the bolls opened after the first frost, and during the next few weeks, Goldie, along with the other pickers, slung the long canvas bag over her shoulder, put on her cloth gloves and knee pads, and headed to the fields where they plucked cotton from the bolls until her fingers, arms, and shoulders ached and she could no longer feel her knees. The full wagons were driven back to the gin where a large vacuum tube sucked up the cotton and extracted the seeds and hulls. The cotton came out in bales wrapped in burlap. The cotton-picking season didn't end until the new year arrived.

When she could, Goldie practiced trick riding. She still hadn't seen Harry since he had vanished from the show many months ago, and she tried not to think about him. Other cowboys flirted with her, and she flirted with them. If Harry couldn't stick around, she guessed it meant he was no longer her boyfriend.

As the rest of the country was celebrating the arrival of 1913, Goldie and the other 101 Wild West performers started preparing for a new season. She figured she'd better go see her mother before the non-stop schedule of life on the road began, so she took a couple of weeks off and boarded the train that would take her from Bliss to Chicago.

Her mother was still in show business, working with her dogs in vaudeville, and living in a flat near downtown Chicago. The train ride home was awfully tame compared to the gambling and drinking on the show train, but Goldie found people to talk to who enjoyed her stories about cowgirling with the

101. However, it was the telegram that she kept pulling out of her purse and carefully unfolding to read again and again that kept her occupied the most.

"That's just foolishness," her mother declared when Goldie proudly showed her the telegram. Of course, that was the reaction Goldie had been expecting, even though she was hoping for something else.

"But this is the big time, ma. This is my dream."

"Oh, come on, Goldie. You've been in show business long enough to know these things don't just happen—"

"Yes, they do. They do happen," Goldie was close to tears, but she managed to control her voice and asked Allie defiantly, "Aren't you gong to say congratulations?"

"No—"

"Now, Ma, I'm gonna do this, and there ain't nothin' you can do to stop me."

"Why would he make an offer like that to someone he don't know? How'd he ever hear of you? Huh? It jus' don't make sense."

"Sure it does. The Miller Brothers are famous, and I been ridin' with 'em for a while now." Then Goldie had another thought. "Maybe he saw one of those flickers I was in." Or, maybe, she thought to herself, he had talked to the Mulhalls. Charley had told her last time she saw him that she had become a really good rider, and Louise had nodded her agreement. If the Mulhalls thought she was good, that had to mean something. And they knew Buffalo Bill. Well, the whole world knew Buffalo Bill. He was probably the most famous person in the world—he'd played for the queen of England. He'd been in theatrical plays and flickers, and he had had his own show forever—the original and the most famous of all the Wild Wests. And before that he'd been an Indian scout and a buffalo hunter, and he'd won the Medal of Honor. She couldn't turn this down. Everyone knew who Buffalo Bill was and wanted to see his shows. *No, she couldn't turn this down.*

The Buffalo Bill Wild West show grounds in Europe, ca. 1891.

"I don't think so. It's just foolishness, that's all," Allie shook her head as she repeated herself and stomped into the kitchen. Goldie looked at the door in disbelief. She couldn't say no. She took a step after Allie, anxious to convince her, but realized she was too angry—anyway, it was her life—*I'm going to be somebody, and this is my chance at the big-time.*

"I'm goin' out," she yelled at the door. "To the telegraph office. I'm gonna take the job."

Her only regret would be leaving all her friends at the 101, especially the cowgirls. They were close, like the sisters she had never had, but this was her big chance, and she wasn't going to let it gallop past her, no matter what. Besides, everyone in the business moved around from show to show. Probably some of the people she'd been working with on the 101 would move on to the Buffalo Bill Wild West with her.

Buffalo Bill Historical Center, Cody , Wyoming; Gift of Thomas P. Isbell, P.69.1512

When she arrived at the telegraph office, breathless because she had almost run the entire way, she wired a letter to Buffalo Bill Cody, the Buffalo Bill Cody, that she would accept his offer to be a Lady Bronc Rider for the upcoming season.

Buffalo Bill wanted her to meet the show in Philadelphia for rehearsals before the opening of the new Convention Hall. But the trains were sidelined due to the catastrophic flood in Dayton, Ohio, in March which killed four hundred and twenty-eight people and destroyed twenty thousand homes. Just when it seemed hopeless, and her mother was telling her that it was a sign that she shouldn't go, she received another telegram from Colonel Cody. He had obtained special access for her to ride the train with the workers who were finding and repairing the tracks through the rubble left by the floods. So it was just Goldie and one other woman, another cowgirl named Rose Henderson, on

Pawnee Bill Lilly and Buffalo Bill Cody created the Pawnee Bill Wild East and Buffalo Bill Wild West. Goldie rode with the Two Bills show in 1913.

Buffalo Bill Museum and Grave, Lookout Mountain, Golden, Colorado

the long, arduous trip east. The two women became friends, playing cards and chatting away the tedious hours. The train stopped almost every few feet, and then it followed the workers who cleared the way. Sometimes Goldie and Rose got off and walked behind the slow-moving mass of metal.

Finally they made it.

As she stepped onto the platform in Philadelphia, a tall, stately man in buckskins strode toward her. Another man behind him looked familiar, but Goldie's eyes were riveted on the great man with the well trimmed goatee and shoulder-length white hair.

"Now, you must be Miss Goldie," he pronounced in sonorous tones, taking her hand in both of his, and Goldie noticed his beautiful, even teeth and his radiant smile.

"Yes, sir, I am. It's wonderful to meet you, Colonel Cody, and...oh, my!" Harry was the other man. She didn't think she'd ever see him again. He'd disappeared from the 101, and he'd never written. Granted, it wasn't easy to write to show people on the road, but you could always put a notice in the Billboard, and he hadn't even done that. And now here he was...with Buffalo Bill.

That was just the beginning of the surprises.

She'd been with the show about a week when Colonel Cody asked to see her. She had hoped that she would know some of the performers riding with the Two Bills show this season, and sure enough, she and Lulu Parr were the lady bronc riders. Lulu was a bit stand-offish, but at least she introduced Goldie to the other girls, and just the fact that Goldie had ridden with Lulu, such a famous cowgirl, gave Goldie instant acceptance and respect with the other performers. She had spent her time so far with the show getting to know the bucking horses, each with its peculiar ways of upending its riders, and practicing the tricks she would be performing. She had had just enough time in Chicago to sew a new riding skirt, and she was particularly proud of its lengthy fringe. She was as ready as she could be for the new season, and she assumed the Colonel wanted to talk to her about the schedule or the broncs.

They were meeting in the lobby of the hotel where the performers were staying until they boarded the train that would be home for the next few months. Buffalo Bill stood up when she approached him and held the chair next to his for her. She wasn't used to that kind of chivalry.

"Now, Goldie," the Colonel began as he took a sip of bourbon from a small glass sitting on the little table next to his chair. "Harry here tells me that you're to be married. And I thought I might like to give you a grand wedding. Would you like that?"

He might as well have shot her. Married? What in the world did Harry tell him? Goldie turned away from the great man, pretending to look for something in her purse and trying to stifle her surprise. Her mother had tried to tell her something wasn't right about Buffalo Bill's telegram. Well, this was it. And now a lot of things made more sense.

Even though she was a newcomer to the show, she'd already learned that all was not well with the Colonel's business. He'd lost millions of dollars and was in debt, which was why he'd had to join with Pawnee Bill and his Wild East Show. She'd even learned how to ride the elephants in the Wild East Show because everyone was expected to do what they could to help out. And, the Colonel was no longer the daring young man who had made the Wild West famous. At the age of sixty-seven, he was getting old, and his health was declining. He had announced that, for the first time in thirty years, he would not be riding horseback in the show. Instead, he would be in a fancy trap behind a team of spirited horses. This was another of his 'farewell' tours, and Goldie had been wondering if it might truly be his last. Although rumors always flew through the cast and crew, everyone who worked for Cody admired him and believed that if anyone could pull himself back up to stardom and millions in box office receipts, that person was the legendary William F. Cody, known in show business and around the world as Buffalo Bill. He had first announced his retirement at the end of the 1910 season, and now he and Pawnee Bill had a plan to do two more years of farewell tours, stopping at every city Buffalo Bill had ever played, but only once. Cody was confident he and his partner would clear a million dollars.

What the show people working for him didn't understand was just how disastrous the 1912 season had been. Competition from the 101 was stiff, with the 101 doing its best to put Buffalo Bill out of business by staying one step ahead of Cody's show, playing cities on Cody's scheduled route before Cody arrived. And, hardly anyone with the show knew that Cody's mining investments weren't paying off at all, in fact, they were draining the great man of more and more of his quickly diminishing money every day. So the Colonel came out of retirement again in 1913 for one more season, this season, financed in part by a loan from Harry Tammen of The Denver Post.

At the moment though, he didn't look like a man who was down on his luck and trying to save his show. He was an august figure with his flowing white hair, his tall boots and erect posture.

Goldie knew show business and she knew that a wedding during a show would be a good draw, and, of course, she wouldn't say no, but she sure wished she'd had some say in the matter. She'd certainly have her say with Harry.

"I was thinking that Madison Square Garden would be the place to do it." Buffalo Bill took a puff from his pipe and wagged his finger at her. "Well, girl, what do you think?"

"That would be wonderful, sir, thank you."

"All right then. That's settled. You'll need a special outfit, so you just ask some of the Sioux women if they'll do some beading for you. Think about making something with color, maybe a nice red, we want everyone to see the bride." He waved her away.

"And, Goldie, darlin'—"

"Yes, sir?"

"Congratulations, girl."

"Thank you, sir."

How could Harry do this to her? When he disappeared the last time, she had done her best to forget him. Now she knew how the Colonel had heard of her. It was Harry. He got her this job with Buffalo Bill by promising the old man that there was a wedding in their future. She could hardly think straight as she walked slowly back upstairs to her room.

Well, so what if Harry got her the job? It was hers now, and it could be her big break. And maybe it meant that he really wanted to be with her. But she couldn't help being angry with him. It was her life. Without even being aware that she was crying, she wiped away the tears.

As angry as she was with Harry, she could feel excitement creeping into her emotions and taking over. She was going to be married. She had to tell her mother.

⟿ TEN ⟾

Steppin' Up

NOT ONLY DID SHE HAVE A WEDDING to think about, but she
had two performances a day to keep up with. And then there
was the publicity for the show. Cody had arranged for the cowgirls to be interviewed by the newspapers in New York about
just about anything. Often, he invented a story that he knew
would appeal to an east coast audience. Hardly any of his stories
were based on even a shred of truth.

One of the stories Goldie clipped out of the newspaper for her
scrapbook ran a picture of her underneath the headline: *Cowgirls
Can't See Why 5th Ave. Girls Dress as if Run Over by a Truck.*

*Miss Goldie Griffith, only woman who ever applied for the job
of policewoman in San Francisco and got it, twisted her pretty face
into a wry look of puzzlement.*

'Whew-w-w!' *she cried.* 'It's easier patrolling a beat in 'Frisco
than trying to cross Fifth Avenue any afternoon!'* Although Goldie
had applied to be a policewoman in San Francisco, she was
never hired, but that didn't stop her from embellishing the incident for publicity for the Wild West.

When the Buffalo Bill Wild West was in New York, Goldie was sent to the police station to 'look after' a starving horse that had been found. Cody told the newspaper that she was the daughter of a neighbor rancher of Cody's in Wyoming and that she was taking the horse home to the ranch. She cut her picture from the publicity stunt out of the newspaper and pasted it in her scrapbook.

The Sterling family

Arline Palmer, who describes herself as a 'lady Cossack rider' and tears over the tanbark like a small whirlwind, thinks modern clothes prevent exercise, and that lack of exercise is what causes most of the ills flesh is heir to.

Arline is about as big as a pint cup, but her small body is sturdy and hard as nails. She would rather ride a horse backward, forward, upside down and downside up than go to a million pink teas. Her hair is the color of a wild western sunset and she has a pair of dimples that a society bud would give her best crystal-embroidered frock to possess.

'We girls,' she says, 'make it a study even out on the plains to look as pretty as possible.'

Reporter Zoe H. Beckley quoted cowgirl Lillian Compton saying that cowgirls are far from the rough-and-tumble tomboys that many easterners think them. *She prefers to draw no odious comparisons, but she thinks the girl of the plains can hold her own when it comes to modesty in dress and manners. 'We keep ourselves wholesome and healthy and happy by exercise and friendship with natural things—earth and wind and weather and horses...'* said Miss Compton. *'I may be wrong, but it seems to me there is a good deal of energy worked off in the east, and perhaps in all big cities, through mad clothes and social excitement. All girls are at heart alike. It is the surroundings that make them grow different. The trouble is in too much sameness...'*

The cowgirls didn't have to worry much about sameness in New York. They definitely stood out in any crowd of city folks.

What they were worried about was that the city of New York had declined to issue a permit for the show's parade. To their surprise, on the first Saturday night in New York, Colonel Cody told the cowgirls, "You girls rest up tonight, because we're gonna to do a big parade tomorrow." The girls all looked at each other, but no one said anything. No one ever talked back to the Colonel, even though they all knew that he had been denied a permit to parade on Fifth Avenue.

Buffalo Bill met the cowgirls in the morning. With him were some of the Indians and a few cowboys. Everyone was dressed out for a parade, but it couldn't be a parade, thought Goldie, because there was no band and no wagons. Cody told them to spread out, "so's we won't look like we're paradin'. We're gonna see the sights. Come on, girls, look pretty."

Cody pulled his buggy up next to each of the cowgirls and told them in a low enough voice that no one else could hear, "We're goin' to Grant's Tomb. If you can, ride on up the steps. We'll be sure to get in the newspapers if you can do that." Since Grant's Tomb attracted more visitors than even the Statue of Liberty, it was a good choice for publicity for the Wild East and Wild West.

Goldie looked back at the thirty-two-story-high minaret-like tower and the spinning statue of Diana as they left Madison Square Park and the arena where they would be performing and where she would be married. Around her, the streets were crammed with people out enjoying one of the first warm days of spring. The Colonel had arranged for a few reporters to ride with them, and they flirted openly with the cowgirls.

As word spread ahead of them, more crowds lined the street and applauded each of the cowgirls, dressed like every Easterner's dream of the West in fringed, supple lambskin or calfskin outfits, loaded with beads that clicked with every movement and twinkled in the sunlight. Goldie loved her new big black hat that she had proudly purchased in St. Louis with a saved-up dollar. It provided ample shade for her eyes and face from the bright sunlight, and as Popcorn, her horse for the day, pranced down the street, she thought: *This is so much better than making those flickers.* The beaded fringe on her glove swayed back and forth when she raised her hand and waved at her admirers. She clicked to Popcorn who liked to show off for the crowd as much as the girl on his back, and he began high-stepping in front of the clapping throng. The reporters who had joined the procession walked and ran alongside the horses with their pads of paper and pencils and lots of questions for the cowgirls. It was a seven-mile trip to the monument, and as Goldie approached, she could see that the crowds that had come to see the marble and granite tribute to President Grant were now streaming outside to watch the first performers to arrive at the monument's base.

Ahead was the grand staircase leading up to the colossal columns and the entrance to the tomb. The Indian Carlo Miles, Colonel Cody's short, stocky valet, paused next to her just before he prodded his horse into a fast trot. "Come, Goldie. Look, no one sees. Follow me." Goldie's horse didn't take too much nudging to follow the gallant valet who wanted his employer, whom he adored, to play to packed audiences while they were in New York City. And Carlo was right. No one realized what they were doing until they were at the bottom of the stone steps, and then it was too late. Carlo prodded his horse up the first couple of steps. Popcorn took one look at the imposing staircase and tried to turn around, but Goldie turned his head and patted his neck, urging him ahead. He lunged at the bottom step, and once he'd landed his feet, he charged ahead, pouncing at each step and occasionally skipping one. In some ways it was like riding one of the bucking ponies. At first, Goldie held her breath, but as Popcorn lunged again and again at the stairs, she started breathing again, although she didn't dare look up until they were at the top.

She liked Popcorn; they trusted each other and seemed to have an unspoken agreement that they could work together like long-time partners. She worked with several different trained horses that belonged to the Wild West, but Popcorn was her favorite, and she was glad she was riding him today.

At the top, the two ponies wanted nothing more than to start back down to earth, but she and Carlo managed to get the anxious horses to weave around the columns so they could take

Carlo Miles, Buffalo Bill's valet who rode up the steps of Grant's Tomb with Goldie, was a pretty fancy dresser himself. Here he wears leather chaps with metal ornamentation and fringe, a cowboy hat, leather gloves, a bandana and cowboy boots.

Denver Public Library, Western History Collection, Z-7479

a few minutes to wave their hats at the cheering fans who had gathered along the sides and at the bottom of the massive staircase. Goldie was having fun. Popcorn did a spin that almost unseated her, and she let him start back down. Going down was terrifying. She was frightened that Popcorn might slip and fall on the polished stone—both of them could be hurt badly. She gulped and then heard a roar from the crowd at something Carlo, dressed in his tribe's finest, and his horse, Big Ears, had done. She remembered—she was performing. So, in spite of her terror, she sat up straighter and smiled at the jubilant fans who were clapping and cheering for every step the horses attacked and won.

Like all the Wild West mounts, Popcorn and Big Ears were accustomed to crowds and applause. What they weren't used to was the immense stone staircase in the middle of New York City. When they finally clattered to the landing, Goldie made Popcorn do another spin for the adoring fans. She needed to regain some of her composure for the last frightening set of steps, but Popcorn did not want to stay on those stairs any longer than absolutely necessary. She nudged him down and did her best to make it look like they did this all the time. She could feel his relief, and she was sure he could feel hers, when they clattered down the last few stairs. They had done it! Goldie couldn't stop grinning, and the crowd couldn't stop clapping and exclaiming about the audacity of the two riders, an Indian and a cowgirl.

It seemed like the whole police department had arrived by the time she and Carlo reached the bottom and rode into the middle of the adoring crowd. Colonel Cody was standing in the back of his buggy, leaning on his walking stick but looking as grand as ever, talking to the police officer who seemed to be in charge. He waved Carlo and Goldie over to them. "You know, I told you not to do that," he said sternly in a loud enough voice that the police officers could hear him. "You know better than that."

Like Goldie, Prairie Rose Henderson rode bucking broncos in the Wild Wests. Here she's pictured on "Brandy" at the Pendleton, Oregon, Roundup in 1922.

Published by Pendleton Drug Co., Photographic Study Collection, Dickinson Research Center, National Cowboy & Western Heritage Museum, Oklahoma City, Oklahoma

"Yes, sir," said Goldie.

"Yes, sir," said Carlo.

"All right then, we'd better head back. We have a show to put on." She knew the Colonel had been just making a show of telling her and Carlo that he had told them not to ride up the steps to Grants Tomb—he had too big a heart to ever bawl out anyone who worked for him—he had to do it so the show didn't get in trouble with the police.

Before they started back to Madison Square Garden, all the cowgirls, cowboys, and Indians lined up for a photograph in front of Grant's Tomb. Above them was a sign that read: Let Us Have Peace.

"Come and see us at the Madison Square Garden, folks," the Colonel boomed over and over to the crowd as he turned the buggy around to leave. "Bring the children. It's a show you won't forget. A true depiction of the Wild West in all its glory! Bring the aunts, bring the uncles. Come see us!"

Goldie shook her head when he exhorted the children to come to the show. Many of these children couldn't afford to come to the show, but she knew the kind-hearted Colonel would be giving several free shows for children in orphan homes and others who couldn't otherwise afford to come. The Colonel had such a soft spot for children that anytime he saw a couple of small boys lying on their bellies with their heads under the edge of the big top, trying to get a glimpse of the fantastic show inside, he would pull them out by their pants legs. And then he would walk them around to the front of the tent and tell the ticket taker to let them in for free.

Crowds lining the street welcomed them back down Fifth Avenue and all the way to the arena. It had been a long day, but one that Goldie would never forget. It would become one of her favorite stories, and it did make the next day's newspapers, just as Buffalo Bill knew it would.

A few days later an extra performance of the Two Bills' show was scheduled. Colonel Cody and the French stage star and now film star Sarah Bernhardt had been friends since Buffalo Bill's visit to Paris in 1888, and now they were both playing in New York, but they hadn't found a chance to get together. So Cody ordered a special matinee performance and invited the members of the Sarah Bernhardt Company to the show.

Goldie was exceedingly grateful that she was working for someone as great as Buffalo Bill, and that he was taking her wedding, which was just a few days away, very seriously, consulting with her almost every day about some detail or other. In the weeks since Goldie had accepted Buffalo Bill's offer to host her wedding during a show, she and Harry had hardly spoken. The show kept them both busy, and when they did see each other, it seemed that Harry wasn't interested in hearing about the wedding plans. His disinterest confused Goldie and left her tearful.

But one of the cowgirls told her that Harry's behavior was normal for a cowboy—none of them liked making plans for social events. So Goldie stopped worrying about Harry and started enjoying her few remaining days as a single girl. She thought it had to be just about the most glorious spring ever in New York.

Unfortunately, those glorious days came to an end the day before her wedding when she was thrown off her horse and into the grandstands.

⤞ ELEVEN ⤝

Straight out of a Fairy Tale

AFTER HARRY'S VISIT TO THE HOSPITAL and his pronounce-
ment that she was healed enough to continue with the wedding,
everything happened fast. Colonel Cody sent a car to bring her
from the hospital to Madison Square Garden, and Goldie
arrived at the arena just minutes before the photographer. There
was no time to change into her fancy red leather wedding outfit
with the beaded steers' heads and long fringe before the photographs were taken.

Harry helped her onto her horse. She wasn't sure she was
going to be able to swing her leg over the saddle, but Harry
pushed her up so fast she didn't have a chance to complain
about the pain. She felt a little nauseous, but there she was, sitting on her horse. They were under the grandstands, and the
show had already started in the arena. Harry was on her right,
Eva, her maid of honor, was on her left. Buffalo Bill was next to
Eva, and Pawnee Bill was next to Harry. "So this must be the
bride," said the Reverend Ryan, the preacher Buffalo Bill had
found to do the ceremony. Ryan briefly shook Goldie's hand. It
hurt to lean down to him, but Goldie didn't want to be rude to

Your Presence is Requested
At the Marriage of
Miss Goldie Griffith,
Lady Athlete, Showgirl, and Broncho Rider
to
Mr. Harry Walters,
Trick Roper and Bronc-Buster
at the
Madison Square Garden Arena
May Ninth, Nineteen-Hundred and Thirteen.
Hosts:
William F. "Buffalo Bill" Cody
Gordon "Pawnee Bill" Lillie
Entertainment to Follow by the Combined
Buffalo Bill and Pawnee Bill Wild West Shows
of World Renown.
In Live Attendance:
Cowboys, Cowgirls, Genuine Indians, and
Rough Riders
of Splendid Accomplishment.

Goldie's wedding invitation

The Sterling family

the man who was going to perform her wedding ceremony. She sat back up in the saddle, the reverend opened his book and stood before the mounted wedding party, and the photographer's bulb flashed.

The photographer retreated, and Harry helped her dismount before he jumped back on his horse. The wedding wasn't until the quadrille, so she had time to change into her new wedding outfit. She limped towards the tent, hoping one of the other cowgirls would be able to help her. She couldn't lift her arms above her head and wondered how she would pin her hair. She'd managed to get a few pins in before the photograph, but she needed to do a better job before riding full speed across the arena.

Thankfully, Eva had ducked out of the stagecoach hold-up scene and was waiting for her. They had to be quick. Goldie gulped down a couple of swallows of the laudanum the doctor had given her before she left the hospital. "Take this when you need it. But be careful, I wouldn't suggest taking it and then riding a horse—or driving an automobile." Goldie was pretty sure she wouldn't be driving an automobile, and she decided against telling the doctor she was getting married in a few hours on horseback. She was sure she wouldn't need the little bottle, but she took it anyway to be polite. She was tough enough to ride bucking broncos, and she'd spent much of the last two years bloody and bruised from her falls, how bad could this be? After getting on her horse for that damn photograph, she knew how bad it could be, and she welcomed the soothing liquid as it slid down her throat. Ten minutes later, Eva helped Goldie onto her horse. This time, it didn't hurt as bad. The laudanum had calmed her stomach, and her head actually felt clearer. The doctor's little bottle was working its magic.

As the cowboy band played a rousing march from the Civil War, Goldie and Eva reined their horses toward the arena. Goldie's outfit was heavy, but it was beautiful, and it was showy. Hundreds of beads of all colors swung from the fringe, and the black and white ones that had been beaded into steers' heads on the rich red leather by some of her Sioux women friends reflected the arena lights, sending twinkling sparks into the night air. Everything on her red wedding outfit was fringed and beaded: two layers on her skirt, her sleeves, her shoulders, and her gloves. Even her boots gleamed, and her big-brimmed black hat shaded her eyes from the lights.

From the moment she spurred her pony into a full gallop and pulled him up in a small cloud of dust next to Harry, it seemed like she was riding on a wave of tumultuous emotion. She was delighted and eager to be a bride. Her apprehensions when Buffalo Bill told her he'd give her a dream wedding had vanished. Her mother's misgivings and doubts about Harry seemed farfetched—she and Harry were the perfect couple, and it was her destiny to be married during this Buffalo Bill show. She wanted to have children with Harry. Not right away, of course, but when she couldn't ride bucking broncos anymore. Right now, they needed both her and Harry's pay to make it, but someday, when they couldn't ride bucking broncos in shows like this anymore, Harry would take care of her and they would live in a real house, maybe on a ranch, and have a family.

The band finished playing, and the crowd in the grandstands hushed, waiting for Reverend Ryan to start. A cowhand stood beside him, ready to hold the megaphone to the preacher's lips so everyone in the stands could hear.

(Next page) The official photo of Goldie's wedding didn't show Buffalo Bill. Harry is at left, then Goldie, Eva Fisher, and Pawnee Bill. Reverend Ryan, standing in front of them, performed the ceremony. This photo was probably taken before the ceremony itself because Goldie is not wearing her wedding outfit, and the group isn't in the middle of the arena.

Buffalo Bill Museum and Grave,
Lookout Mountain, Golden, Colorado

The newlywed Mrs. Goldie Walters posed for this photograph.

Buffalo Bill Museum and Grave, Lookout Mountain, Golden, Colorado

Under her, her pony trembled. In front of them were the packed grandstands, and it felt like all the eight thousand people were looking at her.

Her breath came in short rasps. The hair on the back of her neck prickled, and she didn't dare take her eyes off the preacher as he said his part. When she and Harry said their "I do's," Harry reached for her hand, and the crowd stood stomping, whistling, cheering, and applauding. She was too sore for Harry to pull her over to his horse, as they had originally planned before her accident. Instead he leaned over and kissed her. Behind them, the throng of cowgirls, cowboys, and Indians had gathered from the all the acts in other parts of the arena, and they spurred their ponies in unison. They rode in furious circles around the wedding party, whooping and shooting blanks in the air. A few pairs of old shoes were thrown upwards too, for good luck. Goldie blinked back tears. Still holding hands, she and Harry rode to the stands where Goldie's family waited to greet them with glasses of champagne and hearty congratulations. As the smoke from the gunfire cleared, a luminous half moon the color of a just-sliced peach popped over the top of the grandstands.

It was the most perfect May evening in New York. Humid, but not sticky like it would be in the next few summer months. The crisp early evening air gently dried the tears on her cheeks as she and Harry raised their glasses of champagne. She was surrounded by her friends and family, and the most famous person in the world, Buffalo Bill, had just given her away in a storybook wedding. She knew she would forever remember Colonel Cody's resonant "I do" when the preacher asked who gave this woman to this man. That was the moment she'd been aching to achieve all her life—to be somebody. She'd made it. She'd made herself a cowgirl, she'd learned how to ride, and now she was married and part of the most famous show on earth. After the show, Buffalo Bill Cody himself was going to host her reception in his personal tent. She didn't know anyone else who had achieved that honor.

And Harry was pretty famous himself. She glanced at her new husband, a well known cowboy who had ridden with all the famous shows and worked as a stunt rider in the flickers. Two glasses of champagne had loosened his usual taciturn expression. He was smiling at her mother. Now that she and Harry were married, Goldie figured her mother would have to learn to at least get along with her new son-in-law. And, Goldie wondered, would she like her new mother-in-law? Harry promised they would go to Texas at the end of the show season to meet his family. Unlike her, he had lots of brothers and sisters, and Goldie hoped at least one of them would feel like the sister or brother she'd never had.

Harry nodded at her. It was time for them to leave the arena. She blushed when she thought about the rest of the night. She might be too bruised and sore for Harry's attentions on their wedding night, but she decided not to worry about it. They had their whole lives before them.

~~ TWELVE ~~

Luck Runnin' Kinda Muddy

SHE LOOKED DOWN AT HER IMMOBILIZED LEG and then up at her friends. This was just the most rotten luck, someone had just said. She couldn't agree more.

Dreadful, rotten luck. She'd only been married six days. And now she was in the hospital, again, and the show was going on without her.

At least she'd managed the wedding. Six days ago, when she woke up in the ambulance that was carrying her from Madison Square Garden to Bellevue Hospital, all she could think about was the wedding.

Now she was stuck in the Homeopathic Hospital in Wilmington, Delaware, and every inch of her body hurt even worse than it had six days ago. She was afraid to look in the mirror at her face because everywhere else she looked she was black and blue. The sympathetic faces surrounding her bed didn't help her mood much.

"Arline will be here with you," Eva said, as she sat beside Goldie on the bed, ignoring Goldie's winces from the pain that shot up her leg when the bed moved. "And Bill—and I think Eunice is going to stay on a couple of days too."

"What's wrong with them?" Goldie knew no one would stay behind unless they were hurt pretty bad.

"Bill has a broken ankle. Eunice isn't too bad, but Arline will take a while to heal up." Goldie remembered vaguely that Arline was dragged under the coach until Harry could get the mules pulled up. "She's got one of the biggest ol' cuts I ever seen in her head, almos' scalpt, and another one right here." Eva dragged her finger across a couple of inches of skin above her right eye. The cowgirls knew that sprains and bruises would heal up and never be noticed again, but cuts on their faces might show up forever and could be bad for the paycheck. Goldie felt sorrier for Arline than she did for herself. Eva had brought a couple of newspapers with her, and Goldie read later that Buffalo Bill had tears in his eyes when he told the reporter about Arline's injuries. Another account said the tears were for Goldie. She cut the stories out and kept them for her scrapbook.

It would be good to have a friend staying behind with her, Goldie conceded to herself. She was still curious about the accident. Everything had happened so fast, and she didn't remember much of it.

"What about the stagecoach? Is it a total wreck?"

"Naw, some of the hands think it can be put back together, but if you ask me, it was so rickety it oughta end up in the woodpile," said Sam, one of the cowboys fidgeting at the end of the bed. Goldie was truly sorry to hear the coach could be repaired. She had hoped no one would ever have to ride in it or on it again.

A nurse bustled into the room and looked dismayed to see so many people. "Okay, everybody out. This is a hospital, not a social event. Shoo, all of you. NOW."

"Bye, honey. We'll keep your saddle warm for you," Eva squeezed her hand and stood up.

Sam slid to the side of Goldie's bed and slipped a flask under her pillow, winking as he solemnly said, "See ya, kid. The boys took up a collection and got a little somethin' for you. For later."

"Thank you, Sam. Shit, thank you, everyone," Goldie was close to tears, and her voice cracked. "Me and Arline will catch up with you soon, you'll see."

After all the goodbyes and see-you-soons, the room seemed too quiet, and Goldie burst into tears. The performers really had taken up a collection for her and Arline, and Bill and Eunice. They had spent a small part of it on the flask under Goldie's pillow, and she wouldn't have to worry about the hospital bill. She couldn't believe what wonderful friends they were and how lucky she was to be working with them. She was going to miss them until she could re-join the show, and at the moment she felt truly sorry for herself as she drifted off to sleep.

When she woke up a few hours later, Harry was sitting in a chair beside the bed. "How're you feelin'?"

"Okay, I guess."

"That was quite a tumble."

"So I hear. I heard you were a hero, though."

"Whaddya mean?"

"The boys said Arline might have died if you hadn't got those mules to pull up."

Harry's fair face turned white and his bony shoulders sagged. "None 'a you woulda got hurt if I hadn't hit that rut." Goldie knew that was true too, but she didn't see any sense in making him feel any worse, so she tried to cheer him up.

"The fellas say the coach was already breakin' up, long before it hit anything."

Harry stood up and began pacing the room. Like all cowboys he had spent enough time busted up in the hospital that confining rooms made him nervous. Goldie could see the hospital's white walls between his bow legs. Finally, sighing as if he'd made a difficult decision, he sat down on the side of the bed, and Goldie groaned. He took her hand and patted it. She sucked in the smell of the pomade he used to keep his hair in its proper place. It reminded her of their first kiss.

"I gotta move on with the show."

"Sure, I know that." Goldie felt tears coming but willed them to stay put.

"You'll be up and aroun' in no time. Be back with us soon, I know it. You're tough, and I'll be missin' my wife, so you come back as soon as you can." As he pecked her cheek with a dry kiss, he too slipped something under her pillow. And with that, her husband picked up his hat and was gone. She realized she had been hoping he'd stay with her—after all, they'd been married less than a week. But they were in show business, and the show always had priority. Harry was ten years older than she and he'd been a cowboy forever and had his share of accidents, too. She was sure he knew what he was talking about—she'd be back with the show soon.

After the sound of Harry's boot heels faded down the corridor, Goldie closed her eyes, but she couldn't get the accident out of her mind. The scene, now that she could put it together with the information from her friends, kept replaying itself in her head. Harry was driving the coach during the hold-up for the afternoon show, and he'd talked her into riding beside him. As she climbed up on the seat, she was happy that Harry was the driver, a difficult job that took a lot of skill. She felt safe beside him. The hold-up scene had gone well enough, and afterwards, Ernest, who played the man shot in the hold-up, was still on top of the coach.

They were just rounding the arena when the wheel got stuck in a rut. Goldie was tossed off from her seat next to Harry. Passengers Alexander Lawanda and Eunice and William Demott were thrown clear, but Arline, who was riding inside with them, got pinned under the coach when it tipped over on its side with a sickening crack. The mules kept pulling, and Arline was dragged along until Harry could bring them to a stop.

Cowhands scurried over to them, although other performers who were working in far parts of the arena were at first unaware of the accident. Doc Cassidy thought that Goldie's leg was broken, and then she remembered being lifted onto a stretcher and brought to the hospital with the other injured. The show, of course, didn't stop, even though some people thought it might and started to leave.

The story about the accident in the Lancaster newspaper quoted Buffalo Bill: *The performance will go on just the same this afternoon and this evening in Lancaster. That is something that entertainers have to prepare for, and another stage coach, one we carry for emergency, will be used, until the old Deadwood vehicle is repaired. The old coach that caused the accident yesterday has caused many accidents during its years of service on the plains...Our doctor with the outfit reported to me this morning that the patients are resting easy, and that their hurts have been a little exaggerated. Their substitutes will appear here this afternoon, and the performance will not be one bit marred. They themselves will appear in a day or so I am reliably informed.*

After Harry left, she asked a nurse where they were keeping Arline. The nurse promised to take her to see her friend sometime the next day, but that wasn't soon enough for Goldie. The visit with Harry had left her feeling empty. She needed to commiserate, to make plans for when she could get back on a horse, to talk more about the accident, and to smoke one of the cigarettes Harry had left under her pillow—she needed to be with another cowgirl.

As soon as the nurse was out the door, Goldie swung herself out of bed, ignoring the pain as she carefully pulled her lame leg over the edge. Crutches were hanging on the wall, and Goldie hopped over to them on one foot.

She wanted to see her pal today.

Goldie closed the door to Arline's room after she hopped through it. Arline's eyes opened wide when Goldie collapsed on the side of her bed and pulled the crutches up beside her.

"How bad am I?" Arline wanted to know. Goldie leaned back, inspecting her friend. Her face was starting to swell, and Goldie knew it would be blue with ugly bruises for a while. The cut that Eva had described was indeed long, but Goldie figured Arline's big hat would probably do a good enough job of hiding it.

"Well, all in all, considerin' everythin', I think you look like you're ready for a society ball." Arline sighed at the obvious lie. Giggling with anticipation, Goldie pulled the pack of cigarettes out of her hospital gown, and the two of them lit up. They compared injuries and stories of the wreck, and Goldie was relieved that Arline didn't blame Harry for what had happened. Their reunion was short-lived. A nurse whisked into the room, sniffing loudly, and fiercely told them to put out their cigarettes. Fortunately, Goldie had tucked the pack under Arline's pillow, and the nurse didn't find it.

As soon as Arline could get out of bed, the two cowgirls spent their days sneaking smokes, spiking their coffee, and telling the other patients tall tales of their cowgirl feats. When all that got boring, they raced each other on crutches up and down the hospital halls. The nurses were constantly reprimanding them and reminding them that they were in a hospital. "Quiet, please." "No smoking, ever." "Why can't you act like ladies?"

(Next page) Harry is on the right on the stagecoach with the six-mule team in the Two Bills show. Goldie is on her horse with her hand raised to her hat. Mabel Cline is on the horse next to Goldie. Goldie landed in the hospital after being thrown off the top of one of these stages in the Two Bills show.

Buffalo Bill Museum and Grave, Lookout Mountain, Golden, Colorado

Just to prove that they weren't ladies and had no intention of ever becoming ladies, Arline leaned towards Goldie and said, "Wonder how they'd feel about a little shootin'?" in a loud stage whisper that carried the length of the hall. Nurses stopped mid-stride, and patients looked alarmed. Goldie and Arline laughed so hard they had to hang onto each other so they wouldn't topple from their crutches. While she was holding onto Arline for support, Goldie surreptitiously whapped her crutch against the wall. The resulting loud bang made everyone in the hall jump and scatter, sending Arline and Goldie into more spasms of laughter.

The hospital released its unruly guests early, and eight days after their wreck, Arline and Goldie boarded the train to catch up with the Two Bills show. It was a few more weeks before Goldie could hop from her crutches into the saddle. She hadn't broken her leg as Doc Cassidy feared, but she had torn a few ligaments, and they took about as long as a broken leg to heal. It wasn't until the show headed south again that she felt like her old self and strong enough to ride in both shows every day.

∽ THIRTEEN ∽

A Leaky Sky

CARLO APPEARED AT THE OPENING to the women's dressing tent. He cleared his throat, and then announced in what for him was a loud voice: "Colonel Cody asks you to come to his tent. Now. Before the show." The Indian bowed at the waist and disappeared into the drizzle.

Goldie shrugged into her black slicker. The weather was miserable, and it had been miserable for weeks. Her newly healed leg ached in the damp and cold weather. When all the girls had their slickers on over their show outfits, they sloshed in a group through the mud to the colonel's big tent.

The freezing drizzle dripped off their hats and onto their noses and the tips of their boots. Even the cheerful tinkling sound of their spurs was muffled by the constant drumming of the rain on their hats. The usual pandemonium of camp with its trumpeting elephants, braying burros and roaring camels was only muffled by the downpour. The cowgirls all knew what was waiting for them in the Colonel's tent. He had taken to having Carlo mix up a big bowl of hot rum toddies for them before the show. He thought they needed the fortification before spending an hour and a half in the elements, especially since the crowds had been so sparse, even though the show advertised protection from the near-constant rain under the cover of huge tarps the workers strung over the seats. The show was losing money as it wound its way through the South—not only because of the rain but also because the price of cotton was down, which meant a lot of people couldn't afford entertainment.

The Colonel's tent had an extra fly which helped protect the inhabitants from the hot sun and storms like today's. The heavy board floor was laid in sections and covered by a rug. They were in the front section, the office, and Carlo had moved the couch and chairs to the outside perimeter of the room. The dripping cowgirls stood around the big punch bowl Carlo had put out on the Colonel's desk, an ingenious contraption of detachable legs of gas pipe, a board and a box.

Goldie touched the punch bowl with reverence. It wasn't just a big punch bowl, it was the silver bowl Queen Victoria gave Buffalo Bill when he performed for her in England. The Colonel, Goldie thought, was taking good care of his employees. She didn't think any other boss would care enough about his people to make sure they were 'fortified' before a performance in the rain. The Colonel himself joined them and said hello to each cowgirl, nodding and joking his way around the tent, hopeful that the hot toddies would prevent them from taking colds.

The mud in the arena was slick, and the ponies sometimes had a difficult time staying upright. Everyone had taken more spills. They were always cold, wet, tired, and aching. The Colonel had just rejoined the show after spending a few days in the hospital in Knoxville. While he was gone, another cowgirl had joined their ranks. Her name was May Shaffer.

May had applied to be a cowgirl, but the show turned her down, saying they only had an opening for a teamster. So she and her boyfriend Leonard Sasseen dressed her up to look like a man, and she was hired. She'd been driving an eight-horse team for

ten days when she sprained her hand. As soon as Doc Cassidy
saw the hand, he knew it didn't belong to a man. In Buffalo Bill's
absence, they called Pawnee Bill, and he told her she could join
the show—as a cowgirl. Now she was riding in the show with
Leonard, and Buffalo Bill was back from the hospital.

The constant downpours also made seeing well enough to
shoot accurately a problem. Goldie thought it was a small mira-
cle that the Colonel was such a sure shot in such rotten weather.
He was no longer shooting the specially made balls from the
back of his running horse, but it didn't matter much to their
audiences that he was sitting in a carriage. It was still a sight to
see the famous marksman pick the targets off one after another,
as fast as his man could throw them in the air.

There were three people who could shoot like that. Buffalo
Bill himself, Annie Oakley, and Princess Wenona. Even though
Edith and Vern Tantlinger also had amazing sharpshooting acts
with the show—Vern shot from his trusty bicycle—it was the
Colonel shooting from the back of his charging white horse,
Wenona, who also shot from the back of a running horse, and
Annie, who didn't ride or rope, but who could shoot with deadly
accuracy over her shoulder and at a dead run, who could bring a
crowd to its feet, gasping for breath.

Annie had retired from the show long before Goldie joined
it, although, like many celebrities, she joined them for a few
performances as the show wound its way north, then south, and
then north again and finally west from its opening in
Philadelphia.

Princess Wenona could drink like a man and loved the fast
life. Her real name was Lillian Smith, and she used the stage
names of the California Girl and Princess Wenona. She certainly had at least some Sioux blood, but most of the tales generated
for publicity, like the one that said she was the daughter of a
Sioux chief, were just that, exaggerated tales for publicity. She
always said she started shooting at the age of seven, and since
then her feats were many. Lillian could hit a plate thirty times

Goldie's friend signed her photo, "To Goldie, From her Best Pal, Mabel Cline."

Buffalo Bill Museum and Grave, Lookout Mountain, Golden, Colorado

in fifteen seconds with her pair of Winchester rifles from the back of her pony Rabbit. Then she would break ten glass balls on strings swinging from a pole without a miss. When she was with the show, even more glass balls had to be made than usual. The man in charge of making the balls dipped an empty mold into a bucket of boiling tar, then into a bucket of cold water. An extremely thin, hollow black ball came out. Then he dipped the balls in whitewash so the Colonel or the Princess could see them better. Wenona's tar balls were about four inches in diameter. The hard-partying woman was always the last to leave the Colonel's tent and the punch bowl.

Even though the attendance at the shows in the South was abysmal and their spirits were low, the performers in the Two Bills show still gave their all twice a day, every day, except Sunday. Every part of their workday was harder in the rain and wind. As soon as they started unpacking, everyone went to work to get the camp set up as quickly as possible so the people who had tickets to the show could wander through before the main events started in the arena. The Indians collected poles, and the women put up their own little city of tipis, pulling their possessions out of suitcases stuffed to overflowing. One tent was erected for the 'high school' and trick riding horses, another for the broncos. Grazing areas were roped off for the herd of bison, and separate areas were created for the other stock.

Constantly coming and going from the men's dressing tent were the dapper Japanese, the dark-skinned Mexicans, the skirted, dark-haired Singalese with their hair done up in knots and their long, silky mustaches, the uncouth Cossacks, the powerfully built Armenian acrobats, practicing their tumbling feats, and the usually deadpan American cowboys. The Dahoman people stayed apart in their own groups of typical Arab tents. In spite of the constant rain and high winds, the show's numerous tents still had to be put up and taken down every day, often blowing apart as soon as they were up, and the performers still had to

A couple walks through an Indian village behind the scenes at the Sells-Floto Circus and Buffalo Bill Wild West Show. The village was set up under a large show tent.

Denver Public Library, Western History Collection, Z-7410

ride their horses in the dangerously slick mud and blinding downpours.

Finally, the Two Bills show escaped the rotten weather when their train turned north towards Chicago. Goldie started looking forward to seeing her mother again, even though her mother didn't like Harry and didn't let an opportunity slip to tell her daughter that she thought he was a scoundrel. As if her wedding hadn't had enough disasters, Allie had added to Goldie's stress with her constant harping about Harry, or as she usually referred to him, "that Hiram." Harry hated his real name and had changed Hiram Sterling to Harry Smith or Harry Walters for the show. After the wedding, he explained to Goldie that his brother's name was Walter, so they just needed to add an 's.' Although Goldie had started the tour as Goldie Griffith, she was now more often billed as Goldie Walters.

After the wedding, Harry and Goldie moved to the married people's car in the train. Harry called the Two Bills' tour their 'honeymoon.'

⤞ FOURTEEN ⤝

The Truth

"I DIDN'T HAVE NO CHOICE."

Goldie had waited a week to talk to him. Every day, several times a day, she had opened her mouth to ask him, but she managed to stop herself. She waited until the show stopped in a town where they would stay for a couple of days in hotel rooms instead of sleeping out or on the train. They needed privacy if she was going to get Harry to talk. Tonight, she told him. No dinner, no sex, nothing until he told her about his past. It was her mother, of course, who found out about it. Allie spent a lot of time visiting the show when they played in Chicago. At first, Goldie was so angry with Harry she could hardly speak to him. She couldn't decide what made her madder, that he had done something like that or that he hadn't told her about it. Then she was angry that he hadn't noticed how angry she was. Then she decided she wanted to hear it in his own words; she wanted him to tell her about it himself.

So tonight she confronted him, told him that her mother had found out from some of the show people that he was wanted for murder.

Harry started pacing the room, fingering his holstered gun. She'd seen his temper, and she was apprehensive about what he might do next. She tensed when he turned back to her, but instead of exploding, he squinted at her as if he didn't believe what she was saying. "Your ma has always hated me. You know that. She made that up to get rid of me." Goldie stared at him until he looked away.

"I don't think she made it up. She said almost everyone knows about it. How come everyone else knows about it, but not me?" She brushed at her wet eyes, not wanting to cry. "Why didn't you tell me? We're married and married folks aren't s'posed to keep secrets."

As he paced she worried he would actually pull his gun out, but she had hers too, and she found herself touching her gun when he touched his, hoping that both of their guns, or at least Harry's, were still loaded with blanks from the show and not real ammunition.

He paced, and paced. Finally he sat on the edge of the bed and pulled her over next to him. "You know how much I love you. I jus' didn't want you to know about it. It's not something I'm proud of." Goldie nodded and gripped his hand in hers. Once he started to talk about it, it was a stampede of words.

"It was a long time ago. I was jus' a kid, I didn't know that all this would happen, and that it could hurt you too." Goldie brushed away more tears.

"Did your ma tell you that they tried me six times?" Goldie shook her head. "They did. I went broke, and then they were going to break my family. I jus' couldn't do that, not to my family." Goldie realized she had never heard him talk about his family. He'd mentioned a brother, Walter, and he'd said his father owned a grocery store in Texas, but that was all she knew about his past. *Why hadn't he told her more?*

But now knowing how important his family was to him made her actually feel proud of him.

"They had me under $3,000 bond when they set trial number seven. Number seven. It was jus' too much for a man to stand up to. I skipped out. Went to Nevada, then started doin' the shows, and, well, you know the rest."

"But what did you do?"

"You mean the *murder?* That's what they called it. A homicide. But that's not what it was. Never what it was."

"Then what was it?"

"He was gonna kill me if I didn't kill him. That's the god-honest truth, Goldie. Carroll Whitt, that's who it was, he owned a blind tiger across the street from my stable. The saloon was illegal enough, but he also ran dog fights for people to bet on, and my bulldog was always beatin' his. I guess he just couldn't stand it, you know. One night I come down to the stable and there was his dog fightin' with mine. I had a boy workin' for me, and we got the dogs apart—it wasn't easy—and then in walks Whitt. He decides to take it out on my boy, says he robbed him of a win against my dog, and slaps 'im for helpin' me separate those dogs." Harry stopped and sighed and patted his gun again.

"I told him to lay off. He knew I coulda' beat 'im in a fight, so he went home, and it looked like it was over. But then a friend came by later and tol' me that Whitt was goin' round town tellin' folks he was gonna kill me." She could feel his muscles tense through his shirt.

"Next mornin', jus' as I come in my yard, he come by. He unhooked the buttons on his coat and put his hand in his pocket. I knew what that meant, hell, ever'body knows what it means when a man puts his hand in his pocket at a time like that, so I took cover behind one o' them posts in my barn. He dared me to step out."

Harry kissed Goldie's ear and stood up, wandering over to the double-hung window. He slid the top of the window down, leaned out and gulped the cool night air. He seemed to be reliving that day, and Goldie didn't dare break his mood. She had to know what had happened. The chilly outside air was rushing into the room, and after a few moments of silence, Harry pulled his head inside, smoothed his hair, and closed the window.

"He pulled his gun. My rifle was still there on my saddle an' I slid it out. Then it was jus' him or me. I shot him first, right over the back of my horse."

Goldie shivered.

"Got him right in the forehead too. As you know, I'm not a bad shot." No, Goldie thought, you're one of the best I know, and now she knew one of the reasons he was so tough, and so quiet.

"He was a Mason, and, you know, in Texas that means somethin'. I wasn't no Mason, all I had was my business, and I tried to keep to my own business, until that happened. No jury—*not one of 'em*—" he looked at her sideways, "could decide if I was guilty or not, so after all that, I left." He started pacing again and then checked to see what her reaction was to his story.

"Do you think I was wrong?"

Her answer was immediate. "No, no, never. Of course you had to do it."

(Next page) Like this couple competing in a Roman Race at Frontier Days in Cheyenne, Wyoming about 1920, Harry and Goldie often rode in Roman Standing races in Wild Wests, and later Goldie and her second husband, Tim (Doc) Cameron competed in Roman Standing races and trick riding contests in rodeos around the country.

Ralph A. Doubleday, photographer. Photographic Study Collection, Dickinson Research Center, National Cowboy & Western Heritage Museum, Oklahoma City, Oklahoma

ROMAN RACE FRONTIER DAYS, CHEYENNE, WYO.
(DOUBLE DAY)

"Someday they'll forget the whole thing, and then I can go back home. But for now, I've got you, if you'll still have me."

"Of course I will." She blew her nose on a handkerchief. "But I don't understand. How come they could send you to trial so many times?" Harry pulled her up off the edge of the bed and kissed her. "Remember I tol' you ol' Whitt was a Mason?"

Goldie nodded.

"Masons never let go, and they got all the power in Texas. All the lawyers and the judges, they're Masons. At least half all juries was Masons. And the Masons hated me 'cause I kilt one their own."

"Are you wanted jus' in Texas?"

"Yep, jus' in Texas."

Goldie sighed with relief. Now she knew why Harry always disappeared when the show got near Texas. At least if they stayed out of Texas, everything would be okay.

"Cheer up, sweetheart. It's still our honeymoon." Goldie smiled at him, happy that the air was clear between them.

"Hungry?"

She nodded. So many things were obvious to Goldie now. All the times Harry disappeared without a word. The shrewd looks and respect of the other cowboys. Why he was always chosen to ride the fence line in Los Angeles. The rumors her mother had heard. Her heart felt like it would burst. Now that she knew about his trouble, she wanted to do everything she could to help her husband.

She picked up her hat and followed his jingling spurs to the stairs.

⚯ FIFTEEN ⚯

Gratification in a Pin

GOLDIE WAS FEELING MUCH HAPPIER since the show had left Chicago and she'd finally heard the truth about Harry's trouble. Arguing with her mother about Harry was draining, and she felt her energy return as the train headed west again.

She spent hours sewing on the new Sears and Roebuck machine that was one of their wedding presents. Mostly she sewed up outfits for herself and some of the other cowgirls, and occasionally she made a fancy shirt for Harry or one of the other cowboys.

She was working with a new horse, teaching him to gallop in a straight line as she gradually moved more and more of her weight to one side of the saddle. She thought he was going to be good, and she was thrilled that she was going to have a dependable pony that she had schooled on her own. They were developing the essential bond between rider and horse for trick riding. If something happens to its rider, a good trick pony will stop, or at least will go out of its way to not trample its fallen rider. She was still the head cowgirl for the bronc-riding, and the falls didn't bother her as much now that her leg had healed and the bruises from the stagecoach fall had finally all disappeared. Her roping skills were improving every week, and the crowds seemed to be enjoying the show more as they headed west.

She was enjoying Harry's romantic attentions, and she'd forgiven him for not telling her about the murder in Texas. Everything in her world was right, and she was proud that Colonel Cody had come to depend on her for his hairpins.

Although Goldie couldn't see many faults in Cody's character, she did notice the great man was rather vain. He wore his hair long in the show and he covered a bald spot on top of his head with a toupee. Sometimes he would complain that his long hair was too hot, but he said, "It's my livelihood." His audiences expected to see the great man with long, flowing hair. He was fussy about his clothes, and Carlo, his striker, the army's word for valet, was in charge of making sure the Colonel always looked as dapper as possible.

One afternoon Carlo knocked at the cowgirls' car, asking if anyone had some hairpins. The Colonel needed them to pin up his long hair so it would stay under his hat when he went into town. Goldie produced the required items, and after that Cody himself asked her for them again a few times. The next time the show stopped in a big enough town, Goldie bought a half-pound of the short limber hairpins. They were light, so the bag was pretty big. Triumphantly, she brought them back to the show and rushed to Buffalo Bill's private car.

"I found some hairpins in town, sir, and I bought you a whole bunch."

The Colonel looked aghast at the bag. "You take them right back. I want to thank you heartily for your concern, but when I want them, I'll ask."

So Goldie packed the bag of hairpins in her trunk, and if she wasn't dressed when the Colonel appeared asking for them, she'd just reach her hand through the canvas with the pins.

Sometimes when the Colonel went into town, he took the cowgirls with him. He often was invited to the lovely homes of a city's wealthier women, and when he could he extended the invitation to the cowgirls, and, sometimes if the home was big enough and the hostess kind-hearted enough, to some of the cowboys as well. He believed his girls would learn some of the necessities of city life over tea or a nice supper with the society women, and he knew the city women were fascinated by the cowgirls.

Goldie figured she was in a lot of those women's scrapbooks because they almost always liked to have their pictures taken with the cowgirls, usually grouped around a column on a porch, or in the exquisitely maintained garden, or on the grand steps outside the front door. She learned that even people with money liked to hear her talk and enjoyed listening to her opinions about culture and society, and sometimes even politics. She found that by reading all of the newspaper, not just the articles about the Wild Wests, she had even more opinions to share. Although she could tell the society women led an easier life than she did, she wouldn't have traded with them for anything. She liked sleeping in the cramped, overcrowded train car with her cowgirl pals before she got married, or now, when the weather was good, under the never-ending stars of the Western sky with Harry snoring beside her. She liked working hard every day and playing hard whenever she could. The houses the Colonel took them to were beautiful, but they felt as claustrophobic as the movie business. Neither of those lives was for her.

The Two Bills show continued on its way to Denver with drier weather and better attendance. The longer days of summer got hotter with every show. Goldie had been so wrapped up in worrying about Harry's past and fighting with her mother over it that she had all but ignored the gossip floating through the show people while they were in Chicago. Apparently a lawyer for the United States Printing and Lithograph Company had called on Pawnee Bill and demanded that the show pay at least some of its bill. Colonel Cody still owed them $16,000 from the 1912 season, and so far they had printed $40,000 of the

$50,000 in advertising they had promised Cody for the 1913 season. But since they hadn't been paid anything yet and it was July 1, the lawyer told Pawnee Bill that the printing company was prepared to attach the show for the debt.

Pawnee Bill promised to send $10,000 on account if the printing company would let the show run two more weeks. Finally out of the economically depressed South and the rain and the wind, the show was making more money. Goldie hardly noticed that the crowds were slighter than the ones that had attended the 101 shows the year before. She felt safe and, for maybe the first time in her life, cared for. Buffalo Bill knew every one of his employees and cared for them like he would his children. Cody was the best boss she had ever worked for, and she felt she could relax and enjoy being a bride and a cowgirl.

❧ SIXTEEN ❧

Between a Rock and a Hard Place

"WHOA, HOLD UP THERE NOW. WHOA, I said." Goldie's calls to
the mules were finally heeded. Sometimes they thought they
knew more than she did. Together they had been learning the
little things that made the job easier, but this time Goldie wanted to try not pulling up quite so close to the hydrant. She
looped the reins over the brake and stood up, stretching her
aching back. Climbing backwards off the wagon seat, she
jumped the last two feet to the ground. She unfolded a few
lengths of the heavy hose and dragged it over to the hydrant.

The boys who had watched the whole procedure on her
last trip were there again, pointing and laughing from across
the street. Goldie ignored them, but she did say hello to the
few passersby who greeted her. Some of them were used to seeing her at the same time every day, and it was almost like seeing old friends.

Goldie went back to the sprinkler wagon that had two
tanks mounted on its bed, side by side. She dropped the rest of
the folded hose on the ground and screwed one end into the

first tank. Then she hefted the big wrench out of the back of the wagon and went back to the hydrant. She screwed the other end of the hose into the hydrant, and then she used the wrench to unlock it and turn it on. The gushing water made the folds in the hose pop open. When the tank was almost full, she ran over to the hydrant and used the big wrench to turn it off. Then she unscrewed the hose from the tank and attached it to the other tank and filled it.

The mules waited patiently. They were her old friends from the show, used to working together pulling the venerable Deadwood stagecoach around the arena at top speed. These days they pulled the heavy, full water tanks slowly through the Denver streets with Goldie urging them on. Fortunately, it was only two blocks from the stable in Overland Park to the Overland Hotel, in front of which sat the closest fire plug. Most days Goldie longed to be able to walk into the hotel lobby and get a room with a bath.

The wagon with the tanks that could hold hundreds of gallons of water for sprinkling on the dusty streets belonged to the city, and Mabel had taught her how to fill the tanks and then to let the water back out into the stock troughs. Goldie made three round-trips a day for three waterings, starting at dawn. She made three and half dollars for her work during the day. Then she would take the six mules back to the stable, feed them, and let them rest for an hour. At six she harnessed them up and put them to work again, hauling another load, and she finished up at 7:30. For the night work, she got paid another dollar and a half. By the time she got the mules out of the harness, watered and fed, she was dead tired. But she felt good—every dollar she made was pooled with what other performers could make. The money was used to feed the showpeople who were still in Denver.

The work was back-breaking, but every morning when she climbed up onto the driver's seat and threaded the reins through her fingers, Goldie felt pleased with herself. She was doing a job that hardly any other woman had ever done, and she knew the stock depended on her for their water. Fortunately, the mules were usually pretty stoic about the work and there wasn't much danger of a runaway, but it still was a trick to maneuver the long line of mules and wagon through the streets of Denver, and she was proud that she could do it well.

Everyone had been looking forward to Denver. Baths in a hotel instead of in a bucket in a tent. A city big enough to pick up a few needed items. Bigger audiences at the shows.

They arrived on Saturday night, and Cody told the cowgirls he wanted to take them on a ride the next morning. Just before dawn the cowgirls joined Cody, who was ready to go in his phaeton. The extremely light buggy was fast, and the group made a bit of a stir as they headed out of Denver. Occasionally, the Colonel would stop to invite awed spectators to the show. As always, he had extra tickets in his pocket for children and handed them out freely.

The day was going to be hot, and the cowgirls savored the cooler air as they left Golden and climbed higher and higher on the road that kept turning back on itself in endless switchbacks. Occasionally, they stopped to take in the views, but the Colonel urged them on, saying the best was yet to come. Finally, the road topped out; they had reached Point Lookout, the top of Lookout Mountain above Golden. Spread out below them was the city of Denver and plains that stretched to Nebraska. Wildflowers bloomed in streaks of red, blue and yellow across the green and gray grasses. The pine trees smelled like they were frying in the mid-day sun. The girls took their lunch bags and left the horses to graze. They all sat together, putting Buffalo Bill where they could hear him. He was in a storytelling mood, and while they ate he told them about chasing buffalo across the plains, shooting his tar balls for Queen Victoria, and performing on the stage in New York.

Goldie had to admit the view was breathtaking. She took a final look around as the Colonel stood and waved expansively. He took a deep breath. "You know, I think you can see all the way to Wyoming from up here, don't you think?" He squinted into the clouds organizing for an afternoon thunderstorm. "It's beautiful, just beautiful here. This would be a fine place for a person's grave." Goldie thought it was an odd thing to say. The Colonel, she knew, was now sixty-eight years old, and although his health wouldn't allow him to ride horseback in the shows anymore, he was still flawlessly shooting all his targets from the phaeton, and she knew he never stopped thinking about the show and how to promote it. Goldie felt lucky to have had the chance to work for the old man with a heart of gold, and, as they gathered their horses and prepared for the trip back to town, she was sure he wasn't talking about his own grave. He couldn't be. He was slowing down, obviously, but he wasn't old enough to be talking about dying. Not yet, anyway.

Two nights after the trip to Mount Lookout, just as the final act was drawing to a close, Goldie saw the Colonel do something odd. Frantically, he waved one of the men to him, said something to him, and the man spurred his horse into a dead run. She couldn't tell who it was and went looking for Harry.

"Harry took off. Said to tell you that he'd catch up with you later," one of the other cowboys told her.

"What happened?"

"The sheriff came with his men, and the Colonel tried to get to the treasury wagon, but they got there first." The man wandered off, shaking his head.

Goldie was afraid. Her husband was running from the law, and the law had come to the show. Then the importance of what the cowboy told her dawned. The sheriff had the treasury wagon. All the receipts from the show were in that wagon. This was bad—worse than the hundred days they lost money in the South when rations had been cut in the dining tent and many of the Indians had deserted rather than go hungry.

Sure enough, there was no breakfast, just coffee, and the whole company was supposed to meet up with Cody at noon in the arena. Through a megaphone, and with a pained look on his face, the Colonel addressed them. He stood on the announcer's platform and looked like he hadn't slept all night. His long hair blew around his face, and even his handlebar mustache and goatee, usually meticulously cared for, looked matted and tired.

As you all know, I'm sure, the sheriff was here last night." He stopped and coughed, and, with, it seemed, great effort began again. "He has attached our receipts from last night's show, and, it pains me to tell you, this morning he took possession of your trunks too."

Everyone, it seemed, gasped at once. First the show's money and now their street clothes and their personal possessions were off limits. And it was even worse for many of the cowgirls. For married couples working for him, the Colonel had instituted the practice of holding the woman's pay in the treasury. The couples lived off what the husband made during the season, and then they would have the wife's pay for the off-season. This would have been the first year that Goldie would have had that extra money at the end of the season, and she had been looking forward to it.

"At present I do not know where we will be or how we will eat, but I will find a way. For now, I have made arrangements for the stock to go to a stable in Overland Park. I am so, so sorry, folks, but we will triumph again, I promise." Although his voice was strong, a hand had to help the Colonel down from the platform. He seemed to have aged another ten years in the last day. The showpeople drifted away in clumps of four or five.

Goldie felt tears threatening, but told herself it was just hunger. She'd be all right. She'd been hungry before—and survived. Some of the people around her were talking about Buffalo Bill's partner Major Lillie—Pawnee Bill—with disdain. "*He* didn't stick around to help, you notice." "Yeah, I hear he high-tailed it outta town already." "Guess the heat was too high for his *lily* constitution." "He could pay the bill jus' like that," the man snapped his fingers, "but, no, instead he runs." Goldie found herself feeling more than disdain for Pawnee Bill.

It was the printing bill. The printing company in Chicago had finally had enough, and when Pawnee Bill did not send the $10,000 as he had promised, the sheriff confiscated whatever assets the show had. Lillie could have saved the show by paying the bill from his private funds, but he knew that Harry Tammen of The Denver Post had been after Buffalo Bill for a long while, and he knew that Cody had signed a contract with Tammen to join his Sells-Floto circus the next year anyway. Cody couldn't pay the bill because he had deeded his only negotiable properties, the North Platte ranch, valued at $100,000, and the Irma Hotel, worth $75,000, to Major Lillie. Cody was willing to transfer the properties to the lithograph company, but Lillie was not. Tammen, always the businessman, saw his chance to put competitor Pawnee Bill out of business once and for all after the show's disastrous summer season, and he joined forces with the lithographers to send the sheriff without warning to serve an attachment on everything in sight. Getting rid of Pawnee Bill would make Tammen's new property, Buffalo Bill, much more valuable, and Tammen got his wish when Pawnee Bill Lillie fled to New Jersey.

Goldie thought it was typical of Cody to think of his animals first, and to find shelter for them first, but she was worried where they would all end up. Hardly anyone had enough money to pay for more than a few meals, and that wouldn't last long if they all shared what little money they had, as she was sure they would.

How would they all get home? Train tickets cost money, and the Colonel, it seemed, was fresh out of that.

They were due in Colorado Springs in a couple of days, but they never made it. Instead, Goldie found herself looking for a different kind of job.

"SIR, I COME TO ASK for the job drivin' the water sprinkler."

"That's awful hard work for a girl." Mr. Nesbeth was in charge of the stock now. Mr. Cook, who had been sent from Trenton, New Jersey, by the court, had taken over the management of the show. He'd hired Mr. Nesbeth and Mr. Duffel. It had been a rough two weeks. The stock had been moved to the stable in Overland Park, and a couple days later the performers had moved into the stable too. They were sleeping in the stalls on hay and washing their clothes out at night since they had only what they were wearing the night the sheriff arrived. Meals were few and far between. When they had food, trapeze artist Lamyra cooked for them. Colonel Cody was trying to raise money to help them, but he wasn't having much luck. A friend sent him $500 to help out, and Cody spent it all feeding his employees.

After Mr. Cook's announcement that everything in the show would be put up for auction in September, everyone who could drifted off or went home. But many of the showpeople were penniless. Mr. Cook made arrangements for the Indians to return to the Pine Ridge reservation, but even with that a number of them had to sell their show costumes to make the trip. Everyone's remaining money was put together, and the decision was made that the Indians and children would be taken care of first. A troupe of young boys, who had been billed as boy scouts, started their long walk back to Chicago, and the money the other performers gave them for the trip didn't last long. They gave exhibition drills where they could in exchange for a meal or a place to spend the night. Starting that third week in August in Denver, they marched through Nebraska's weltering heat, finally arriving in Chicago on October 14.

Several shows were planned to raise money. Some of the circus performers from the Wild East show were going to perform that evening at the city auditorium. Goldie had offered to do a wrestling exhibition in the show.

Everyone was already angry when they heard that H.H. Tammen and F.G. Bonfils of The Denver Post also filed an attachment with the court. Tammen wanted his loan of $20,000 to Buffalo Bill back. The show people wanted to know why now? Talk about hitting a man when he was down. If Tammen could have waited just a week or two, he could have had his money. Receipts had been up as the show traveled west, and the performers were sure Tammen and Bonfils attached the show to stop it in Denver. The newspapers estimated that 300 to 500 people from the show were stranded in Denver without any means of support. With nothing else to do, show employees wrote over 200 indignant letters to the Billboard. Only one of those letters was critical of Buffalo Bill. Rumors were rocketing through the groups of stranded showpeople that Tammen and Bonfils were solely responsible for stopping the Two Bills show and taking their clothes, money, and livelihood.

On Saturday night, attorney Omar E. Garwood told the newspapers that bankruptcy proceedings would be started against the show unless something was done to aid the 250 men who stormed his offices seeking relief. The next day, the same angry mob of hungry employees of the Two Bills show, almost all with bedrolls under their arms, gathered in front of the office of The Denver Post and demanded that they be fed. Many said they had had nothing to eat for 12 hours. Traffic was blocked, and the police reserves were called. When the crowd was dispersed, the show employees were provided with meal tickets at the safety commissioner's office. Some were fed from the municipal lodging house, but most were cared for at Father Burke's mission at Sixteenth and Blake streets.

Harry had reappeared, much to Goldie's relief, and he was given a job helping with the stock, but the show was forbidden to take the stock outside the stable in Overland Park, even to the Platte River, which ran behind the park, to water them, so the hands had been hauling water to the stable from the river for not only the ponies and mules, but also for the elephants and giraffes and sacred cows that were traveling with the Far East.

Since no one could take a horse outside the park, the cowboys and cowgirls entertained their numerous visitors inside the park. And they got a lot of visitors, sometimes people who wanted to help, sometimes people who were curious about them, and sometimes old friends. One visitor was Mabel McDonald, who had performed with several Wild West shows. Goldie was fascinated when Mabel explained her current job of driving a sprinkler.

Thinking about Mabel driving a wagon loaded with water up and down the streets, sprinkling down the dust, gave Goldie an idea. If Mabel could do it, so could she, although she figured she'd have to have six mules instead of the two Mabel drove and haul much more water with each trip she made, but it sure would be a much easier way to water the animals. She approached Mr. Nesbeth and Mr. Duffel that afternoon.

I'm a hard worker. I can do the work, you'll see."

"Well, hmmm." Mr. Nesbeth stroked his chin with one hand and adjusted his glasses with the other.

"I think it's a good idea," Mr. Duffel said. "The animals need more water than we can haul in a day." He nodded at Goldie. "I'll talk to the people working with the city. See what we can do."

"Oh, and, sir, if you can, I sure would like the same pay you give my husband." Goldie said it as if he'd be a fool not to, which was what she believed.

"Yes, and what was that?"

"Five dollars a day."

She got it. The muleskinning job and the pay. It was a windfall. A dollar a day was good money—although less than she made as a cowgirl—and this was five times that.

THE NEXT DAY, SHE CUT THE STORY out of the newspaper that one of that day's visitors had kindly left with her, folded it up and put it under a rock on the hay bale she used for her things. If she ever got her trunk back, she would put it in her scrapbook.

GIRL "CHAMP" WINS WRESTLING MATCH

"Kid" Farmer and Miss Griffith shook hands and the match was on. The audience enjoyed it hugely and evidenced its pleasure when Miss Griffith threw her opponent and was declared winner.

Before the curtain descended "Kid" Farmer extended to the audience the thanks of the circus people.

We thank you from our hearts," he said, "and hope you will never again have to attend a benefit for unfortunate circus people. We were let upon the mercies of your citizens and we thank the Denver people for what they have done for us."

The lariat throwers, the Cingalese dancers and the wrestlers refused to take any share of the receipts of the performances. They said they did not need money so badly as do the laboring hands and the smaller "fry" among the performers.

The newspapers had promised that Denver had never heard a rag-time song by Russian Cossacks in the Russian tongue, *but they say it listens good and looks fine when a native dance is set to it.* Another highlight of the show was a hilarious comedy sketch by Conley and Abel illustrating the making of a bed in a circus sleeper car. Carlo Miles and Montana Earl, who was billed as the champion trick roper of the country, twirled and spun their 60-foot lariat ropes into circles, squares, diamonds and other figures.

The circus and Wild West performers were joined by local cabaret entertainers, and admission to the Sunday afternoon performance was 25 cents. The Denver Auditorium charged nothing for the venue, so all of the proceeds could be used to help the show people get home or to other jobs.

By the time the auctioneer banged his gavel on the show's possessions on September 15, only a few of the show people

Buffalo Bill on his beloved Isham.

Buffalo Bill Museum and Grave, Lookout Mountain, Golden, Colorado

remained at Overland Park to take care of the animals, including Goldie and Harry.

Goldie's old bosses with the 101 Wild West, Colonel Joe Miller and his two brothers, came to the auction. Zack Miller bought seventy-eight of the best show horses, including the great buckers Hightower, Pueblo, Lamar, and Omaha, for an average of $61 a head. They also purchased the "big end of their arena stock, all of the wardrobe and costumes, the lighting plant, and considerable other stuff," wrote Joe Miller. "Was very sad indeed to see such a grand and big outfit like that finish as it did."

Cody himself didn't want to go to the auction. A good friend of Cody's, Colonel Bills of Lincoln, was in town for the sale and offered a ride to Cody in his automobile, but Cody declined, saying that he could see everything else in the show auctioned off but he couldn't bear to see Isham, the faithful horse that had carried him for over twenty years, bought by strangers.

What Buffalo Bill didn't know was that Carlo had sold his saddle and other personal effects so he could buy the horse and give him to Cody. What Carlo didn't know was that Colonel Bills had the same idea. The two men bid against each other for Isham until the price reached $150, and Carlo had to stop, muttering under his breath, "If the man who bought that horse don't give him back to Colonel Cody, I'll steal him tonight and take him back myself."

When Bills met with Cody after the sale, Cody asked, "Has Isham been sold?"

"Yes, he has," Bills told him.

"I hope whoever it was will treat him kindly."

"I'm sure he will, since his owner is none other than his master of the last twenty years."

"You mean...?"

"Yes, sir. Isham is yours again."

Bills reported that tears slid down Cody's cheeks.

✾ SEVENTEEN ✾

A Disappearin' Act

GOLDIE AND HARRY HAD TO DECIDE what to do next. Harry told her that he wanted to sign on with the 101 while the Millers were in Denver. Goldie was pregnant, and she thought about signing up too, but then she changed her mind. She wanted to go home to Chicago to be with her mother until the baby was born. Most of her friends continued riding, even on the bucking broncos, until a couple of months before they gave birth, but Goldie was tired after the months of living in the barn at Overland Park and driving the sprinkler wagon. She decided to do a few more shows and then to go home.

So they parted ways, like many show couples who couldn't always find work together. She boarded the train for Chicago, and Harry, who was now billed as Harry Smith, headed south with the 101 to Oklahoma and Texas.

In the past, when one of his shows got close to Texas, Harry had made himself scarce. But as time went on, it seemed that no one was looking for him anymore. He thought he was safe when the train headed into Texas after the shows through Oklahoma, and for a while his luck held. But on a rainy day in Houston, cowboy Milt Hinkle stepped down from his gray horse to find the guns of two big detectives pointed at him. Because he was wearing white angora chaps, the detectives mistook him for Harry. Someone pointed out that they had the wrong man and waved towards Harry. Harry tried to duck under the sidewall of the tent, and one of the policemen aimed his gun at him. "For some reason," wrote Milt later, "I bumped into the cop as he pulled the trigger. The bullet hit Harry in the left leg high up, but it didn't stop him. He made his way to the stock cars."

As the cowboys loaded the horses into the cars, Chester Byers and Amos Clayton put Harry in an empty boxcar that was marked dead-head to Chicago. They gave him two bottles of milk and some bread, and he arrived four days later in Chicago.

Goldie cut the bullet out of his hip and patched him up as best she could. Allie wasn't happy at all about having "the scoundrel" staying at her apartment. Fortunately, Harry was tough, and his wound healed quickly. He left as soon as he could, kissing his pregnant wife goodbye, and he managed to arrive in New York City before the S.S. Varsara, loaded with personnel and stock from the 101 show and bound for Argentina, left the dock on November 1. Vern Tantlinger was the arena director, and other crack performers from Buffalo Bill's show were on board, including Bill Pickett, Chester Byers, Lulu Parr, Jane Fuller, Mabel Cline, Ed Bowman, and Iona and Milt Hinkle.

Harry never did write Goldie while he was gone, but she read about the voyage in the newspapers in Chicago. The weather was so stormy and the Atlantic so rough that everyone was seasick. Passengers came down with smallpox, including trick roper Hank Durnell, who was so sick he stopped eating and refused to leave his bunk. When some of his friends dragged him up on deck for fresh air, he begged them to throw him overboard. He eventually recovered, as did Bill Pickett, who was so sick he later said it was only by thinking of his wife and children in Oklahoma that he survived. Four of the Indians traveling with the show were not as lucky. After days of chills and high fever they died and were buried at sea.

Twenty-eight days later the show finally reached Buenos Aires. Ed Arlington, who owned part of the show, managed to sneak everyone off the ship after bribing the health officials. The stock, however, was victim to a livestock inspector who found out that one of the show horses had glanders, a contagious and often fatal disease. The official ordered all the livestock shot and burned. Pickett said a prayer of thanks that he had left his prized mount, Spradley, at home in Oklahoma. New stock had to be purchased, and several of the cowboys, including Milt and Harry, were dispatched to find what they needed.

After all the setbacks, the show was a tremendous success. Arlington placed lots of favorable newspaper coverage ahead of the show, and in some locations it was so popular he scheduled three shows a day.

After the last Sunday night performance of the show in Buenos Aires, Milt was leaving for Reginald Casey's ranch, where Milt and the other cowboys had bought the stock to replace what the show had lost when they arrived in Argentina. Ed Bowman and Harry were going with him, and they started to drive Milt's stock out of the horse tent when Arlington appeared and demanded $100 for a feed bill. Milt lost his temper because Arlington had used Milt's horses for free during the show and now wanted money for their feed. As the boys started to leave with Milt's horses a couple of gauchos tried to stop them, and Ed Arlington yelled out, loud enough for all to hear, "Harry, you know you're wanted in the United States for murder, so you'd better watch what you do."

Harry snapped back, "And I'll be wanted for murder in this country, too, if you don't get out of my way!"

In his later years Milt was known as one of the foremost storytellers of cowboy tales and for the wonderful way he could embellish them, but Goldie said she actually believed this one "because it explained a lot that I never could understand." Milt recalled later that it was at that point that a friend of Harry's stepped into the fracas. "Harry had made several friends while with the show, but one in particular that he went around with. They had been to parties together and got to be pretty good pals…First, Harry's pal told the gauchos to get off their horses, and then he mounted and rode over to me. He took my 30-30, and I saw that he also had a pistol." The police had arrived, and so had ranch owner Casey. "When Casey spoke to the police, they stepped back, so we rode out of the park with no more trouble," Milt recalled. Milt said he found out later that Harry's friend was "one of the lieutenants of the well known Butch Cassidy gang" who had moved to Argentina.

According to Milt's story, after Harry and Ed dropped Milt and his stock off at the Casey ranch, Milt gave each of them a good saddle horse. Harry and Ed rode on with Harry's friend, Andrew Duffy, formerly known as Harvey Logan or Kid Curry, to his spread near Bahia Blanca, where they broke horses and skinned wild cattle for their hides.

GOLDIE THOUGHT IT WAS THE LONGEST off-season of her life, and one she would like to forget as soon as possible. She didn't want to be a burden on her mother. Although Allie was happy to have her pregnant daughter stay with her, Allie's new husband wasn't as welcoming. Goldie thought the man was taking advantage of her hard-working mother, but the two women finally agreed to a truce not to argue about their husbands, and they settled into an almost-comfortable routine. Goldie took a job in a café to help with the expenses because her new stepfather refused to pay anything to help his stepdaughter. As far as Goldie could tell, he was gambling too much to even pay his share of the expenses.

She'd been thinking about her return to show business. Chicago seemed colder and windier than usual without Harry and her friends, although at least some of them had written. She hadn't heard from Harry. When she read about the ill-fated crossing of the Atlantic, she worried that Harry had been one of the sick or dead, but she hadn't heard a thing. Maybe he'd left for good this time—she didn't know. After days of mulling it over, she'd written to Colonel Cody.

Now she couldn't wait to see the grand old man, and she imagined him puffing on his cigar, sitting in the lobby of the La Salle, waiting for her. She thought about the excitement of being in the arena, the crowds, the horses, even the ones that bucked her off. She thought fondly of the Colonel, and how nice it would be to work for him again on his tour with the Sells-Floto Circus in the spring—after the baby was born.

She re-read the Colonel's telegram for about the hundredth time. *Dear Goldie, Your letter received and you will be taken care of if you still want to come with our show, at the salary you mention in your letter. Fred Hutchinson, our manager, tells me that he has engaged Finn and Arline. Now Goldie I will be at the La Salle Hotel, Chicago after Wednesday next for a week. Call on me there. Love to you all, W.F. Cody.*

But that Wednesday came and went, and Goldie's life didn't change. The Colonel's plans had changed, and when he wrote to tell her, Goldie decided she would stay in Chicago and work in the café until the baby arrived.

Harry was still in South America when his son was born. He was there when Goldie named the infant Russell, and he was still gone when the baby died a few days later. She and Allie buried the baby boy by themselves, and they cried together over the loss. Goldie wasn't sure she wanted to see Harry ever again.

The news traveled fast through the cowgirl community. She got several telegrams, and, Goldie had to admit, they had helped.

It was the telegram from Lucille Mulhall that put an end to her depression and sparked her fire to get back to work. Lucille was offering her friend a place in her vaudeville show. Goldie

S. F. DUTTON, PRESIDENT

THE ALBANY FIREPROOF ANNEX
EVERY ROOM WITH BATH

THE ALBANY
DENVER, COLO.

Dec. 7, 1913.

Goldie Griffith,
7 E. 22nd St., Flat 3,
Chicago, Ill.

Dear Goldie :-

        Your letter received and you will be taken care of
if you still want to come with our show, at the salary you mention
in your letter. Fred Hutchinson, our manager, tells me that he
has engaged Finn and Arline. Now Goldie I will be at the La Salle
Hotel, Chicago after Wednesday next for a week. Call on me there.

Love to you all,

Goldie thought she might go back to work for Buffalo Bill after the Buffalo Bill Wild West and Pawnee Bill Wild East—the Two Bills Show—went broke in Denver, and when she asked him for a job, this is the reply she got.

The Sterling Family

wired an immediate reply: *Yes.* Even Allie thought that 22 weeks on the road would be good for her daughter, and she encouraged her to start working on a new outfit right away. Goldie sewed and cried every day until she left Chicago for the first rehearsal with the Lucille Mulhall Girl Rangers. She decided to return to the road not as Goldie Sterling, or Goldie Walters, or Goldie Smith, but as Goldie Griffith, using her maiden name.

She waved good-bye to Allie and settled in her seat, and the train pulled away from the station and picked up speed, the sights of Chicago rushing past her window. Goldie rocked to the familiar thwack, thwack, thwack of the train car's wheels on the tracks below her, whisking her off to a new adventure, a new chapter in her life. She put her handkerchief away and looked for someone who might enjoy hearing a good story to make the train trip more enjoyable. She figured she'd cried enough. Maybe she wasn't meant to be a mother, but her life as a cowgirl was waiting for her.

Lucille Mulhall Girl Ranger Tour—Goldie poses in front of the poster for Lucille Mulhall's vaudeville show at the Pantages theater in Tacoma, Washington.

The Sterling family

⟩⟩ EIGHTEEN ⟨⟨

A Girl Ranger

CLEVER HORSEWOMAN RIDES INTO FAME, claimed the newspaper headline. Goldie cut the story out and pasted it carefully into her scrapbook. The most famous cowgirl of her time, Lucille Mulhall, had left her vaudeville show to go to the Stampede at Walla Walla, leaving the show in the capable hands of fellow cowgirl Goldie Griffith.

Goldie had learned a lot about her friend Lucille as they traveled to their first engagements around St. Paul and then into Canada. Lucille and Charley's father, Colonel Zack Mulhall, was with them almost all the time, and he rarely let Lucille out of his sight. Goldie didn't mean to eavesdrop, but one day as she walked down the hall in the hotel past Lucille's room she overheard Colonel Zack shouting at his daughter. "You will do as I say and forget about that man." Goldie couldn't see him, but she could imagine the stern old man's big white mustache quivering with rage. Lucille, her hand clenched into a fist, was leaning towards her father. Goldie thought she might try to strike him, but instead she heard a quiet, "Yes, papa." Goldie scurried away as fast as she could. She really didn't want to be in the middle of a family fight—she suffered through enough of them with her own mother—and she felt sorry for Lucille. A few days later, Lucille asked her if she didn't have a letter to post, and Goldie was confused. But she saw Lucille's pointed look at her father's back and played along and said yes, as a matter of fact, she did. This was a ruse they continued to use several other times to get away from the old man for an afternoon.

Goldie found herself accompanied by Lucille and Charley on her "mission" to post a letter and "see some of the sights of St. Paul."

Charley grabbed Goldie's camera as Louise drew a letter out of her coat. "I want a picture of this," he told his sister gleefully.

"Charley Mulhall, you're going to get me in trouble."

"No more trouble than you've been in before. And it's Goldie's camera, I don't think the Colonel will ever see any of the pictures. Right, Goldie?"

Goldie looked from brother to sister.

"Okay, hold it right there," Charley pointed Goldie's camera at his sister, but she ignored him.

"What's up with her?" Goldie asked him, watching Lucille's back vanish through the post office doors.

"She's looking for a letter from Homer." Goldie didn't know who that was. "Homer Wilson, you know, he was the manager of our vaudeville show forever. Lucy's sweet on him. She has to be sneaky about it because it don't matter who the poor girl falls for, pa finds a way to break it up. Just look at what happened with Martin." Goldie had heard of Martin Van Bergen. She'd read a description of his voice in the newspaper as having a "captivating tone quality and appealing sweetness." She knew Martin had performed with the Mulhalls' stage show.

"Well, actually, Martin wasn't the first, but he sure made the Colonel mad. Lucy thought she could marry the poor sap and keep it a secret. She used the Colonel's real name, Vandeveer, for the paperwork, but, of course, he found out— and he was furious."

Charley handed Goldie her camera and gave her a boost up onto the wall next to the stairs of the post office. "You know she has a son?" Goldie shook her head. "Yep, sweet little William. Let's see, he'd be about five now. She never sees him."

Goldie didn't have to ask any more questions because Charley was still in the storytelling mood. "He's with Martin's parents. Sister Lucille isn't good for anything but the stage or the arena. And the Colonel will never let her do anything else. She's too valuable." Goldie found herself staring at Lucille as she came out of the post office.

"Come on, you two, I want to see some of the sights." Charley and Goldie followed her across the street. Charley's hand brushed Goldie's shoulder as he reached again for her camera.

"Let's get a picture of Lucille, shall we? No mail from Homer?" Lucille put her hand in her coat pocket and cocked her head, faintly smiling at Charley's humor. The two white feathers on top of her hat shimmered and tickled the air as she shook her head. "Right then. Let's get another picture—this time my two favorite gals in their fantastic hats. How 'bout over there?" Charley was pointing at the cannon in front of the courthouse. Obligingly, the two show women struck a pose.

Goldie was thinking more about Charley's hand brushing her shoulder than she was about Lucille's past. All the cowgirls had pasts. Almost all of them had flings with different cowboys. Some of them got married, and then a lot of them got divorced. Including Charley, who was rumored to have been married to the aloof Lulu Parr and divorced in a single month. Lulu said Charley had deserted her, but after hearing about Lucille, Goldie had to bet that the Colonel had something to do with it.

Goldie thought bitterly about her own husband. She understood why so many of the couples she knew got divorced. Did

Harry have a blanket companion when he was hiding out from everyone, including his wife? She didn't want to think about it, and threw herself into some serious flirting with Charley.

From St. Paul, the Girl Rangers next traveled to Canada. They played in Winnipeg, and then took the long, long train ride to Edmonton. Goldie took pictures of the troupe on the baseball field in Edmonton, where they took on some locals between shows before moving on to Victoria and Vancouver. The company was small, seven of them in all, with as many horses, and a steer billed as a "Genuine Texas Long Horn."

At every show they had to unpack all the theater props and erect the portable fence the Mulhalls had devised to hang from the fly loft and fasten between the stage and orchestra pit. They laid a thick rope mat on the floor and stretched ropes above it to make it look like a corral, and the "fence" prevented accidents if the bucking bronco got too rambunctious during the performance. Because of all these preparations, and the need to clean up after the horses had been on stage, the Girl Rangers were always the last act of the vaudeville bill.

Their thirty-minute show started with the curtain slowly rising on a sunrise scene. Charley was asleep next to his sleeping horse. Colonel Zack tossed a couple of roosters onto the stage, and they crowed. Then a live coyote wandered onto the stage, attached to a piano wire that was invisible to the audience. When the Colonel made a funny little whistling sound it stopped and howled. Most audiences had never seen a live coyote, and they were enthralled. Next the longhorn steer plodded on stage. He also was attached to a piano wire. Charley woke up and rolled a cigarette with one hand, a trick he had to learn for vaudeville, lit it, and got up, ready to ride. Then a cowgirl, in the first weeks played by Goldie, rode onto the stage, calling out, "Here comes Lucille." More cowhands, including Lucille, rode into the scene, to the tune of 'Gypsy Love Song,' only they sang 'Cowboy Sweetheart.' Lucille performed her roping act, includ-

Lucille Mulhall Girl Ranger Tour—A passerby takes a second look at Goldie and Charley, maybe a reaction to their matching, unconventional hats, as they pose for a picture in front of a Pantages Theater during Goldie's tour with Lucille Mulhall's Girl Rangers show.

Buffalo Bill Museum and Grave, Lookout Mountain, Golden, Colorado

ing roping Goldie, who appeared again, riding a running horse. Then Lucille took Eddie C., her horse, through his tricks.

Charley was always a smash hit when he rode the bucking Buzzard X, a horse the Mulhalls had trained specially to buck on the small stage. Buzzard X was a hit everywhere—he squealed when he was saddled, bawled when he bucked, and he bucked frighteningly high, weaving as he did. Some of the city folk complained when they thought the horse was squealing because he was being hurt, so the Colonel took to putting announcements in the newspapers of the cities they played, saying he would pay a thousand dollars if anyone could find a scratch on any of the show's horses. When humane society

Lucille Mulhall Girl Ranger Tour—Above: Goldie took these pictures of Charley in St. Paul, Minnesota. Below: Goldie, left, and Lucille Mulhall at the post office in St. Paul.

The Sterling family

Lucille Mulhall Girl Ranger Tour–Members of the cast and crew relaxed with a visit to the ballfield in Edmonton.

The Sterling family

officers would come to examine the horses, they would find them healthy and happy, including the squalling Buzzard X, who was just like the other horses until someone saddled him. For the stage work, the horses were shod with rubber shoes so they wouldn't slip, but that didn't stop Buzzard X from putting on an exhibition accompanied by his crazy snorts that always elicited muffled screams from the audience which feared the bucker could jump off the stage into their laps at any moment.

Lucille and Charley left the Girl Rangers for a while to perform in a roping contest in Walla Walla, Washington. When that happened, Goldie took Lucille's role in the show. After Lucille won the title of World Champion Steer Roper, her father was always promoting her and booking her into rodeos and shows that made more money than her vaudeville act. Most of the extra money Lucille and Charley made in the rodeos went into maintaining the Girl Rangers' performing troupe and the stock, both of which had to be housed and fed between engagements. Interest in the Wild West shows was declining, and even the famous Lucille Mulhall was attracting fewer and fewer people to her vaudeville show, especially now that audiences could go to a movie theater to see one of their Western heroes or heroines in a heart-stopping flicker.

After Lucille and Charley left the show, Goldie did Lucille's trick riding and roping, and for the finale she rode the squealing Buzzard X on the narrow stage while the rest of the company was yelling and shooting blanks from their revolvers.

In Seattle, for the part of the act when Goldie needed to ride in fast, she found she could get a good start from the far side of an alley back of the theater. She rode on stage through a wide door with a low top. But on the last night of the engagement, she forgot to duck and ended up with fifteen stitches in her head.

The tour with Lucille's show ended in San Francisco, and as soon as they arrived Goldie started looking for another job. She rode with the Society Circus, and she applied to the San Francisco police department to be a policewoman. She had always wanted to be a policewoman, ever since she had talked about it to that newspaper reporter in New York and let him think it had been one of her jobs before she joined Buffalo Bill's show. The San Francisco newspaper reported: *Saturday morning it was when Miss Goldie announced to the world her yearning to be a cop. She announced it to the Civil Service Commission in a mighty business-like way. "I desire to take an examination and join the police force," she announced severely to the clerk in the civil service office. "I can vote, and I can ride, and I am just as well fitted to be a uniformed officer as any man." ...She is thoroughly and absolutely convinced that she can jail drunk and disorderly persons, break up fights, arrest robbers and other horrid men who would try to disturb the peace and quiet of San Francisco, and do everything in the lines of policing that any mere man cop can do.*

The authorities couldn't find anything in the city's charter or its laws where policewomen were mentioned, so the city

Miss ...Idie. Griffin Wants to Become Cop and Asks for the Job

Miss Goldie Griffin, who asks chance to become a police woman.

City Attorney Debating Eligibility of Women for Such Posts

MISS GOLDIE GRIFFIN, horsewoman, athlete, sometime actress, and young and attractive to boot, wants to be a police woman in San Francisco. Also she perfectly don't care a good piece of fudge who knows it. She has made application to be a police woman, believing that she can walk a beat just as well as any member of the city's finest, and she intends to walk that beat if there is any way that she possibly can do so. She is thoroughly and absolutely convinced that she can jail drunk and disorderly persons, break up fights, arrest robbers.

When Goldie applied to be a policewoman in San Francisco, she was performing with a western show that made more money for charity than any other up to that time in California. The money raised was donated to orphans and poor children, and the show was sponsored by several high profile, high society organizations. The prominent women who were involved with the show also were involved with the push to get policewomen on the San Francisco force. Immediately after the last show closed, Goldie, who by then was a celebrity in the city, made her application to be a policewoman. Unfortunately, the city "fathers" weren't ready to hire women, but Goldie's application was big news. In interviews with local newspapers, Goldie declared that she could do the job as well or better than any man. According to Lee Sullivan, historian for the San Francisco Police Department, Goldie's public announcement allowed for the eventual incorporation of women as police officers.

The Sterling family

Lucille Mulhall Girl Ranger Tour—Goldie, Charley, Milt Rankin, Maud Meyers, and an unidentified member of the cast in Oakland, California.

The Sterling family

Lucille Mulhall Girl Ranger Tour—On board the Princess Charlotte on the way to Tacoma from Vancouver, Goldie and Charley, at right, pose with other members of the cast.

The Sterling family

attorney looked into Goldie's proposition. He ruled against her, and she didn't get the job, but she did get a good bit of publicity as the first woman to apply for a job as a cop in San Francisco.

The tour with Lucille Mulhall's Girl Rangers had been exhilarating, and she'd regained her confidence after the devastating loss of the baby and Harry's disappearance. He'd never even seen their baby, but she'd managed to get through those dark days by herself. She wasn't sure she could ever forgive Harry, but she hadn't seen him in so long it felt like he didn't even exist, and that made the pain more bearable. She was doing all right taking care of herself, although she had a feeling that he would turn up sooner or later.

Allie came out to San Francisco to celebrate the end of the successful tour of Lucille Mulhall's Girl Rangers with her daughter, and the newspaper reported, *Miss Griffith is a St. Louis woman whose equestrianism has won her honors in theatres as well as in the tented arena. Her recent San Francisco visit resolved itself into a family reunion as her mother, Mrs. Allie Crites, formerly in professional ranks, came on from St. Louis and Chicago to greet her, and several functions for theatrical and former frontier days co-workers served to start a flow of reminiscences at these jolly get-together parties.*

Lucille Mulhall Girl Ranger Tour—Colonel Zack Mulhall posed for Goldie on the train, above, and with a couple of friends, below center, during the tour.

The Sterling family

Lucille Mulhall Girl Ranger Tour—Above: Mr. Lee, Lucille Mulhall, Maud, Goldie, and Charley Mulhall in Tacoma, Washington. Below: Charley and movie star Duke R. Lee.

The Sterling family

When the Girl Rangers were playing near Los Angeles, Goldie and Charley took a short side trip to visit with Tom Mix, the top cowboy of American silent films. Goldie and Charley are on the right, posing with Tom and Ollie Mix and their two girls.

The Sterling family

While visiting with Tom Mix, Goldie and Charley took some time to visit Mixville, in Glendale, California, where many of Mix's 300 movies were filmed. Here Goldie hams it up for the photographer. Both the stagecoach and the building were used for Mix's famous stunts.

The Sterling family

❧ NINETEEN ❧

Prairie Dog Court

SHE WAS HUMMING TO HERSELF as she picked the dishes up from the table. Harry's much younger brother Walter, or Buddy as everyone called him, had just arrived in Denver, and the three of them had had a pleasant dinner at the table in the kitchen. Buddy had gone out for a ride, and Harry was in the other room, figuring out how long it might take to sell the stacked hay he had bought for $1,400. First they needed to find someone who could haul it to their barn. Harry's back, which he'd injured when a horse kicked him in Oregon, was better for now, but both she and Harry believed his days of bronco riding were over. When they busted up this last time, he had started this horse-selling business at the stockyards, and after he got the business going, he came to get her. Once again, Goldie had forgiven him and came back to Denver with him. They borrowed the money to buy the little house, and Goldie felt like things were finally going right.

She was pregnant again. It had been a rocky two and a half years with Harry, but when they made up this last time, it

The Pin Heads were some of Goldie's friends who also worked the Sells Floto shows. Often the Wild West was one of the acts in a circus show, and Goldie had many friends who continued to perform with circuses after the demise of the Wild Wests.

Buffalo Bill Museum and Grave, Lookout Mountain, Golden, Colorado

seemed like it was going to stick. She was working the Sells-Floto show, but it was the end of the season, already mid-December, so she was home, home in Denver, working at the Stockman's Club to help support her mother who had moved to Denver after divorcing her husband. Goldie had always known her mother's new husband was no good, and finally Allie had seen through the scoundrel.

Goldie had thought plenty of times about divorcing Harry, but she wanted so badly to make their marriage work. And now she thought it was possible. She found it hard to believe that she was putting dirty dishes in a sink, and not only that, it was *her sink,* in *her house.*

Buddy sauntered into the kitchen, carrying a glass ceremoniously to the sink to be 'helpful.' He gave her a friendly punch in the shoulder, and joined his brother in the front room. The two men laughed at something, and there was a knock on the back door. It creaked loudly as Goldie opened it and invited Art Wachter, the tall, burly horseback patrolman at the stockyards, to come in. He pulled off his big hat, and dabbed at his forehead and balding head with his bandana. He was glistening with sweat despite the cold outside. He looked anxiously at the doorway to the other room. "Harry here?"

"Hi, Art. Come on in," Harry called to his pal. They had been friends since Harry had started selling horses at the stockyards, and he always told Goldie she could count on Art if anything happened to him. As Goldie ran water into the sink, she could hear them talking, and then it got quiet. Too quiet, she thought, and the hairs on the back of her neck prickled. She turned the water off and walked into the other room to see what had happened.

Harry had a funny look on his face. "Goldie, they're gonna take me back." Goldie shook her head. She didn't understand.

"Hold on here just a minute," Buddy started, but Harry interrupted him. "Now don't start nothin', Art's a friend o' mine, and he's jus' doing his duty." Goldie knew then what it was about—the old murder charge.

Art grimaced. "I gotta to take him in, none of us got any choice here. The law's the law."

"You take care of everything, Goldie," Harry said as he swung into his jacket, and Art followed him out the door.

Goldie grabbed her coat off the rack standing next to the door. "Wait, I'm coming with you. You take care of everything here, Buddy." She thought Buddy looked like he was going to swell up like a poisoned pup, but he nodded.

The three of them rode in the police car to the station. Goldie tried talking some sense into Art—explaining that Harry had already been tried six times for his supposed crime, but she got nowhere. Harry's past had finally caught up with him.

She asked to talk to Harry before they put him in a cell. She wanted to know what else she could do to help. The deputies let them sit for a few minutes in an interview room, but one of them stood guard outside while they talked. Harry asked her to look after the business and the house. Then he said it might sound peculiar but he believed it would look better for his case if he wasn't married, and if they weren't married, it wouldn't look good if she was pregnant.

"What do you mean?"

"I mean, well, you know what I've told you about Texas. They'll do anything to a man, and it just would be better for you, too, if we weren't married."

"But," Goldie gulped.

"Hey, honey, you want to help me, don't you?"

Goldie could feel the sobs rising from her solar plexus. She knew what he wanted her to do; he wanted her to have an abortion. She'd already lost the baby she'd named Russell and buried in Chicago, and she didn't know if she could stand losing another baby. Harry chucked her under the chin and looked her in the eye.

"Please, say you'll do it for me. You know I love you, and after this is all over, we'll be back together again, and you can have all the babies you want."

Goldie pulled herself together. She'd never been afraid of anything before, and there was no reason to succumb now. If

Harry Walters, right, posed with four other Cheyenne Frontier Days champions. He won his title just months before being arrested and sent back to Texas to stand trial for the old murder charge.

Wyoming State Archives, Department of State Parks and Cultural Resources

Below, the story that appeared in The Denver Post on December 19, 1915.

CHAMPION BRONCHO BUSTER HELD IN DENVER FOR MURDER IN TEXAS

Hiram Sterling, Stockyards Horse Dealer, Is Wanted In Waco for Crime in 1906 for Which He Has Been Tried Six Times, and Jury Disagreed.

Hiram Sterling, alias Harry Walters, 29, champion broncho buster and trick rider of the world, who has been operating a horse and mule exchange at the Denver Union stockyards for over a year, was arrested late yesterday by Detective Cole and Mounted Officer Wachter on telegraphic request from the police of Waco, Texas, where he is wanted for a murder committed in 1906.

The crime with which he is charged took place at Teague, Texas. The victim, according to Sterling's story of the affair, was Carol Whitt, proprietor of a "blind pig," and the trouble which educated to the serious side of life. I can see now where I made a mistake.

"As far as my conscience is concerned, I feel that I was perfectly justified in shooting Whitt because he tried to kill

she could ride a bucking bronco, she could survive this too. She found herself nodding, thinking that it wasn't a good time to have a baby anyway, and fifteen minutes later she told the sheriff that Harry really was her boyfriend, not her husband.

In the next two weeks, she sold the hay, put the house up for sale, sold the horses, sold their few possessions, found a room in a boarding house, and visited a doctor who was willing to perform the illegal abortion. She received a telegram from Harry in Houston, and he'd asked her to bring $150 when she came. After selling everything and paying off the bank, there wasn't that much left. She'd already paid the doctor and bought her train ticket for Houston. She wanted to be there for him during the trial, and she couldn't bear the thought of not going. She only had $25 left. So she borrowed $100 from a neighbor woman, and took on extra shifts at the restaurant so she could earn the rest of the $150 Harry needed.

After the abortion, she cried for two days, so it was actually a relief to take on the extra shifts. Working with her women pals and chatting with customers brought a sense of equilibrium to her life and lifted the cloud of depression that was hanging over her head. When she felt the cloud swirling again, she'd remind herself of Harry's promise: "All the babies you want."

The visit with her mother hadn't helped her depression much. Goldie had hoped to get solace from Allie, but Allie's expression was grim after Goldie told her about the abortion. Allie was living in a boardinghouse not far from Harry and Goldie, and her dislike of Harry had never dimmed. Dinners together were tense, so Goldie had taken to seeing her mother only when Harry was not around. But now, when Goldie needed to believe in her husband who was waiting for her in a jail in Texas, Allie said Harry had every trouble coming to him, that he deserved to spend the rest of his life in jail, that she'd always known he was up to no good. So, instead of solace for the abor-

Goldie's mother, Allie Crites.
The Sterling family

tion that had left her so depressed, Goldie retreated from Allie's room with her ears ringing from Allie's diatribe about Harry's faults. Allie had never understood that Goldie loved her husband. Sure, they'd had some rocky times, but so did every couple she knew.

A few nights later Goldie was surprised to see her mother at her door. It was her last night in Denver. Her trunk was packed with all her remaining belongings, and she was ready to go. The desperation she'd felt when she returned home from the jail that first night was back. She'd been working hard, doing what she could to help her husband, but she wasn't sure it was enough. What if they hanged him?

When Goldie answered the knock on the door she wasn't feeling very friendly—she was in no mood for more arguments—but her mother didn't seem to notice. It was Christmas Eve, and Goldie could only hope that Allie had come by to say she was sorry about what she'd said about Harry and to wish her a Merry Christmas, but she was suspicious because Allie was empty-handed, not even a handkerchief for a gift. Goldie hadn't had time to think about a gift for Allie, but she had figured her mother would understand why. Allie marched in and made herself at home at the kitchen table, and as soon as Allie opened her mouth, Goldie knew her worst fears were confirmed. Allie hadn't come with any holiday cheer.

"You have to hear me out this time, Goldie." Allie was so determined Goldie knew that she would have to listen.

Goldie dropped into the other chair at the table and sighed. "Okay, what?"

"Your husband is a bigamist." Goldie shook her head. Her mother had come up with some crazy reasons why her daughter shouldn't stay with Harry, but this one seemed the craziest of all. "You don't believe me, but what I'm telling you is the truth. He was married in Texas, and he has a wife and a daughter there."

"No, ma, that's not possible."

"Yes, it is, and you know it."

"No."

"Well, you can decide for yourself. I already told Chief Duffield about it, and he sent off to Texas to find out if it's true."

"You did what?" Goldie was furious and started drumming her fingers on the table to keep herself from punching her own mother.

The two women glared at each other. "When did you tell Chief Duffield?"

"When I told him about Harry, about how he was wanted in Texas, about how he dyed his hair—"

"You what?" Goldie couldn't believe it. Her own mother had tipped the police about Harry and was the reason he was sitting in jail in Houston at that moment. The reason she'd had an abortion. Her head roared with indignation. Her own mother! "Get out, get out of my house!" She pointed at the door, and her arm was shaking, but she couldn't lower it until she saw Allie's backside.

"Goldie, you'll find out I'm right about that man. Just wait. Wait and see. I'm right," Allie stomped to the door and slammed it behind her.

Goldie sat down and sobbed. It couldn't be true. Allie had been against him from the beginning, and now she was trying to drive them apart just as Goldie was trying to make everything good again. Would nothing in her life ever go right?

GOLDIE FOUND A CHEAP ROOM close to the courthouse in Houston for her five-day stay for Harry's trial. Her question for the lawyer they hired was how they could try Harry again for something that happened nine years ago, *so long ago*, and that he'd already been tried for so many times. The lawyer thought that was a good question, and told her he thought that this time the judge and jury had to make a decision. He told her not to worry, but she was worried sick.

The seventh trial lasted one excruciatingly long day. Goldie listened anxiously as Harry told his story. Then the Whitt family told their side. There hadn't been any witnesses, so it came down to who the jury was going to believe. Six times before the jury was hung, but this time they reached a verdict. Harry received a five-year suspended sentence. And he couldn't ever come back to Texas. Goldie was relieved. At least he was free. Their life together would never be the same, but she had her husband back. Harry kissed her cheek, shook his lawyer's hand, and she put her soggy handkerchief back in her purse.

They left the elegant courthouse arm in arm, but as they descended the stairs, Harry wrenched his arm away from her. At the bottom of the steps, a stylishly dressed young woman approached them. Beside her was a little girl who looked to

Goldie to be about five years old. The woman smiled posses-
sively at Harry.

"I have your money," Harry told her. Goldie looked from
one of them to the other in astonishment. "Goldie, honey, give
me the money." Goldie pulled the hard-earned and borrowed
$150 out of her purse. Harry swept it from her hand and gave it
to the other woman who threw her head back and laughed at
them before she and her daughter turned around and walked
down the avenue.

"Was that your wife?" Goldie spat the words out.

"Yes, that was Nina. But she's no longer my wife. You know
that, Goldie. You're my wife—my only—"

"I know no such thing."

"Yes, you do."

"How would I know?"

"Didn't you talk to Chief Duffield before you left?"

Goldie just looked at him.

"No? When your ma tipped him off 'bout me, the Chief
said he was gonna add charges of bigamy to the murder charges.
I had the authorities here send him a letter explainin' that Nina
had divorced me. But she also wanted $150 in alimony, so I had
to pay it—if I didn't, I'd be back in jail. You understand, of
course, don't you, Goldie?"

She couldn't believe it. She didn't understand even one little
part of it, and at the moment she hoped she'd never have to see
her husband again. Anything was preferable to the misery she
felt at that moment. She turned and walked away from him.

As it turned out, she didn't have to worry about seeing Harry
for a long time. He disappeared—again—before she even got
back to the hotel, and later she heard from Buddy that he'd
headed for Tijuana, where a new horse-racing track had opened.

∽ TWENTY ∽

No Regrets

UNDER HER PICTURE WAS THE HEADLINE: *Circus Rider Shoots at Husband She Asserts Betrayed Her Love.*

Goldie smiled. So far all the newspaper accounts had got it right. But she really liked this one.

With her only regret that she did not kill her husband, Goldie Walters, 23 years old, is in the city jail for shooting at Harry Walters, champion broncho buster of the world, at 2 o'clock yesterday afternoon in front of his home at 4667 Humboldt street.

Her mother, her baby, her good name she sacrificed for him, she says, and he turned against her, so she says she made up her mind she would have to kill him, as there was nothing left for her to care for in the world. Black-eyed, dashingly beautiful, the young woman who herself has spent her life in circus riding, told her story in the matron's quarters of the jail last night.

The young reporter had faithfully copied down every detail Goldie had given him about the shooting. She'd been in jail four days until her lawyer, Jim Smith, could get Judge Rice to agree to lower her bond to $500. The bond was originally set at $2,000, but Jim had argued that it should be reduced because the charge, "assault to kill," was not a serious one. He'd put up

REGRETS SHE DID NOT KILL HUSBAND

Mrs. Goldie Walters, who shot at Harry Walters, champion broncho buster yesterday, after she had given up all for him, she says, and he had deserted her.

"REGRETS SHE DID NOT KILL HUSBAND." Goldie cut out this Denver newspaper story about her arrest and pasted it in her scrapbook. Although the police referred to her as Goldie Sterling or Goldie Smith, the newspaper reporter wrote about Goldie Walters.

The Sterling family

his own property as collateral for the bond, and the judge had agreed to let Goldie out of jail on a bond of $500.

Although Harry had said he wouldn't prosecute her after she'd shot at him on the street, he'd apparently thought better of that decision, according to the newspaper, when he found out she was bonding out. She shuffled through the clippings until she found it. ...*but fear that she would again attempt his life if given her liberty is said to have caused him to change his mind.*

Her trial was scheduled for May 18, and two months was a long time to wait. She couldn't leave Denver, and her lawyer told her not to go near Harry, so she worked and waited. When she thought about what she'd done, she still wasn't sorry. One of the other headlines, *Wife Regrets Effort To Kill Husband Failed,* had it nailed. That really was her only regret.

She wasn't surprised that there was a hubbub as they all gathered in the courtroom for her trial when that morning in May finally arrived. Goldie guessed it had something to do with Harry. Her lawyer reached over and squeezed her hand. The judge appeared, and everyone stood. After they all sat again, he asked Sheriff Duffield if the witnesses were ready.

"No, sir."

"Please explain."

"Well, sir, I went around last night to notify the witnesses to appear today for the trial, but Mr. Sterling is missing."

Jim reached over and again squeezed Goldie's hand.

"What do you mean, missing?"

"Just that, Judge. His friends think he may have joined a circus."

Judge Rice opened his mouth and closed it without saying anything. He shook his head, looked at the papers in front of him for a minute. Then he asked the prosecuting attorney, "What do you want to do now, John?"

John Rush, Denver's District Attorney, rose slowly to his feet. "Sir, I have no choice but to ask that the charges against Mrs. Sterling be dismissed."

Relief flooded through Goldie.

"This case is dismissed. Mrs. Sterling, you are free to go." Goldie beamed. She was a free woman. A few whoops of congratulations were met with loud boos behind her, but she didn't care. She kissed her lawyer, shook hands with the friends who had come to support her, and left the courtroom feeling jubilant. She stared hard at Harry's friends, the ones who had booed the judge's announcement—they weren't going to intimidate her. She hadn't done anything wrong.

Harry had made her life hell. He told her he loved her, but he never acted like it. He'd ruined her relationship with her mother, and he'd left her destitute. He'd married her when he was already married. Every time she thought about it, she felt so betrayed. She should have listened to Lillie that night in New Mexico so long ago. Lillie was right, Harry was dangerous—not only with a gun, but also with his relationships. She knew she would always love him, even if she didn't know why, and even if she didn't ever want to see him again. And she would always hate him for what he did to her. She was glad she'd tried to kill him. It would have felt so good.

At least there was one thing she could always count on with Harry. He would disappear at the most important moment. Maybe this time it was a little gift to her—although probably he wasn't even thinking about her when he left town. In any case, she was glad this once that he had taken off and left her.

↝ TWENTY-ONE ↜

Meeting the Misty Beyond

"STEP LIVELY," CALLED OUT the master of ceremonies, alternately waving his cane above his high silk hat and tapping it loudly on the white marble floor. The sound echoed above the muffled murmurs of the crowd. "Big crowd behind; step along; hurry up, folks." Goldie slipped past the people in line to see the bronze casket lying in state in the rotunda of Colorado's Capitol building. High above the casket, the Capitol's elegant dome soared skyward, and muted daylight filtered across the room from the many stained glass windows. In two hours, 25,000 people had come to pay their last respects to Buffalo Bill Cody. They started streaming past the troopers from Fort Logan, past the master of ceremonies, and finally past the casket at 10 a.m.

At noon the seemingly endless procession was stopped, and the Colonel's family was given a chance to say farewell. Following them was the delegation of Knights Templar from North Platte, Nebraska, Cody's birthplace. Then Goldie, surrounded by many of her friends, and many other cowboys and cowgirls she did not know, filed past the bier. After they paid their respects, the public was allowed to continue its sad march for another twenty minutes.

Thousands packed the streets of Denver for Buffalo Bill's funeral procession.

Buffalo Bill Museum and Grave, Lookout Mountain, Golden, Colorado

Cody had died four days earlier, when 1917 was only 10 days old. The newspapers were full of reports about the Colonel's last days in Denver. After the disastrous 1913 season, when the Two Bills show went broke in Denver, he had worked some for other shows, including Harry Tammen's. Late in December of 1916 he got sick, but in early January he felt better and traveled across the Continental Divide to Glenwood Springs, a town that had sprung up next to a mineral hot springs, to "take the waters." Two days later he collapsed. He died at his sister's home in Denver, and had lain in state there for four days. The day after he died, the Colonel was the biggest news in the country, stealing headlines from the war.

From the gold-domed Capitol, the funeral procession, led by the horse-drawn caisson, made its way to the Elks' building. Among the motor cars in the procession were the governors of Colorado and Wyoming. Condolences came from President Wilson, Teddy Roosevelt, King George V and Queen Mary of England, and other dignitaries from around the world. Several thousand people walked behind the automobiles in the cold wind, including Boy Scouts, Spanish-American war veterans, two hundred Elks, and Civil War veterans with a fife and drum corps. Among the seventy cowboys who walked behind the caisson were two who had rented a white horse from a local livery stable that looked like Cody's beloved Isham. They led the riderless horse with its stirrups reversed and Buffalo Bill's pistols hanging from the saddlehorn.

Even though a burial service was read at the service at the Elks' lodge, there was no burial. The coffin was taken to Olinger's mortuary where it was put in a crypt until spring. The Denver Post had already begun a drive, called "pennies from schoolchildren," to pay for a monument to the Old Scout on Lookout Mountain. No child was permitted to contribute more than five cents. Goldie thought it was shameful that Harry H. Tammen of The Denver Post, the man who had engineered the financial collapse of Buffalo Bill's Wild West, took over the planning of the elaborate funeral. It was rumored that Tammen paid Mrs. Cody $10,000 to bury Buffalo Bill on Lookout Mountain instead of on Cedar Mountain, above the town Cody had founded—Cody, Wyoming. Goldie's story of the time she had spent with the Colonel on top of Lookout Mountain was cited as proof that Buffalo Bill had changed his mind about where he wanted to be laid to rest.

On June 17 another huge crowd, again estimated at 20,000 to 25,000, began its slow, sad ascent of Lookout Mountain. It took almost three hours for the 3,000 cars and many thousands of walkers to climb the seven and a half twisting miles of the Lariat Trail.

Buffalo Bill had been Brother William Cody, Master Mason, Scottish Rite, Knights Templar, and Noble of Tangier Shrine Temple. His eight pallbearers were Brother Templars, and the services were conducted by Worshipful Master G.W. Parfet of Golden City Lodge No. 1. Everyone attached to the funeral procession seemed to be Masons—the white lambskin aprons were everywhere, on car drivers and policemen, and on men on every corner ready to give directions or help to those in need. It was one of the largest Masonic funerals in American history.

Mrs. Cody announced that all those people who had come to pay their respects to her husband should be able to see him, so they again opened the casket and allowed Buffalo Bill's adoring public to file past in two lines on both sides for two hours. The open, glass-topped casket was shaded from the intense noon-day sun by a large umbrella. Taps was played, the American flag was raised, and a salute of eleven guns, usually reserved for a brigadier general, was fired.

William F. Cody, known around the world as Buffalo Bill, was buried under a pile of stones, and a large sign was nailed to a tree. The next year a stone monument was placed at the grave, and a fence was erected around it. After the death of Cody's wife Louisa in 1921, Cody's niece Mary Jester Allen lobbied to move the world-famous showman's remains to a different site. Places like Cody, Wyoming; North Platte, Nebraska; or Arlington National Cemetery were mentioned. Talk of moving the grave spurred Cody's "adopted son" Johnny Baker into action. The world-famous crack shot had been a long-time performer with Buffalo Bill's shows, and Cody had taken a shine to the young man. In 1927 Baker had the whole grave site redone. A hole was blasted out of the rock, lined with cement, and a steel vault was installed. Ten feet of concrete was poured over the grave. The "new" impregnable gravesite was more attractive, and today it is a major tourist attraction.

But on that June day in 1917, Goldie, and the world, said a final good-bye to the great Buffalo Bill, the man who had changed forever the way Americans would remember and idolize their past. For Goldie, he had been her ticket to fame as a cowgirl, a ride that was cut short when his Wild West went broke in Denver. He'd been her friend and mentor. He'd given her away at her wedding, and he'd been the best boss she'd ever had. She would never forget that tumultuous season of 1913—Buffalo Bill's last with his own Wild West, and Goldie's first and last as one of his Lady Bronc Riders.

⟫⟩ TWENTY-TWO ⟨⟪

A Twisted Tale

GOLDIE HAD BEEN DEPRESSED since Christmas. She was working in a restaurant again, just trying to make ends meet, and the only time she'd heard from Harry was the note that came with a tiny box just after the holiday. *Dear Goldie, This is exceedingly small and not near what I would like to give you for Xmas but please except [sic] it from me that means well—wishing you a Merry Xmas and a Happy New Year. –H*

She thought he might come for the Colonel's funeral, but again she had been disappointed. Instead, here she was, 24 years old, alone in Denver, while her husband was off somewhere, doing who knew what. She knew it was time to get on with her life, even if it had to be a life alone.

She looked again at the little book of photographs she had pulled out of the bottom of her show trunk. Among the pictures from her tour with Lucille Mulhall's Girl Rangers were pictures of Charley. She had cut him out of one picture and written "Some Boy" above his head. There were pictures of Lucille and the whole gang on the baseball field in Edmonton, pictures of

Charley, Goldie, Lucille, and the ruggedly handsome Duke R. Lee, who was famous for his work in the cowboy flickers. There were the pictures from their visit to Ollie and Tom Mix's home in Los Angeles, but the ones Goldie was looking for were on the very last few pages. Charley had sent them to her after the end of the tour. There was one of her putting a letter in a mailbox, and in the picture's white border Charley had written, "I wonder who will get this?" Another photograph showed Charley and a pal astride a screaming hog. Around its edge he wrote, "On the hog in Oklahoma. But Some Ranch." Yeah, she had to agree, some ranch. In the border of the photograph next to it in which she and Charley posed for the camera, he had written, "I hope we will be together again soon—do you?" In the next picture, she was playfully hanging on the shoulder of a friend, and Charley had written, "Don't you think this makes me jealous?"

He proposed to her after that vaudeville tour. Some of the members of the crew had come with Goldie to her mother's in Chicago for Thanksgiving, and after dinner she and Charley took a walk. Of course, she couldn't say yes. She was already married. But she was flattered nonetheless. When you never knew where your husband was, it was good to know that someone else cared.

She traced her finger over the photos again before she put the album back in her trunk. Now she had no one. In spite of that, she was glad that she had decided not to marry Charley. Colonel Zack Mulhall would have been her father-in-law, and she was sure she wouldn't have bent to his will the way that Lucille, and even Charley, did. Lucille may have been the best rider and roper she'd ever seen, but for as long as Goldie knew her she was dominated by her father. Charley had done slightly better at making a life of his own, but Colonel Zack was a formidable force, and Goldie was certain she would have been unhappy as his daughter-in-law. What Prairie Rose told her after Buffalo Bill's funeral verified what she had observed when she worked with Lucille and Charley on the Girl Rangers tour.

Lucille Mulhall Girl Ranger Tour—Was it Charley who wrote around the edges of this photo? *"I hope we will be together soon—do you?"* Goldie pasted it on the last page of the scrapbook of her tour with Lucille Mulhall's Girl Rangers.

The Sterling family

After the funeral on Lookout Mountain, she and Prairie Rose had retired with some of the other cowboys to the Albany Hotel where the Colonel spent much of his time in Denver. When the weather was amenable Cody used to sit ramrod-straight on the steps of The Denver Post building on Champa Street during the afternoons, telling stories to the local boys before retiring to the bar at the Albany Hotel where he continued with the storytelling into the late evening.

Prairie Rose Henderson, center, poses with her pals and fellow cowgirls Kittie Canutt and Ruth Roach.

Wyoming State Archives, Department of
State Parks and Cultural Resources

Rose's outfit was outlandish and fun in Goldie's opinion, but
from the looks shot their way as they ambled up the hotel steps,
Goldie guessed that most of the good folk of Denver disagreed
with her. To them, the outfit Prairie Rose had chosen for the
evening—a short skirt made of ostrich feathers and a heavily
sequined bolero vest—was inappropriate at the very least. The
stares continued as the two women entered the bar at the
Albany. Rose just flashed her big, toothy grin, enjoying her own
spectacle. If they wanted to drink, women were supposed to do it
in their rooms, but the management of the Albany was willing to

suspend the rules for the grieving cowgirls who were used to being on equal footing with men in the arena. The Albany was doing good business in the bar that night—not only were the cowboys and cowgirls tossing a few back as they raised toast after toast to the great old man, but some of the city's most important men had come to the bar to remember Cody—and to watch the cowboys and cowgirls. We're still entertaining everybody, even after Buffalo Bill's funeral, Goldie thought to herself, as she surveyed the small groups of nattily dressed city men.

She and Rose snagged a table in a corner so they could talk. "I think ya shoulda' dumped ol' Harry and jumped on Charley when he asked ya," Rose told her. But Goldie said no, she still thought there was hope for her and Harry. "Bullshit. You never know where he is, you never know what he's doing. At least with Charley you know what yo'r gettin'."

"Whaddya mean by that?"

"Just that. You know."

"Know what?"

"Oh, Goldie, sometimes yor so dense. You really don' know about the Mulhalls?"

Goldie shook her head, and Rose took her elbow and leaned low over the table.

"Okay, so you know Georgia and Mildred, right?"

"Charley's sisters?"

"Yeah, right. Well, not right. Okay, take a deep breath, honey. Ya know ol' Zack Mulhall, so ya shouldn't be too much s'prised. He always ruled his own family like the cock he is, if ya ask me. When the Colonel was workin' for the railroad he met Georgia. This was when she was real young, and she was an orphan and she was workin' in one o' the boardin' houses he used stay at. He felt sorry for her and brung her home with him one time, and they pretty much adopted her, but then after a while they was splittin' the blanket, and, o' course, Mrs. Zack, she din't take too kindly to that, so he moved Georgia back to Kansas City. That's where Charley was born."

Goldie's face must have shown her horror, because her friend plunged on, obviously relishing the details of her story. "That's right, hon, can you believe it? Charley is Georgia's son, not his sister. After Colonel Zack's son Logan died, he went and got Charley and brought him out to the ranch. And Mildred— well, Mildred is another result of the union between Georgia and Zack, but she always called Mrs. Mulhall her ma. I heard Georgia brought her to the ranch right after she was born and gave her to Mrs. Zack to bring up. Don' know how she coulda' done that—I couldna' done it, give up my babies like that."

"But they all live together," Goldie gasped.

"Yep, they do. I do believe that Mrs. Mulhall, what's her name anyway? Mary? Yep, Mary, the saint. Anyone who would put up with all that got's to be a saint."

"Charley never said nothin''bout it. I don't believe it."

"Think about it, hon." Rose shook her blond curls out of her face and fluffed the ostrich plumes in her skirt, fanning them so they would lie flat. She moved her big hat to the edge of the table so she could set her drink down. "Why would he tell ya anythin''bout it? Mighta put'ya right off him, mightn' it?"

Goldie shook her head again, but she knew her friend was right about Charley's family. Little things people had said through the years, little things she'd seen between Charley and his 'sister' made sense now.

"But even with all o' that, I think Charley woulda been a better catch, don' you?"

Goldie just looked at her friend. Rose grinned. "How 'bout another toast? Here's to the cowboys, bless their schemin' little hearts." Goldie had forgotten where she was, but when Rose bumped her elbow so she brought the glass to her mouth, she swallowed more of the liquor. In fact, she swallowed enough that night to not want to get up the next morning.

❧ TWENTY-THREE ❧

A Brave Heart

"Aren't you scared every time you go out there? I mean, I could never do that, never."

The nurse's question broke through Goldie's grief. She wiped her eyes again and blew her nose. The nurse, who was so slight Goldie thought a good wind would blow her over, reached over and patted her arm. Goldie pulled away from her. This little wisp of a woman might know her way around a hospital, but she wasn't Goldie's pal, not like the women she rode with and who often depended on each other to live to see another day.

"No, I never was scairt."

"But didn't you say you broke your leg, and you've been in the hospital plenty of times."

"You don't think about that none. Not while you're on your horse. If your pony thinks you're scairt, then he gets jittery too. That's when there's danger."

Danger and fear—both had been in the arena today. Fred Albans and Steve Girardot had organized several exhibition cowboy performances at Union Park in Denver. A later newspaper account said the exhibitions were being staged for moving picture scenes. Goldie wasn't one of the performers, thank God. She had come to watch the show with a couple of friends. One of them drove the group in his Ford automobile.

A big steel cable was strung in front of some cars that were parked in a circle, and that became the arena. As Goldie and her friends settled in their seats, the assembled cowboys and cowgirls were hootin' at Maggie Wright. Maggie had just won the 1917 bronco busting world championship at Cheyenne Frontier Days, but something had her spooked on this day, and she didn't want to ride.

"C'mon, Maggie. Show us your stuff."

"Hey, champine, get in there an' ride, will ya."

It didn't look to Goldie as if the taunts were having any effect. Maggie kept shaking her head. Goldie watched as Maggie's husband, Ed, grabbed her arm and steered her behind the cars. Curious, Goldie swiveled around in hope of seeing what was happening, but her view of the couple was blocked. A few minutes later they emerged into the arena again. It was obvious to Goldie that Maggie was crying, and her heart went out to her pal. She could tell that Ed had hit her, and that was why she was now agreeing to ride a bronc in the show.

Goldie wasn't sure if anyone else had noticed or not, but the program was quickly changed and Maggie was announced next. She made the best of it. She entered the arena waving her hat and smiling as the crowd applauded her new-found fame as world champion. The bronc stood near the 'grandstand' trembling beneath its blindfold that was held in place by two cowboys. Maggie's husband was ready to help her into the saddle, and Goldie was dismayed to see the horse was hobbled. The stirrups were tied together under the pony's belly, as was sometimes done for cowgirls because it was thought to be an easier way to ride. Maggie had won her championship riding slick, just like the men, but today she was riding her horse hobbled. Goldie always rode slick; she thought it was safer. She'd seen

Maggie (Mrs. Ed) Wright won the World Championship Ladies Bronco Busting contest at Cheyenne Frontier Days in 1917.

Wyoming State Archives, Department of State Parks and Cultural Resources

too many accidents when the stirrups were hobbled and the rider got caught in the gear.

Maggie signaled that she was ready, and she slid quickly into the saddle. The cowboys slid the blindfold off the bucker and jumped out of the way. As soon as the horse felt the weight on his back he circled like a cyclone, and Maggie held on with one hand in the air. He started bucking backwards, closer to the cars and the cable with every upheaval. Then, quicker than anyone could even blink, he was tangled in the cable, and Maggie was tangled with him. He thrashed, trying to break free of the cable, and Maggie was caught in the hobbled stirrups, she couldn't kick free, and then she was down, under the thrashing hooves.

Cowboys on horses herded the panic-stricken animal away from the fallen cowgirl, but it took so long Goldie felt her heart stop. Then she was running into the makeshift arena. She slid to a stop next to Maggie and couldn't believe the blood. Her friend brought his Ford alongside the injured woman. State Humane Officer Morton David helped load Maggie's limp body into the back seat, and Goldie climbed in next to her and held her friend's head on her lap as they sped to the hospital. She'd seen so many accidents, and been in so many accidents, but she'd never seen anything this bad, and she was afraid for Maggie. Her head was bashed in and bound with a cloth that was no longer holding back the flow of blood that was now running into Goldie's hands and onto her skirt, which felt damp and sticky next to her skin. She tried to cushion Maggie's head from the bumps, and she kept murmuring encouraging words, but before they got to the hospital Maggie was gone.

The nurse would never know the whole story. She would never know that Maggie was a true, brave cowgirl, who rode in spite of her bad feelings about doing it today. If only we had all listened to her, Goldie thought. If only Ed had listened to her instead of hitting her.

A purse was collected at the arena and from Maggie's friends, and a special tombstone was carved to sit on the grave of the World Champion cowgirl in Ohio. It had a hat on one end and a rope on the other.

✒ TWENTY-FOUR ✒

The Lost Days

WHEN HER HEADACHE WAS JOINED by a sore throat, Goldie knew she had the grippe. She'd almost been expecting it. Everywhere she'd been, the influenza was catastrophic. On the East Coast, theaters were closed and funerals were limited to fifteen minutes. Stores and factories had to change their hours so that crowding on subways and elevated trains was minimal. Schools were closed all over the country, and almost every state had declared an emergency. Since so many doctors and nurses were overseas tending to the men fighting in the Great War, most of the medical schools had closed, and the student doctors were now serving as nurses. In San Francisco, a law was passed requiring everyone to wear a gauze mask when outside their own homes. The penalty for violating the new law was $5 to $100 or ten days in jail, or both.

And, it wasn't just Americans dying from the Spanish influenza. Young people around the world were infected. The influenza decimated the troops fighting the Great War in Europe, and in India it was estimated that at least six million to as many as sixteen million people died in the worst year of the pandemic, 1918. The flu killed more people than the Great War.

Goldie knew the influenza struck people down quickly, usually starting with a sore throat, a headache, a loss of appetite, and a fever. The fever lasted three to four days, and if it didn't turn into pneumonia, you might be lucky and live.

As she wobbled into the lobby of the Dyer Hotel, her current home while she was in Cheyenne, she wondered if she could make it to her room. The clerk took one look at her and came out from behind his desk to help her up the stairs.

"Is there anyone I can notify for you, Miss Goldie?" he asked, and she wondered if he was asking in case she died. She collapsed on the bed, and the clerk took off her boots and pulled a blanket over her. She could tell she had a fever now because the blanket felt itchy and like it was burning her skin. Her head felt like it was going to explode it was so hot. That was the last thing she remembered.

She felt her head. It seemed okay. She opened her eyes and looked around the room. She was still in the same bed on the second floor of the Dyer Hotel. The curtains were pulled, and somehow she'd put on her nightgown. Her whole body ached. She moaned and went back to sleep.

The next time she came to, she was looking at Harry's face. She was confused. She didn't think he'd been at the hotel with her when she got sick, but her memory of the days before the fever set in were fuzzy. After they got back together this last time, they had traveled to Cheyenne for a rodeo—they'd always had good luck with the prizes in Cheyenne—but then they'd had an argument, and she'd walked out on him. She could remember that much. They had been staying at the new Plains Hotel, far more elegant than the old Dyer, but she could only afford the Dyer after their argument, so that's where she'd booked a room.

When they'd been here in Cheyenne in 1915, Harry won both the trick riding and bronc riding contests, and he'd been named the bronc riding and trick riding champion. That year they had stayed at the Dyer, and she felt like it was more of a home for her in Cheyenne than the pretentious Plains.

"Want some water, champ?" Harry poured some from a pitcher sitting on the dresser and held it for her. Her lips felt parched, and the cool liquid relieved the heat in her throat.

"How long?" she croaked.

"Four days. About the usual." A series of gunshots exploded beneath the window.

"What the—"

"The war is over. Everybody is celebratin'."

"Oh, that's wonderful." Goldie tried to sit up so she could see out the window, but she couldn't even prop herself up on an elbow.

"You need to rest, darlin'."

"How did you find out?"

"That you were sick?"

Goldie nodded.

"The notice you put in the newspaper."

"What?"

"You don't remember? The clerk said you might not. He said you were pretty well gone when he got you to the room. I guess you told him to find me, that I was at the Plains."

"I did?"

"Yeah, you did. I guess it means you really do love me."

Goldie couldn't remember saying anything to the clerk, but Harry gave her the newspaper he'd folded over and left on the dresser.

MRS. HARRY WALTERS REPORTED ILL

Mrs. Harry Walters, wife of Harry Walters of Grover, is ill with Spanish Influenza in the Dyer hotel in this city and is anxious to see her husband, according to word brought to the Tribune office by the management of the hotel.

Walters is world champion trick and fancy rider. He was in

Cheyenne yesterday, at the Plains hotel. It is believed that he does not know that his wife is ill in this city.

She must have said something. Maybe she was talking in her delirious state. That must be it. She closed her eyes.

When she opened them again, she knew she'd slept a long time. A nurse was sitting beside her bed, and she'd brought a bowl of soup. Goldie hadn't thought about food when she woke up and talked to Harry, but now the smell of the soup made her hungry.

"Let's get you sitting up so you can eat, shall we?"

"Sure." Goldie's voice creaked with the effort of talking. The nurse helped her sit up against the bed pillows.

She chattered about the news that the war had ended as she fed Goldie spoons full of the delicious broth.

"What day is it?" Goldie asked. She figured she'd collapsed on the bed on November 6, and Harry said she'd been sick for four days.

"It's November 12. The war ended yesterday. I wish I could say the same for the influenza, but I hear those poor fellows in the trenches and the camps in Europe are still getting sick and dying. It's a worse death than being shot, if you ask me."

Goldie felt herself falling asleep again. "That's all right. You go ahead and sleep all you want. Here, let's make you more comfortable."

Goldie slept off and on for another two weeks. By the end of that second week, she was able to walk outside and seemed to be gaining more strength every day.

Goldie was one of the lucky ones. In the two years the influenza raced across the globe, a fifth of the world's population was infected, and ninety years later scientists estimated that as many as 21 million people died. More than 500,000 Americans died from the Spanish Influenza, ten times as many as in World War I.

Harry stopped by occasionally. It was dangerous to travel as the influenza was still epidemic, so he'd decided to stay with

The Dyer Hotel in Cheyenne where Goldie recovered from the Spanish flu in her second-floor room.

Wyoming State Archives, Department of State Parks and Cultural Resources

Goldie. When she was starting to move around some, he'd given up his room at the Plains and moved in with her. Beth, the nurse, was needed elsewhere all the time, and she'd told Goldie that Harry had stayed with her almost all the time she was delirious. Goldie suspected his new-found devotion wouldn't last, but nevertheless she forgave him for their latest spat and welcomed his move into her room. When she considered her feelings toward Harry, she wasn't sure she loved him as much as she had when they married—too many things had happened since then—but they were still man and wife, and, she told herself, he had taken care of her during the influenza.

During the two years since she'd tried to kill him in Denver, they had broken up so many times it was hard to keep track.

After she tried to shoot him, Harry had disappeared without prosecuting her, so she'd signed up to work for Sells-Floto Circus with Buffalo Bill. Then, after Colonel Cody's funeral, she contracted with Rhoda Royal at Sells-Floto to perform in that equestrian show with the educated horses. Somehow, Harry always found her. They would patch things up, and it would last for a few months, but she never could forget what he'd done.

For a while now, they'd been on the rodeo circuit, and they'd done pretty well. After Harry became the champion bronc busting and trick riding champion in Cheyenne, he took first money at Walla Walla and in Rawlins, Wyoming.

She had learned a lot of the finer tricks of riding broncs from Charley Mulhall and from Harry, and now she was putting a lot of them to use. In Lucille Mulhall's Girl Rangers she had ridden a show bucker, and she knew all his moves by heart. On the road with a Wild West, the buckers were trained—not in the normal sense of the word, but they were encouraged to excel at finding ways to get rid of the load on their backs. Now she'd learned to ride the outlaw buckers at the rodeos that would use tricks like falling back or the side throw or the corkscrew to unload her. Before she'd contracted the influenza, she had started to win some rodeo contests. In Walla Walla she'd won a saddle for bronc riding. She now could "fan" the horse at every jump by swinging her hat above her head. And to think that when she first rode a bucker, she was scared she might die and was sure she'd never be able to raise one hand in the air.

(Next page) Harry Walters (Sterling), shown here Roman Standing, won the trick riding contest at Cheyenne Frontier Days in 1919.

Wyoming State Archives, Department of State Parks and Cultural Resources

HARRY WALTERS WINS CHAMPIONSHIP TRICK RIDING CONTEST, CHEYENNE, WYO, 1919, (4.F.P.CO.INC)

Harry, center, and the other winners at Cheyenne Frontier Days in 1915.

Buffalo Bill Museum and Grave, Lookout Mountain, Golden, Colorado

She'd learned to ride straight up with a close seat—it certainly meant far fewer bruises if she wasn't always thrown in the air above the saddle. Most of all, she'd learned to ride the bucking broncs with style, and that translated into winning money at the rodeos.

And maybe she'd learned to sit up straighter in the wild ride of her marriage to Harry. As the weeks slipped by in Cheyenne and she started walking and riding again with Harry's help, she was confident that this time things were going to be right between them.

When they were both winning at the rodeos they made pretty good money, but it seemed no matter how well they did during the season, they were always broke during the winter. After she recovered from the influenza, they traveled to San Francisco, thinking they might pick up some work. She was pregnant again, and they were broke. In February they learned about the new Kit Carson Wild West show. It seemed like a godsend. Jobs were hard to come by, and all the cowboys and cowgirls who were wintering in San Francisco were eking out a living as they waited for the next show. A lot of them signed up for the new show, including Harry and Goldie. She figured she could ride in the Kit Carson show for a few months, and then head back to Chicago to be with her mother for the baby's birth, which would be in September.

The show worked its way east from San Francisco, playing stops in Nevada and Idaho. Bad luck followed them. It seemed that everywhere they went, customers complained about thefts from their buggies while they were watching the Wild West. Somewhere in Idaho the cowboys got proof that it was Kit's men who were stealing the robes and fancy whips from the buggies. "Kit Carson Jr." was a crook. The cowboys and cowgirls may have been a rough and tumble crowd, but they lived by a strict moral code, and none of them wanted to work for an outfit that stole from its own audience.

"I, for one, I ain't puttin' up with this," Harry told the cowboys and cowgirls who had assembled to decide what to do.

One of the younger kids said, "Well, I ain't goin' without my money." They hadn't been paid anything since the show left San Francisco, which wasn't an unusual arrangement for a Wild West. Often the boss of the show kept the pay in a safe to distribute at the end of the tour. It was a way to keep the performers sober and working until the last show.

The cowboys and cowgirls unanimously decided to quit the show, but they wanted their money. A group was appointed to confront the boss, but when he heard their demand, Kit pulled a gun and told them, "You'll get it when I'm damned good and ready to give it to you." Kit waved the gun towards them, and the cowboys just backed up, not wanting to get in a fight with a loaded gun. When Goldie, who was by then five months pregnant, heard that the boss wouldn't give them their pay, she was furious. She was looking forward to leaving the show soon for Chicago, but without any money it seemed impossible. She kicked at the dust with the toe of her boot and bit her lip to stop her tears. Harry reached through the cloud of dust she was making and grabbed her hand, giving it a squeeze so hard all she could feel was the pain in her fingers. He told her not to worry, the boys had a plan.

Goldie didn't know where it came from, but the boys got their own gun and went back to see Kit, and they got their money. The next night she saw the bills in Harry's hand to prove it.

Harry was grinning triumphantly. "I tol' you we weren't gonna get stuck here. Never again are we gonna be stuck somewheres without our money or our outfits."

Harry jammed some bills into her hand. "See—we got it all."

"What happened?"

"It went jus' like I tol' you it would. The bum gave us our money—all of it."

It wasn't enough to get them to Chicago, but it was enough to get back to Denver.

∽ TWENTY-FIVE ∾

Stirring Up Some Magic

AFTER RUSSELL'S BIRTH in Denver in September, congratulations poured in from Wild West friends, vaudeville and circus friends, and even from William Vaile, Colorado's Representative in Washington from the First District.

But when her son was just three weeks old, Goldie's world collapsed again. She learned that Harry was seeing Lorena Trickey. She had performed in rodeos with Lorena and thought they were friends. Only five-foot-two-inches tall and a hundred pounds, Lorena was named the world champion bronc riding cowgirl that year, 1919, at Pendleton, Oregon. Goldie figured that was when she and Harry got together. Goldie had felt jealous from the moment Harry had left her, in her last stages of pregnancy in Denver, to go to Pendleton. But they had agreed that they needed the money he was bound to win. Then, just after Russell was born, Lorena turned up in Denver, and when she left a few days later, she took Harry with her. Lorena knocked on their apartment door, and Harry came out of the bedroom with a bedroll. Before Goldie could ask any questions, they left the apartment together. They were laughing as they walked out the door, and Lorena had her arm through Harry's. "Don't worry, darlin'," Harry yelled over his shoulder. "I'll be back for my son." But Goldie knew that Harry wasn't ever coming back, and she vowed that he would never take their son away from her.

Life with Harry hadn't been easy, even though Goldie had tried hard to be a good wife. Deep down, she had to admit that she wasn't really surprised that Harry left her. They'd broken up so many times before, but she was always the one who walked out after the vitriolic and sometimes violent arguments. Harry just disappeared whenever he felt like it. How many times had he done that to her? Every time she started to count, she'd lose track in the midst of a rising fog of anger. And what had they argued about? When Harry came back after he had disappeared for several weeks or months, he took charge of the money Goldie had earned in his absence, and then it was all gone. Goldie was resentful and felt that Harry was taking advantage of her, and their money, or the lack of it, was the basis of many of their arguments. Sometimes Goldie flirted with other men when Harry was gone, and if Harry found out, he was jealous. When they argued about it, Goldie would accuse Harry of seeing other women during his travels, and he never denied it. Goldie should have known that Harry would never be the type to settle down and have a family.

Their life together seemed like a jumble of disconnected images that kept replaying in her mind as she nursed Russell and rocked him to sleep. Her surprise when Buffalo Bill told her that she was marrying Harry. The incredible wedding in Madison Square Garden. Her disbelief when her mother told her that Harry was wanted for murder and had another wife and daughter in Texas. Her fierce loyalty to him through the trial. Her anger when Harry's other wife took the money she'd brought to him for the trial in Texas. Her astonishment when she opened her eyes after that awful fever passed and saw Harry

Lorena Trickey was one of the most fearless and famous of the cowgirls.

Wyoming State Archives, Department of State Parks and Cultural Resources

The upper picture shows the band of Sioux Indians giving their dance. middle picture shows some of the noted riders who will participate in events at the Roundup. Left to right: Mrs. Frank C. Miller, Jack ble, Harry Walters and Lorena Trickey, champion woma broncho er of the world. At the bottom on the right is Frank C. Miller, who led the Boosters' party to Denver.

When Harry and Lorena traveled to Denver to promote the Wild West they were working for, this picture appeared in a Denver newspaper. When Goldie put the clipping in her scrapbook, she wrote above Harry's head: "The Goat," and above Lorena's she wrote: "My Friend."

The Sterling family

watching over her. The incredible anger and emptiness she felt as her finger quivered on the trigger before she shot at him. The smoke that filled the street between them so Goldie could no longer see her husband clearly.

The smoke was finally gone. Now she could see that Harry hadn't changed much in the years they had been married, but she sure had. She'd been young, too young, and Harry had taken advantage of her inexperience with men. He'd never even asked her to marry him. He'd just assumed she would. Things were different now. She was different. She had a child, and that changed everything. She couldn't just up and disappear like Harry. He obviously wasn't cut out for family life. He'd proved it once when he left his other family in Texas, and now he was proving it again. It was time she faced the facts. She was going to be raising this child by herself.

A few months later, Goldie heard that Lorena and Harry were going to be in Fort Collins, just north of Denver, for a rodeo, and her friends asked if she was going to take Russell up there to see his father. No, she said. She didn't ever want to see Harry again. And she didn't change her mind when she heard that Harry and Lorena had busted up. She had heard that, instead of spending the months between shows with Harry, Lorena was doing vaudeville skits with her trick horse, Black Baby, at Pantages theaters, probably the same ones Goldie had played as a Lucille Mulhall Girl Ranger. Now that she could see Harry more clearly for the liar and womanizer he really was, she guessed that Lorena probably was playing vaudeville because Harry had either disappeared or he was wintering over between circus show seasons with yet another woman.

Harry's departure from her life was a relief in some ways, but it meant she had to work harder. Before, her paychecks had gone to her mother, and she and Harry lived off what he brought home, but now she had to make her pay stretch to take care of everyone. All that year her mother, who was living close-by in Denver, watched Russell for her, or Goldie took him with her while she worked at a small restaurant near their apartment.

When winter's snows melted into ankle-deep mud and spring bulbs began to bloom, she didn't think she could take life without horses and audiences any longer. She consoled herself that at least she'd be able to go to some of the shows that were coming to Denver, and when she heard that Wortham's show was coming to town, she figured there would be a chance she could visit with some of her old pals who were traveling with the show as performers with Tantlingers' Wild West. She bundled her son up against the cool spring weather, and they boarded a streetcar for the stockyards. And sure enough, here was Edith Tantlinger, hands on her hips, looking Goldie up and down.

"Look at you, my, my, it's good to see you again. And look at this handsome little fella," Edith nodded at Russell approvingly.

"This is Russell. Russell, say hello to Mrs. Tantlinger." Russell gurgled at the cowgirl, and she smiled. "How old is he now?"

"He's almost two."

"Big fella, aren't you?"

Russell nodded solemnly in agreement.

"And where's Harry?"

"I dunno. I don't keep track of 'im."

"Sure you don't. We all heard about him and Lorena. I'm real sorry, Goldie." Goldie couldn't look at Edith, but she nodded. Edith continued, "Bet he doesn't marry her. Harry always did have an eye for the all girls—especially if they were good riders—but you're the only one who roped him into saying the vows." Now that Goldie thought about it, she wasn't sure who had done the roping, but it didn't really matter any more.

She bit her lip and didn't answer. Sometimes Edith's candor was too much. She often felt intimidated around the well educated woman and felt reticent to discuss her personal life with her, unlike the non-stop banter, sometimes very personal, when the single cowgirls were by themselves.

"Are you working?" Mrs. Tantlinger plowed on, oblivious to Goldie's distress.

"I been waitin' tables at a little place next to where we're stayin'."

Edith gave her an appraising look. "Where's your outfit?"

"I don't even know if I can still wear it."

"Of course you can, although now that you say it, you do need to lose some of that extry baby weight." Well, Goldie knew

Goldie poses with some old friends when Wortham's World's Best show came to Denver. Tantlingers' Wild West was part of the company. Goldie became friends with Edith and her husband Vern Tantlinger when they all worked for the 101 Wild West. Edith Tantlinger is next to Goldie. Goldie misspelled Tantlinger when she wrote on the photo.

The Sterling family

Goldie and two friends. This photo was probably taken when Goldie visited with her pals who were performing with Wortham's show when it came to Denver shortly after Russell's birth.

Buffalo Bill Museum and Grave, Lookout Mountain, Golden, Colorado

Goldie worked for Diamond Jack briefly when she lived in Denver. The well known gangster staged a number of rodeos in Colorado.

Denver Public Library, Western History Collection, X-22166

that. She was still carrying quite a few extra pounds from the baby, even after all this time, and she wasn't getting much exercise except for walking while she was working at the restaurant. "You should join the show. It would do you a lot of good to work outdoors instead of inside. That can't be good for you." As always, Edith was taking charge.

"Oh, I'd like that, Mrs. Tantlinger. But I've got my son, and I've got my mother to look after too." Goldie fondled the boy's hair. He had a death grip on her leg and was watching the commotion around him with big eyes. "I can't leave her right now. She needs me too."

"Oh, p-shaw. Bring your son with you. He's big enough to travel." Goldie looked doubtfully at her new leg-iron. "And you can always send your mother money. She can take care of herself. You're too talented to stay at home."

"I don't think so, Mrs. Tantlinger, though it's awfully good to see y'all."

"Come back tomorrow and wear your outfit! I bet all the girls would like to see you in it."

On the way home, Goldie was sure she wouldn't come back the next day, but in the end, that's what she did. She dragged her show things out of her trunk and tried them all on. She wore what she could, and spent another day joking and reminiscing with her old pals. Although she was sorely tempted to sign up with the show before it left Denver, she didn't.

Her jobs never seemed to last long, and she was working in a clothing store when her friend Mabel, who had taught her how to drive the sprinkler wagon when Buffalo Bill's show went broke in Denver, came to see her. A few years before, Mabel had operated her own small Wild West show. She had some exciting news. The Diamond Jack show was looking for riders for its parade, and Goldie jumped at the chance. Diamond Jack, alias

Louis Alteria, was a gangster who had been a member of Dion
O'Banion's gang in Chicago and 'retired' to Colorado. Diamond
Jack had grown up on a ranch in California, and he could ride,
bulldog, and rope. One of the first things he did after he moved
from Chicago to Colorado was to stage a few rodeos in Denver.

Diamond Jack himself led the parade, wearing his trade-
mark red silk cowboy shirt, woolly white chaps, Tom Mix style
cowboy hat, and diamond-studded gold belt buckle.

He scheduled two shows on each of the three days with
bareback bronc riding, trick saddle stunts, a musical chair race,
the cowgirls' race, calf roping, a potato race, trick roping, wild
cow milking, and a wild horse race. A Denver newspaper
reported: Diamond Jack says he's got the original "bad hoss" in
just about a hundred editions, and that his steers have never
seen anything more peaceable than a Mexican revolution.
Alongside the story ran a big picture of Goldie and Mabel in
the parade that started at 18th Street and Broadway and wound
its way into the heart of downtown Denver. The headline above
the picture proclaimed: 'Diamond Jack' and Some Queens.

As she pasted that picture in her scrapbook, Goldie was
flooded with the feelings she had when she sat tall in the saddle
and raised her hand above her head to wave at the people on
foot and in the automobiles along the route during the parade.
The magic she always felt when she mounted her horse and
rode into the arena was stirring inside her again.

↞ TWENTY-SIX ↠

One Last Hurrah

AFTER HARRY LEFT HER FOR LORENA, Goldie worked hard to provide for herself, her mother, and her son, but as the months and years went by she missed being on the road and she missed the better pay she could earn as a cowgirl. She longed for the days and nights on the road and the taxing physical work. After seeing her friends at the Wortham's show, she decided that even if Russell wasn't old enough to go on tour with her, he could travel with her to rodeos, and she signed up for a few, mostly in nearby states. It was a lot of work dealing with all of her gear, the saddles and tack, and Russell and everything he would need for a week or two on the road, but it sure beat waiting on tables in the restaurant.

When Russell was approaching his third birthday, she decided he was big enough to travel with her on a show, so she signed on with Bill Penny. Penny had the backing of the Western Saddle Company for a new Wild West, and he booked twenty-two weeks of county and state fairs before they left Denver.

Eva Fisher, who had been in her wedding, was with the show, as were Hank Durnell, Dutch Foster, and Doc Cameron. Goldie knew that no one else was going to promote her, unlike her days with Buffalo Bill, so she wrote a letter to The Billboard.

Goldie Griffith (Mrs. Harry Walters), the cowgirl athlete, wrote from Denver: "Have been sort of 'lost' in this State the past five years, but will be out with the bluebirds and troupers in spring. While Wortham's World's Best Shows were here last summer I met Mr. and Mrs. Vern Tantlinger, of the old 101 Show, and Lulu Bell Parr and Tefoe, of the old Buffalo Bill outfit, and it made me so 'homesick' I had to start again. I contracted with Bill Penny to ride for him at the Pageant of Progress here last June and found him a square business man; also rode at the rodeo held here—which I understand will be again held this year. There are a few 'hands' around Denver. Everyone (almost) knows Doc Cameron, or 'Tim', as a few knew him in this section. He is here—just as good-natured as ever, also Maynard Church and Bob Clayton. Penny's Wild West, here in winter quarters, is getting ready for the coming season.

The Bill Penny Show was a last hurrah for the Wild West. Everyone knew the Wild West shows were doomed—most audiences now went to the flickers to see stars like Hoot Gibson, Art Acord, and Tom Mix in the thrilling action-adventure stories of the old West, or to gobble up serials like *The Hazards of Helen* with the spunky cowgirl Helen Gibson. No longer did they flock by the many thousands to a Wild West show when it came to their city, not when they could see their favorite Western stars every Saturday, and the live shows suffered.

Jobs for veteran Wild West performers were fewer every year, although some cities were producing their own homegrown rodeos. Goldie felt fortunate to have been hired by the Penny show. She would be doing what she loved, although this time she was a married woman with a husband she never wanted to see again, and she had little Russell to look after. She knew that the carousing and fun times with the other performers were going to be fewer for her as a mother, but nevertheless it felt good to be going on the road again as the show train left Denver.

She was keeping Russell as far away from Harry as she could after he'd left with Lorena. When he and Lorena had come to that rodeo in Fort Collins, Harry had borrowed an automobile and driven to Denver. Goldie was still living in their old apartment. Harry told the landlady that he needed to retrieve some of his personal possessions, and he was waiting for her when she came home from work, juggling baby Russell and a wrapped plate of leftovers from the restaurant. Goldie must have jumped two feet in the air when she saw Harry rocking in the chair she used to put Russell to sleep.

"What are you doing here?"

"I jus' came to see my son. He's lookin' good, aren't you, boy?"

Russell cocked his head and blinked. This was the day she'd been dreading ever since Harry left with Lorena. He'd come to steal her son. She glanced behind her at the door. Fortunately, she'd left it standing wide open. She deliberately threw the plate she was carrying on the floor in front of Harry. The sound of the crash brought immediate screams of alarm from Russell, and Harry threw his arms in front of his face to ward off the flying shards of cheap china. Goldie turned and ran back into the street, holding her son tightly. Russell had started screaming, and passersby looked curiously at mother and son. Goldie jiggled Russell, hoping people would think she was trying to pacify him when really she was hoping that he wouldn't stop fussing and crying out. She whispered into his red and tear-stained cheek, "Make all the noise you want to, Russell, and maybe your schemin' sorry excuse for a father won't want to follow us. That's right, scream."

Goldie re-traced her steps to the restaurant, looking over her shoulder to see if Harry followed. She saw him standing at the door to the apartment house, hesitating as he watched Goldie take his son into the restaurant. He didn't follow them.

Goldie watched him from the safety of the restaurant as he jumped nimbly into the automobile he'd parked on the street and put it into gear. She waited ten minutes just to be sure. Russell stopped screaming when one of the other girls who worked with Goldie came by and tickled his chin. "I thought I forgot something," Goldie answered the girl's arched eyebrow.

Harry's attempt to steal little Russell was a wake-up call for Goldie. It meant she had to be on her guard all the time. Harry had already proved that he could slip in and out of her life, and she was determined he would never do it again. She listened closely to gossip and tried to read between the lines of items about any of the cowboys in The Billboard or any newspaper she could get her hands on. She may have still been officially married to the scumbag, but Russell was hers.

Sometimes, when Russell was being particularly recalcitrant with her about something, she felt like he was a burden she'd rather she didn't have to carry. But she loved him and she knew she was all he had, so she worked hard to protect him from his father. Fortunately, the other show people helped her with him when they could. Usually, the Indians who traveled with a show brought their youngsters with them, and the Sioux who had signed with the Penny show were no exception. Russell did have a few playmates, although time for play was always limited by the constant travel and the show schedules. He learned how to ride a pony and how to help the roustabouts with the tents by bringing them tools or running messages. And Doc Cameron was really good with the boy, teaching him rope tricks and letting him ride with him whenever they could.

Goldie was in a bit of a quandary about what to do about Tim, or Doc as everyone called him. The wiry cowboy with a dimpled chin was an incredible horseman, a person who got along with everyone on the show. But, like Harry, he was someone you didn't want to cross. He was tough. He'd been on the rodeo circuit for years, and he was consistently in the

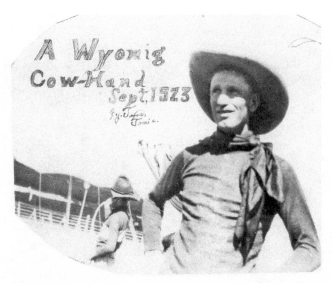

This photo of Doc Cameron was signed "by Texas Tomie." Doc's brother Tom Campbell worked the Wild West circuit with Doc for a short time.

Photo in possession of Campbell family

money. He'd done stunts for Tom Mix, some of the hardest work in the world. He knew just about everything there was to know about horses.

For a while, Doc's brother, Tom Campbell, had ridden with him on the Sells-Floto show, but he left after only a few months, telling his brother he was crazy to stay. Tom thought the work was extreme for the pay, so he went back to ranching. Until she heard the stories about Tom, Goldie hadn't known that Doc's real name was Campbell. She often marveled at the way the light seemed to come right through his clear, pale blue eyes, and she didn't mind that he was starting to get lines around his eyes from the years of working in the sun and wind. Usually he wore a tie tucked into his shirt, and he tucked his pants legs into his fancy tall boots with butterflies stitched into

Above, a close-up of the center of the large photo on the next page shows some of the cast of Bill Penny's Wild West. The show was subtitled 'The Passing of the West,' and it was indeed one of the last of the Wild Wests to tour the country. Above, Goldie is third from the right, in the all-black outfit, and Doc is to the left of her. Next to Goldie (second from the right) is Eva Fisher, who was in Goldie's wedding at Madison Square Garden. She is wearing Goldie's extravagantly beaded, red leather wedding outfit for this photo.

Photos in possession of Campbell family

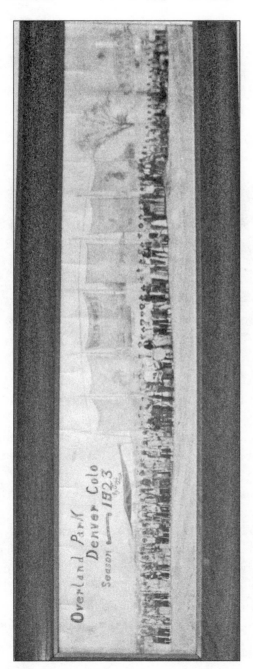

The cast of Bill Penny's Wild West during the 1923 season in Denver, Colorado's Overland Park.

Photo in possession of Campbell family

Doc and Goldie pose with their horse during the Bill Penny Wild West.

Buffalo Bill Museum and Grave, Lookout Mountain, Golden, Colorado

the leather. His tall, wide-brimmed hat was ridged with a big crease that caved in both sides of the top. When he was working, he donned his chaps with the WYO on the sides and sometimes he swapped the tie for a big, dark neckerchief that he wore loosely around his neck and over his white shirt.

But what Goldie liked best about him was that he had always been straight with her.

He too had been married but was divorced in 1920, and he seemed to be serious about making his relationship with Goldie work. She was sure she was falling in love with him, even though she was still married to the non-existent Harry. The last time they talked about it, Goldie told Doc that she was ready to get a divorce from Harry. "I'm raising my son by myself anyway, I might as well divorce the no-good—"

"Stop, don't say it—not around the kid." Goldie bit her lip, and she didn't say anything for as long as she could, which was only about ten seconds. Now that she'd said it out loud, a divorce seemed like a good idea. It was time to move on with her life. In deference to Russell's big eyes full of questions, she changed the subject.

The Bill Penny Show had been playing fairs in the Midwest, and now they were in northern Indiana, making their way towards Logansport, home to two of the new factories that made Bendix and Revere automobiles. Goldie's mother, who was visiting with relatives and friends in the Chicago area, wanted to visit Goldie's show when it came to Logansport. Thank goodness her mother had liked Doc when she met him in Denver just before the show went on the road because since then Goldie and Doc had become almost inseparable.

"Try this," Doc pulled a leather strap out of his pocket and put it around her wrist, tightening it so it restricted the way her wrist could move. She'd been complaining that the reining was hurting her wrist more and more. She'd been wearing a thin leather strap around the wrist, but it wasn't working any more.

"That's better," Goldie said as she tried various movements. "Yep, it's better. Thanks, Doc."

"You can pay me back later, sweetheart."

Goldie ignored his innuendo. "I hope it'll fit under my gauntlets." She was pulling one of them over the new strap, wriggling her hand through.

"Looks like it works fine."

Goldie nodded, concentrating on her wrist, which she was still twitching in different directions to see if it hurt. It was late July, and they were at the Northern Indiana Fair. The Bill Penny Wild West performed two rodeos in the afternoon and evening in the amphitheater in front of the grandstand. The twenty-five Sioux Indians from the Pine Ridge Reservation in North Dakota, the twenty-five cowboys and cowgirls "from Colorado

Goldie, right, and her son Russell pose on top of the stagecoach used in Bill Penny's Wild West.

The Sterling family

Eva (Fisher) McGooken, Tim (Doc) Cameron, Goldie, and Dutch Foster. Eva is wearing Goldie's wedding outfit.

Buffalo Bill Museum and Grave, Lookout Mountain, Golden, Colorado

ranches," and the two carloads of ponies and western steers opened the rodeo with a grand tournament and parade. The rodeo included trick roping, lassoing, fancy rope spinning, riding bucking ponies, and Indian dances. It closed with a realistic stagecoach holdup with the entire company participating.

Fireworks closed out the fair after the rodeo. She and Doc were watching the pyrotechnic display from under the grandstand.

"Hey, sweetheart, when's your ma coming?"

"She should be here next month, on the 27th, when we get to Logansport."

"That would do."

"Whaddya mean, that would do?"

"Well, darlin', I've been thinkin'. Why don't we get hitched?"

"Get married?"

Doc nodded.

"Oh. Well." Goldie twisted on her pony so she was looking at Doc full on. Her smile was as wide as her broad face, and her eyes twinkled with delight. "You know I'd like that."

"Then let's do it. Let's do it when your ma comes. She can be our witness."

Goldie thought about the years ahead raising Russell by herself and about Doc, the quiet, unassuming man, who as far as she knew, had never lied to her and had always been there for her. She knew they couldn't work the rodeos and shows forever, and he would be a good man to settle down with.

"Okay."

"Okay, that's settled then. I'll never let you down, darlin'. We'll have a good life—I know I can make you happy, and you already make me happy."

"Thank you, Mr. Cameron. You've made me very happy today too."

They were married on August 28, 1924, in Logansport. Allie was their witness, and on the marriage license Doc said his

WHY WORRY?

"Beware, Danger." When she put this photo in her scrapbook, Goldie pasted the words WHY WORRY? under it. The picture of her and Tim (Doc) Cameron was taken in 1923 during the Bill Penny tour.

Buffalo Bill Museum and Grave,
Lookout Mountain, Golden, Colorado

name was Timothy Cameron, even though his real name was Ervie Tyra Campbell. Goldie listed her name as Goldie Sterling, and she said her former husband, Harry, was 'dead.' Marshall Beebe performed the ceremony in the courthouse, and afterwards, they took Russell to the park to ride the fancy painted horses on the Dentzel Carousel. Russell, of course, had to reach for the brass ring, and neither Goldie nor Doc was surprised that he won a free ride. Allie took her grandson for an ice cream, and Goldie and Doc headed back to their tent to make their marriage official.

Unfortunately, no one from the show could come to the wedding because the show had gone bust a couple days earlier in Rochester.

The Logansport Morning Press reported: *It didn't go broke because it was no good; the management was not as careful with the gate receipts, maybe, as was necessary to make both ends meet. People who saw performances at Rochester say it is one of the best shows of its kind they have witnessed.* The newspaper reported that Charles Grant, the ex-sheriff and proprietor of the Grant Detective Agency, was made receiver pro tem for the show. Grant paid $45 out of his own pocket to get the show freight from Rochester to Logansport, "where all parties involved hired attorneys." None of the performers had been paid anything since the show left Denver, and once in Logansport they hired a lawyer to attach the show. They figured that was their only chance to get their money. Goldie knew all about attachments. Although it had taken two years, the court had finally decided that the performers with the Two Bills Show should get their possessions returned and 25 cents on the dollar of the money owed to them when the show went broke and was attached in Denver. Goldie hadn't had the money to replace her trunk, so it was a blessing to get it back.

Detective Grant moved the Bill Penny show to Lux field, on the south side of town.

Logansport was a Klan town—even the policemen wore white robes over their uniforms when they were directing traffic, and the show people had to be careful while they were in Indiana, one of the states with a very strong Ku Klux Klan presence. At least in Indiana, the Klan wasn't as violent as in some of the southern states. For that, the performers felt grateful, but they still didn't party or drink liquor in public. The country's Prohibition laws were upheld with a vengeance by the Klan. Goldie and Doc had been apprehensive about listing their previous marriages on their marriage license. The Klan in Indiana didn't take kindly to divorced people. But Doc had told the truth when the clerk asked him if he'd been married before. When Goldie's turn came, she wasn't sure what she was going to say. The word "dead" just popped out of her mouth, and the clerk wrote it down. It was, after all, how she felt about Harry. And, she had to admit, she was a little scared after the stories she'd heard about what the Klan did to divorced women. One divorcée was stripped to the waist and whipped. Goldie just had to hope that the Klan wouldn't find out she was marrying again without a divorce. On the whole, though, she felt safer as a married woman in the company of her husband, especially now that they had to do business with Klan members to make enough money to go home.

She couldn't believe that, once again, she was with a show when it went bust. She'd been there twice before, once with Buffalo Bill and the Two Bills Show, and once with the Kit Carson show. And now with the Bill Penny show.

When they found out that Penny had spent all the gate-receipt money the show had taken in since Denver and there was nothing left, the performers knew they needed the help of the townspeople if they were going to get home.

They got it. Grant arranged for them to do two shows right away. The Klan had a big picnic and celebration already planned for the park at Lux, and he put out the word that the cowboys and cowgirls would be holding a rodeo. Most all the important people and the people with money in Logansport belonged to the Klan, which in many Indiana towns was like a social club, and they all turned out for the shows. For maybe the first time, the Bill Penny Show made really good money. It was only enough, however, to send the Indians home, and the performers decided that was their priority. Everyone, including Goldie and Russell who were sad to see their friends head back to the reservation, went down to the imposing Pennsylvania Depot to say good-bye. Next they sent off the two juveniles who had been performing with the show—Demaris and Cecil Kennedy. She was a trick rider, and her brother rode broncs.

The performers paid their attorney with two ponies and two steers. Goldie's mother stayed only long enough to see her daughter married, and then she, too, headed home to Denver on the train.

Eventually, the performers scraped together enough money for the rest of them to buy train tickets. Before the last of them left town, the performers wrote to the local newspaper: *We, the undersigned, wish to thank Harry Gruenoch, Mike Fansler, W.H. Porter, president of the City National Bank, citizens of Logansport and the members of the Ku Klux Klan, for all donations and considerations extended to the stranded laborers and performers of the Bill Penny Wild West Show. We also wish to especially thank the management of the Spencer Park and Barney Heronemons. Signed respectfully, Tom Allen, Mr. and Mrs. Fred Motts, Tim Cameron, John Carrington, Goldie Walters and son Russell, Mary Sunshine, Leslie Remington, Cecil Kennedy, Chuck Worth.*

Goldie, Russell, and Doc were headed back to Denver, but they only had enough money for tickets to Oklahoma. In Tulsa, the newlyweds found jobs in the oil fields. Two years later, they finally made it to Denver.

Part 2

Ranching
1924–1927

To help make ends meet, Goldie led groups of tourists on horseback to Arapaho Glacier. Trips to the Continental Divide were dangerous even in the summer because of sudden thunderstorms and sun that could make you snowblind. During an interview, she commented on this picture, "I always did sit crooked in the saddle."

The Sterling family

❧ TWENTY-SEVEN ❧

The Offer

THE SNOW WAS COMING DOWN HARDER, and Doc and Russell stomped into the house, shaking gobs of wet snow off their jackets and hats. Goldie set the table, and the three of them sat down to eat.

After Russell drifted off to sleep, Doc fixed them a couple of drinks to celebrate the new year, and they toasted the arrival of 1926 and their new life.

"What do you think, Mrs. Cameron, can we make this work?"

"If anyone can, it's you, Doc. You know everything about ranching, and I can help."

"I know that—"

"Well, you know, we can't rodeo no more. We're too busted up. You had to retire. There's no money left in it anyhow."

"Speak for yourself, woman. You know, I—"

"Do you think you can work with Doctor Moore?"

"Yep, I do. We've already talked some about it."

"I know that," Goldie said impatiently. What she wanted to know was what Doc thought about the doctor. Her Doc and

Goldie, left, and her friend, "the Swede," Esther Olsen Pedro. Goldie
wrote, "My sweet friend, Esther O. —G.W."

Buffalo Bill Museum and Grave, Lookout Mountain, Golden, Colorado

Doctor Moore had talked incessantly on Christmas day when the doctor had brought them up to the ranch, and as much as Goldie had tried to talk with them, it was obvious that she didn't know much about the ranching business. So she'd had to content herself with talking to the woman doctor's son, Alf. The man seemed endlessly fascinated with her life as a cowgirl, and Doc didn't seem to notice how much interest Alf was taking in her.

What was it? Maybe six months ago? Dustin Farnum, the famous Broadway and film cowboy actor, was on stage in Denver in a play she attended with her friend Esther Olsen. After the play, many of the theater-goers were standing in groups outside, socializing, smoking, and deciding where to go next. "This was western. Why weren't you in on this?" a man from the stockyards asked Goldie.

"Oh I got enough to do," Goldie told him. A tall, good-looking man detached himself from the group next to theirs and joined them.

"Hello, Esther."

"Oh, hello. Everyone, this is Alfred Moore." The two cowboys who had been talking with them looked the new man up and down, noting his cowboy boots, cowboy hat, and his city overcoat, and wandered away as soon as they could after shaking his hand.

"Hello, Mr. Moore," Goldie said and extended her hand.

"Please, just call me Alf. I couldn't help overhearing what your friend said, and I was just too curious. I had to know. What is your name?"

"Which name do you want?" Goldie teased him.

"What do you mean?"

"Well, I've got my own name, my show name, my rodeo name."

Seeing his confusion, she continued, "My maiden name is Griffith. I was married to a Sterling, we used the name of Walters, and in show business we used the name of Smith. Now I'm married to a Cameron."

"Oh, I see."

"Goldie's one of the best riders you'll ever meet," Esther told Alf. "She rode bucking broncs for Buffalo Bill in his Wild West, and she's been in scores of rodeos. She's the real thing, a real cowgirl."

"Well, I always did love animals, any kind of animal, but especially horses," Goldie said, smiling and cocking her head in appreciation of her friend's praise. "Do you like horses, Mr. Moore?" she asked the darkly handsome, self-assured man who reminded her of Colonel Joe Miller with his lush mustache and stately, almost severe manner.

"Oh yes, very much. I ride whenever —" He was interrupted by a woman calling his name. "I've got to go, but it was very nice meeting you, Mrs. Cameron. And very nice seeing you again, Miss Esther." Mr. Moore tipped his white cowboy hat at them, revealing his salt and pepper hair, and returned to his original group. Goldie and Esther wandered off to catch the streetcar home.

That fall, Alf Moore occasionally dropped by the restaurant where Goldie worked to talk with her. He liked hearing her stories of the Wild Wests and rodeos, and she had enough stories to keep him entertained for hours. He had done quite of bit of riding too, mostly in the Nederland, Colorado, area.

On Christmas Eve, Mr. Moore knocked on the door to Doc and Goldie's apartment on Colfax, just across the street from Franklin School, where Russell would be starting soon.

"How did you find out where I live?" Goldie asked Mr. Moore after she'd introduced him to her husband and her son.

"That girl you're always chumming with, Miss Esther, she told me. I hope you don't mind."

"No, no, of course not."

The three of them chatted about the weather and the holiday, but Goldie was still puzzled about why Mr. Moore had come to her home.

"I brought my mother with me," he said.

"Where is she?" Goldie asked quickly, looking guiltily at the door as if she might have forgotten to let her in.

"She's in the car."

Goldie couldn't believe the man would leave his mother in the car on such a cold night. "Why don't you bring her in?" Alf went back outside and returned with a well-dressed, ramrod-straight old woman who looked slightly disoriented.

Alf introduced his mother as Dr. Alice Moore and told them she had been asleep.

"I do have a habit of going to sleep in the car," Dr. Moore said with a gentle smile. She took off her hat, and Goldie took her coat. Her gray hair was wound into a tidy bun at the nape of her neck, and her eyes, which now had regained their focus, swept the room.

"My son has told me all about you, and I came to offer you a proposition," she told Goldie and Doc after she sat in their best chair.

"I have a ranch up near Nederland. My brother owned it, and when he died it came to me. I've got a boys' camp that I run up there in my brother Tom Tucker's name, but I also want to run some cattle."

Goldie had poured coffee for their guests, and Dr. Moore sipped at the hot drink before she continued.

"I want someone to go in with me, and I thought I'd talk to you about it. My son says you know a bit about ranching."

"Yes, ma'am, I do," Doc told her. "I was brought up on a ranch, and I been workin' with horses and cattle all my life."

Goldie was confused again. "Why don't you take it over, Mr. Moore?" It seemed to her that Dr. Moore's son was amply qualified for the job.

Alf looked slightly distressed. "I already committed to ranching elsewhere when this opportunity came about."

His mother nodded. "Yes, it's too bad Alfred can't do this for me. But he will be around for a while if you need anything and I can't help you."

Dr. Alice Moore is identified both as "Miss Moore '97" and "Mrs. Moore" (she is fourth from the right) in this photograph of an autopsy performed by Dr. Mugrage. This photograph may have been taken when Dr. Moore was in medical school at Gross Medical School in Denver in the late 1800s.

Denver Public Library, Western History Collection, Z-2187

"'Course," Goldie murmured. "Didn't mean to interrupt."

Dr. Moore looked at Doc and Goldie again to make sure she had their attention. "I need someone to be my foreman. Do you think that might interest you?"

Doc looked at Goldie, and she could tell what he was thinking. This could be the chance of a lifetime. She nodded, and let the two of them talk, her mind wandering to other things, like what made Alfred Moore decide to come here tonight, Christmas Eve, with his mother. Shouldn't they have been at home with their family?

When they had decided that Dr. Moore would come by the next day, Christmas day, and run them up to the ranch, the old lady stood up to leave.

"Would you like to come around tonight with me, my dear?" Goldie had no idea what she was talking about, but she thought she should say yes, so she did.

The chauffeur jumped out of the big black Packard Eight and made a space in the back seat so Goldie could sit next to the doctor. Alf climbed in the car next to the chauffeur, and they took him home first. Goldie knew that Alf liked her, and she had noticed that she felt a warm glow just thinking about him. She was careful not to look at him. How quickly her life had changed again. Just when Doc had decided to retire from the rodeos and stunt riding and she thought she would finally become a housewife, Alf dropped by with this opportunity. Now it looked like she and Doc wouldn't have to leave behind a life with horses and stock, riding and roping. Whatever Alf's feelings for her were, he had changed their lives. She would be riding again—soon—and she felt the magic stirring in her gut.

The car was full of baskets for Dr. Moore's poorer patients, and she explained that it was getting difficult for her to get in and out of the car, and she'd asked Goldie to come along for that purpose.

Between their stops, Dr. Moore quizzed Goldie. "Do you like living out?"

"Yes," Goldie said, "I do. Always have liked the quiet. I don't like a lot of excitement."

"And what about your son? How old is he?"

"He's just seven, and he should be starting school."

"Nederland has a fine school. That's where you'll have to take him."

"Oh, that's fine. I'm sure he'll like living on a ranch."

Goldie had never lived year-round on a ranch before. She really didn't know what it would be like to be 'living out.' She'd grown up in show business, and show business had been her life.

Well, she hadn't known how to wrestle or box or fence when she took her first job with Blanche Whitney, and she didn't know how to ride when she got her job with the 101 Wild West, and she'd learned how—even when she thought for sure she'd die the first time she got on a bucking bronco. She had become a successful athlete as a wrestler and then one of the country's top women riders, almost always in the money at the rodeos, and she'd ridden with Buffalo Bill. If she could do all that, she sure as hell could learn how to ranch. And she could learn to like the quiet.

~ TWENTY-EIGHT ~

A New Year and a New Life

THEIR NEW LIFE STARTED WITH THE NEW YEAR.

Before the sun came up, they threw saddles and tack into their automobile next to the rest of their negligible belongings. They had only recently decided to settle down in Denver, leaving the rodeos behind, and they hadn't had a chance to gather much in the way of possessions yet. On Christmas day, Dr. Moore had brought them up to Nederland from Golden and Black Hawk, but today they decided to take the road from Boulder up Boulder Cañon.

Off to the east, the sun rose over the plains as they drove out of Denver towards Boulder. In Boulder they stopped for coffee and to warm up. As they left Boulder behind and began climbing the narrow cañon road to Nederland, the sun finally climbed high enough in the sky to warm their black Ford Model T. Once deep in the cañon, the road was shaded and covered with patches of snow, or, even worse, ice, which made the drive nerve-wracking.

After about four miles, Doc pulled the automobile into a pull-out for passing vehicles and got out to stretch and water a tree. Goldie shivered and pulled the blanket tighter around her shoulders. She tugged at her soft felt hat, trying to get it to cover her ears. These days her golden-brown hair was not so golden, and she kept it pinned back, although she allowed a soft wave on one side of her still-round, girlishly plump face. She frowned with worry as she turned to look at Russell curled up in the back seat, using one of their saddles as a pillow, his straw-colored hair spread against the well-used, soft leather.

"Hurry up, Doc. It's cold."

The slight man squeezed back inside the automobile, tossed his big hat into the back so it missed Russell, and re-arranged the blanket on his lap. It was so cold inside the Ford his breath was white.

"You're not sayin' much today. You feelin' okay?"

"I'm good, Mr. Cameron. It's just cold." Her husband arched an eyebrow. Goldie hoped her use of the more formal "Mr. Cameron" instead of her usual, more familiar Tim or Doc would catch his attention. Automobile trips were fine in the summer, but when the roads were covered with snow and ice and the temperatures were this low, Goldie preferred a horse. They drove around rocks and holes in the winding road, occasionally almost doubling back on themselves. Doc honked the horn before the blind curves, in case another vehicle might be coming their way. When they did meet another machine or a wagon, the vehicle going downhill had the right of way, but, if they could, both would slow and look for a pullout. The bridges seemed endless, and Goldie worried about ice on them. Russell woke up, shivering and full of questions about their new home, but Goldie could only guess at the answers. As the Ford slowed to chug up what they would later learn was Eagle Rock Hill, Goldie hoped that would be worst of it. She was glad that her husband was such a good driver. They had both learned to drive in the Wild West shows when they started playing polo with automobiles instead of horses, and driving a speeding machine after a ball quickly made fearless drivers out of the cowboys.

Just past a sign that read, "Road Built by Tom Tynan's Road Gang, 1913," they stopped beside a wagon that had pulled up at a fifty-gallon half-barrel overflowing with water from a pipe coming out of a spring in the mountain. Their radiator had been steaming for the whole last mile. The two horses were gulping noisily, and the father and son who had been in the wagon were now re-arranging their load while they talked to a family of four that had stopped working when the strangers arrived.

"Howdy, folks," the man who lived in the nearby cabin greeted Tim and Goldie.

"How-do." Tim answered for all of them. Russell scampered out of the car and stood in front of the barrel, watching the horses drink, backing up only when one of them eyed him suspiciously.

"Need some water in your radiator?"

"Prob'ly should. It's not over the top yet, but it's pretty hot." They had already stopped twice to fill the radiator at other barrels that were set out just for that purpose. "How far to Nederland?"

Oh, you got about another twelve or so to go."

"How's the road the rest of the way?"

The other two men exchanged glances. "Well, it's not too bad, once you make it through the Narrows."

"What's that?"

"Well, sir, the Narrows start just up the road a bit, and the road it gets narrow in there."

"And steep," the wagon man added.

"Not too steep for your horses?"

"Well, not usually. But today we've got a bit of a load. We'll be takin' it pretty slow."

Goldie looked more critically at the horses hitched to the wagon and realized they were in fact light-duty saddle horses, probably not used to pulling loads up steep roads.

"I'm hopin' we don't have to spend the night out. Too cold for that," the wagon man said, running a hand down the back of one his horses, which already looked pretty worn out. Goldie bet that they would push their horses to make it the rest of way today.

The Narrows were indeed narrow. The cañon walls rose in vertical columns from the right edge of the road, and they were even taller on the other side of the river, which spewed noisily through ice caps on the rocks. The sun disappeared behind the tall cliffs, and the temperature dove another five degrees. One false move and their automobile could dive into that freezing water. Goldie told Doc to slow down at least a dozen times even though she knew they needed the speed to get up the hill. At one point they met a wagon headed down-hill, and Goldie shushed Russell so Tim could concentrate on getting out of its way.

Once out of the Narrows the road wasn't as steep, although they had to stop a few more times to fill the radiator and ice was becoming more common on the bridges. Doc brought their machine almost to a stop before every bridge, and they crept across, hoping the tires wouldn't slip too much in the wrong direction.

After they passed Ted Green's store in the town of Tungsten below the dam, they climbed one last hill that zig-zagged to the top of the dam. From there they could see Nederland nestled under the snow-capped peaks. At their feet was Nederland Lake, a white expanse of ice that ended miles away in the first buildings of the little town. The road wound its way around the lake's coves, and, finally, they drove into Nederland. They were almost frozen, in spite of all the blankets. The sun had been replaced with gray clouds that were getting darker by the

A postcard showed how inviting the road up Boulder Canyon could be in the summer during the 1920s.

Kay Turnbaugh

minute. At least here in Nederland there were a grocery store, a livery, a few hotels and restaurants. They thawed out and picked up some groceries at the Tanner Brothers store. After a lunch of sandwiches, they parked the automobile at the Moore Livery. They had arranged for four horses to be left there for them, and they saddled three of them and packed their most necessary belongings on the fourth animal. Snow was floating on swirls of air as they took the road west out of Nederland toward the tungsten mining town of Cardinal, where they would take the right track, just as Dr. Alice Moore had shown them only a week before on Christmas day. The road was blown bare of snow in places, and in others drifts almost blocked their passage. Goldie was happy they had left their Ford in Nederland, and she realized they would probably hardly ever drive their automobile on this rough road, winter or summer. The machine was fine in the city, but up here it was almost useless.

Nederland's Wolftongue Mill in 1929. The mill building is at left. Also shown are ore processing sheds, houses, and Boulder Creek. From 'The Mining Review,' Salt Lake City.

By the time they arrived at the log house, dusk had turned into night, and the snow was serious, as was the wind that blasted them with hardened snow crystals blown up from the drifts. Stiff with cold, they climbed off the horses. Goldie grabbed Russell's hand to make sure he didn't blow away, but he pulled back in disgust. Some dry wood had been laid in next to the house, and Goldie got a fire going in the stove while Doc and Russell unsaddled and unpacked the horses. It had been a long day. The house was quiet except for the crackling of the fire in the potbelly. She emptied the ashes from the cookstove and got a fire going in it too. As the oven warmed up, she stirred up some biscuits. They had splurged and bought steaks at the grocery store, and she got them ready for frying.

After she put the biscuits in the oven, she sat down and looked around the kitchen. This would be her home for the five

years of their lease with Dr. Moore, and she thought that maybe she was finally going to be the housewife she'd always dreamed about after all. She would cook and clean, take care of her husband and her son. She would scour the newspaper for tips about keeping house and live the life she'd been denied while she chased the Wild West star. Of course, she would also help her husband with the cattle and ride whenever she wanted to. She was sure this was going to be the perfect life. She sighed with contentment.

──────────────[NEDERLAND, COLORADO

TIM CAMERON—RANCH MAN AT TOM TUCKER

Following is a partial list of the merit awards given at the Tom Tucker Ranch:

Fisherman	Hiker	Packer
Archer	Forester	Guide
Artist	Handiman	Woodsman
Astronomer	Leather Worker	Marksman
Athlete	Life Saver	Botanist
Metal Worker	Birdman	Blacksmith
Bugler	Miner	Mountaineer
Camper	Photographer	Boatman
Signaler	Carpenter	Surveyor
First Aider	Swimmer	Roper
Dramatist	Whittler	Entertainer

Any camper may select from these or other activities.

Merit Awards for Games

A sensible portion of each day in camp is given over to football, baseball, tennis, treasure hunts, and a host of other games of fellowship, skill and pure fun. Merit awards are given for accomplishment and participation in games, and a reasonable proportion of such awards is allowed for Advancement.

PAGE   ELEVEN

A page in the Tom Tucker Ranch brochure. Doc is pictured on horseback as "Tim Cameron—Ranch man at Tom Tucker."

✐ TWENTY-NINE ✐

Enjoying the Quiet

DRIFTS DRAPED THEMSELVES OVER THE TRAIL. They looked benign and as beautiful as sculpted sand dunes until her pony stepped into them. The wind-packed snow broke into hay-bale-sized chunks with each laborious, lunging step the horse made. In some places he went in above his knees.

Behind her, Russell sneezed. His small gloved hands were clutched around her waist, and she absently rubbed them with her free hand. Their progress toward the school bus was slow today, but they had started early, so they should make it. The wind had howled mercilessly all night, as it did many winter nights. The nights in this country were often clear and starry, but they were not often still, and when the wind blew, it packed snow into every crevice, every hole, every trail that had been hard-fought to break the day before. The wind shrieked above them as it bent the treetops, and around them tree trunks creaked ominously. The gale picked up snow and swirled it in blinding mini-hurricanes. She'd told Dr. Moore that she liked the quiet, but if this was the old lady's idea of quiet…

Russell sneezed again. Damn it. She was worried about him getting sick. When she had promised Judge Lindsey that she'd keep him in school she'd had no idea how difficult that would be. In spite of what she'd read in the newspapers, especially lately, about Judge Lindsey, she liked the man. Lindsey had reformed Colorado's juvenile court system, and he was always putting the children first in his decisions, which seemed to make some of Denver's powerful people hate him. Goldie thought Judge Lindsey had been fair in his decisions when she divorced Harry. She'd finally pursued a divorce after she and Doc moved to Denver. Doc knew how fearful she was of Harry's threat to take Russell from her, and he convinced her that the right thing to do for Russell and their new family was to divorce Harry in a court of law. That way, Russell would belong to her legally, and the three of them could get on with their lives without having to constantly look over their shoulder for Harry. Goldie finally agreed with him, but she knew she would never stop looking for Harry over her shoulder.

During the divorce trial, Harry fought hard to keep Russell, telling the judge that Goldie wasn't a fit mother, that she had tried to kill the father of her child. Harry said that Goldie was nothing more than a cheap carnie who had never even been to school, an accusation that fired Goldie into spitting rebuttals and scathing accusations of her own. After a day of listening to Harry and Goldie argue about their respective worth as parents, the judge awarded their child to Goldie and extracted her promise to send Russell to school. Early in the year Russell would turn seven years old, Judge Lindsey sent Goldie a letter, reminding her of her promise. If she hadn't made that promise, she wouldn't be here struggling through the blowing snow, taking Russell to the damn school bus.

This was the Camerons' second winter on the ranch, and it seemed to be more difficult all the time to keep Russell in school. Every day she and Doc got up before dawn. One of them revived the potbelly stove, and the other got the cookstove

Nederland in 1926, about the time Goldie and Doc moved to the Tucker Ranch northwest of town. The water level in Nederland Lake was low. The Wolftongue Mill is at the front right.

Kay Turnbaugh

going. Most days she didn't want to get out of bed, and she snuggled deeper under the massive pile of blankets as long as she could. Before she could make the coffee, she had to get the coffeepot unstuck from where it was frozen to the stove. As soon as the kitchen was warm, they got Russell up. Usually Doc had to shovel a path through the new snow to the outhouse, and after they'd all made the trek out there, they had breakfast. After breakfast, Doc and Russell shoveled and stomped a path out to the barn, and as soon as Goldie had cleaned up from breakfast she joined them and saddled Blackjack. He had the longest legs and was one of the strongest horses on the ranch, attributes needed to posthole through the snow which in places could drift chest-deep. The school bus picked Russell up on Caribou Road at the fork of the track to Cardinal, where it loaded up all the miners' children before it turned down the hill toward the Nederland school.

Doc helped boost Russell up behind her in the saddle, and they started their cold journey to the bus.

"Why do I have to go to school, ma?" Russell shouted over the wind.

"Because you have to."

"But you didn't go to school. You could teach me."

"No, honey, I couldn't teach you everythin' you learn in school. You know that."

"But, ma—"

"Maybe next year we'll move into town for the winter. Would you like that?"

"I guess."

The two of them were quiet as Blackjack pushed his way through a deep drift.

"Ma, Billy's havin' a birthday party next week. Can I go?"

"I don't think so. We have too much work to do. You know that." She had to shout the last over the deafening wind.

Russell sneezed again, and Goldie was happy to catch a glimpse of yellow through the swirling snow. Her son would

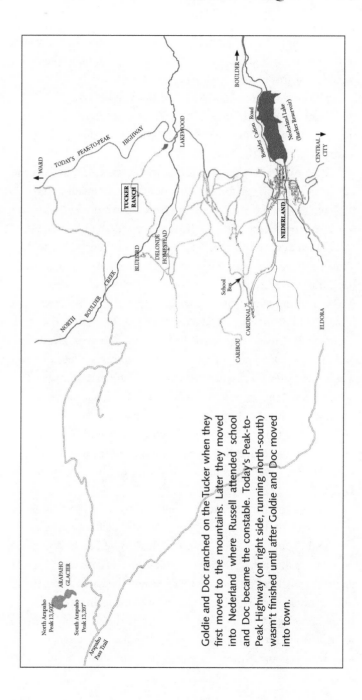

Goldie and Doc ranched on the Tucker when they first moved to the mountains. Later they moved into Nederland where Russell attended school and Doc became the constable. Today's Peak-to-Peak Highway (on right side, running north-south) wasn't finished until after Goldie and Doc moved into town.

soon be wrapped in a blanket on the bus, headed toward a warm schoolhouse, and she could turn back to the ranch where she too could warm up before starting her day's work.

"I'll see you here when the bus drops you off, okay?"

Okay." Russell slipped off Blackjack and almost got lost in the deep snow. But in a few steps he was in the bus, and Goldie waved goodbye to the bus driver.

After two years they had found the rhythm of living on the ranch. When spring came, they would leave Russell behind at the ranch with the cook and ride their horses down to Denver or Evergreen to meet the train that carried their new herd of cattle. Last year it had been just Tim and Goldie, which was an almost impossible amount of work trailing the thousand head back up to the ranch by themselves. Usually, you needed one puncher to every two hundred and fifty or three hundred head of cattle. That meant that Goldie and Tim had to do the work of four trail drivers to get their herd home. This year, Dr. Moore had promised that her son Alf and maybe another hand or two would help them. They had fifteen-hundred head on order. The doctor leased the government land for grazing the cattle all the way up to Arapaho Glacier, so once they got the herd to the ranch, they let them wander the high country and fatten themselves up until fall, when they reversed the process, rounded them up and trailed them back down to the stockyards in Denver.

Last year, when the April snows got so deep the mail truck couldn't get to Eldora, Ward, or Caribou, at least the road to Cardinal could be opened. The mail had to be taken from there on horseback up to the mining town of Caribou, and Goldie knew that at least on part of that journey the carrier had to get off his horse and hang onto its tail, following in the track the horse broke. And then, a few days later as the deep snow began to melt, the side of the road in Boulder Cañon caved in on a man who was navigating his automobile through a herd of cattle. Fortunately, he braced himself, and his machine landed on its wheels in the gully below. He could get his Lincoln touring car back to the road, but he had to drive very slowly because his steering wheel was damaged. Goldie and Doc hadn't even heard about the accident until they'd managed to get to Nederland a couple of weeks later. The news made them glad that they used Coal Creek Cañon to drive their herds to and from Denver. It was no less steep, but it had more open places for the herd to get off the road.

During the summer, Doc had hands to manage and he gave talks at night to the boys who came to the Tom Tucker summer camp. He was the head wrangler for the horses, and in charge of the boys' activities that had to do with either horses or cattle, so he was busy all the time, day and night. Alfred Moore would be back again this summer, leading groups of tourists on horseback to Arapaho Glacier from his Moore Saddle Livery business in Nederland. His trips started from the Tucker homestead, which Russell would be passing about now in the school bus. She put Alf out of her mind—he wouldn't be back in Nederland until June.

To pick up some extra money, Goldie also led groups of tourists who signed up with the Kite and Glacier Route to see Arapaho Glacier on horseback. If it was just a group of ten, she'd take them up by herself, but if there were more, she'd get Doc or one of the hands to help her. They charged each person five dollars, a fair price considering that it could be a dangerous trip, and it was hard on the horses. From Boulder the group came up the cañon in a Kite and Glacier taxi, one of the seven-passenger canvas-top touring cars. Glen Sherman drove the Cadillac. Jack Gilman drove the Lincoln. Seth Armstead drove the Packard. Starting up the cañon road they would point out the Cañon-Park dance hall; the Alps Lodge; the Public Service Generator Plant; the El-Vado village; the Red Sign Mine; Eagle Rock and Wiley's Place where you could get gasoline at the top of Eagle Rock hill; the Old Toll House just below the waterfall; the village with a store and gasoline station at the falls; the Eureka Mine; Eckels Resort which had a boarding house, skiing, skating, and dancing; the Perfect Tree; and Castle Rock. Near the Perfect Tree were ponds where fish were raised to put into Boulder Creek. Finally, there was Ted Green's store at Tungsten. In the summer, a sign propped up against the store's porch read, "We Have Pop On Ice, But We Don't Know Where Mom Is."

Goldie met the taxis full of tourists in Nederland with a string of saddled horses. When they let the horses out to graze at night, she'd spend the early morning hours rounding them up. Once she got them all together in the corral she'd saddle them up and lead them into town. Tanner Brothers provided lunches of sandwiches and pickles for everyone, and Goldie picked those up too before she met her group and they started their day-long ride.

The famous glacier they came to see almost touched the Continental Divide, tucked into the cliffs just under North Arapaho and South Arapaho peaks. It nestled there in the rocks above treeline, like a sparkling white oasis in a sea of barren rocky peaks, a harsh landscape broken only by tiny colorful lichen and small clumps of tundra flowers.

Alf took her to the glacier during her first summer on the ranch. He was born in Nederland, and even though he'd spent most of his years growing up in Denver, the mountains and horses were in his blood. He always came back to Nederland and the surrounding mountains, running a livery in town, or ranching. Anything to be with horses and out in the open. He'd taken lots of people to the glacier through the years. Everyone wanted to see it, either on foot or on horseback, but the trip could be dangerous, Alf told her. Make sure your clients bring extra warm clothes and hats. The summer sun glinting off the snow could make you snowblind. Fierce thunderstorms could suddenly appear on the Divide and bear down on the unsuspecting in a matter of minutes. She'd seen lightning strike so close that the earth shook and horses scattered in terror.

She was daydreaming about dainty blue columbines nodding beside waterfalls that poured from under melting ice shelves and creeks that splashed over and around big rocks and lapped at lush green tufts of grass when she and Blackjack arrived at the ranch.

She could smell the smoke from the chimney before she could see the house, and breathed deeply. Smoke meant a warm house was waiting for her. She unsaddled Blackjack and left him with the other horses in the barn.

While she was delivering Russell to the school bus, Doc watered and fed the horses. This time of year, it seemed like there was always repair work to be done, and just keeping the house warm was a constant chore. Wood that they had dragged out of the forest the previous summer had to be cut to length and chopped into pieces that would fit into the potbelly and the cookstove, and then it had to be brought into the house. Water had to be pumped from the well and hauled inside for cooking and washing. Goldie had come to appreciate the cookstove in their new home. The water reservoir held about four buckets of water that she could use for cooking and doing dishes. On bath day, she heated two buckets of water on the stove and used another to cool the water to the right temperature. She could leave beans on the stove all day, and she learned to can venison. Everyone hunted to have enough to eat year-round, and Goldie and Doc were no exception.

Goldie poured herself the last cup of coffee from the pot on the stove and lit a cigarette. She had started smoking when she became a cowgirl. Like so many things the cowgirls did and the way they dressed, it was necessary to play to the fantasies of their audiences. Their fans thought that all cowboys and cowgirls smoked, so she started smoking. Doc was bent over a cowhide he'd laid out on the table.

A view of part of Caribou Ranch today. Even in May the Indian Peaks can be white from a spring snowstorm.

Kay Turnbaugh

"Whaddya doin'?"

"I thought I'd make you somethin' for a Christmas present."

Christmas was a couple of weeks away, and they were all looking forward to the weeks of no school. Goldie had cut down a small tree and hauled it in the house over the weekend, and the three of them had strung popcorn and decorated it. She stood with her back to the stove, gradually thawing out from the ride to the school bus and finished her cigarette. She watched as Doc used a small knife to painstakingly cut a few inches of the hide. He'd started in the middle and was making a pinwheel.

"What is it?" Goldie wanted to know.

I don't know if I should tell you before Christmas."

"Oh come on, you can tell me. If you're going to be workin' on it here in the kitchen I might as well know."

"Hum." It seemed that was all Doc was going to say, so she gave up for the moment.

"I told Russell today that we might move into town for next winter."

"Did you?"

"Well, I know we've only just talked about it a bit, but you said it would be better for him."

"Thinkin' it's a good idea and findin' the money to do it are two way different things."

"I know. But I'm so afraid he's going to get really sick on days like this. It's horrible out there."

Tim straightened up and stretched his back. He gave her an affectionate peck on the cheek. "You really want to move into town?"

"Well, yeah. I think it might be a good idea. Just for the winter. I could come up on the weekends and help out. It's just...Russell." Mr. Cameron looked at her sideways and raised an eyebrow. She turned her back on him and walked over to a window, watching the snowstorm outside. She loved her husband, but Alf Moore's attentions had turned serious after they moved to the ranch. Now she and Alf tried to get away for an afternoon whenever he came to the ranch. If she was living in town part of every week, it would be easier to see him. She was pretty sure Doc didn't know about Alf, but the way he'd just looked at her made her feel guilty.

"I gotta keep 'im in school. You know that. I promised the judge."

"I remember." Doc sighed behind her. She turned around to watch him.

He was inspecting the work he'd done on the hide. "I was talkin' to Mike Shellhaas last time I was in town. He said he thought we might be able to get a good deal right now on a house—maybe buy one for back taxes. He tol' me how to find out who hasn't paid their taxes by goin' to the courthouse. I was thinkin' I'd check it out next time we're in Boulder. If we can swing it, we can get somethin' in the summer."

"Oh, that would be wonderful, Mr. Cameron. But why didn't you tell me?"

"It's hard pokin' a word in edgewise sometimes."

"You don't mean that, do you?"

" 'Course not."

"Good. Then let's talk about somethin' else. Like what you're doin'." Doc smiled and bent over the hide again.

"Well, see, this will eventually be one long string of hide. Then I can weave it together, and make you—"

"A lariat?"

"Yep."

"Oh, that's really great," Goldie's smile was big. She'd been needing a new lariat, so it was a perfect gift. "Will it be ready by spring to drive the herd?"

"Yeah, I figure I can work on it at night when we're snowed in."

Goldie patted the hide appreciatively, and the cowboy squeezed her around the waist. In spite of the howling wind and the sideways snowstorm outside, she felt peaceful and happy, and she set about making them sandwiches for lunch.

Their gift to Russell that year was Goldie's old bronc saddle. Doc had decided the boy was getting too big to ride in his mother's saddle. It was time Russell handled a pony on his own. Harry had used the saddle, and then she'd used it for her bronc riding, and at times Doc had used it for riding buckers too. The saddle didn't have much of a swell to make it easier to ride bucking ponies, so they had taken it to Denver to get a new swell. Russell seemed pleased with the gift, but he informed them that when he was grown up all the way he was going to be an engineer on a boat, not a cowboy.

⫷ THIRTY ⫸

Expiation

WHEN SHE LOOKED UP she expected to see Russell jumping off
his pony, but instead she saw an empty saddle.

"Russell?" How could he have slid off that saddle so fast
that she didn't even see him? "Russell?"

Angry now, she picked up Digger's reins. They were muddy
and dirty.

"Oh no! Russell!" She was screaming his name, but there
was no answer. She ran for the barn and threw a saddle on
Blackjack, thinking only of her boy and what might have happened. Almost blind with worry, she tossed her whip over the
saddle horn. She picked up the reins to Russell's pony and urged
Blackjack to pick up the pace as soon as she was in the saddle.

Russell was a good rider. But he never took to it like Goldie
had. Now that he was old enough, he saddled his own pony and
rode into town to school. This spring it was his job, on his way
home, to check for stray cattle, and if he found any, to herd them
back to the ranch. While he was at school, he left the pony at the
Shellhaas place. Doc and Mike Shellhaas had become friends
over the last few years. Goldie had been welcomed by his wife

(This page and next page) Goldie's son Russell wanted to be a
miner as a young boy growing up in Nederland.

Buffalo Bill Museum and Grave,
Lookout Mountain, Golden, Colorado

Elsie and their daughter Marguerite, who was in high school when Doc and Goldie first moved to the ranch. Marguerite and her mother often dropped by the Camerons' cabin on the ranch when they fished near Lakewood, and sometimes they would give Doc and Goldie a couple of trout for dinner.

Goldie didn't have much time to socialize in town, and she wasn't the type to join the Rock and Garden Club or the Ladies Aid, and in the boyish Marguerite she found a kindred spirit, although this winter, now that she'd graduated from high school, Marguerite was across the Divide teaching school. Goldie didn't think her friend would take to being in a class-room with a group of children all day and didn't give her long as a schoolteacher, although she was glad Marguerite seemed to have found happiness with the young woman she had brought home last weekend. Goldie had known several cowgirls who preferred women to men, and she didn't see anything wrong with that, so long as they kept to themselves. There were people who wouldn't speak to women like that, but that seemed silly to Goldie. What people did in private was up to them.

She kept urging Blackjack to pick up the pace. She hoped she wouldn't find her boy unconscious and bleeding, but that's exactly what she expected. She had been so determined to have Russell—she had even thought that having a child would fix what was wrong between her and Harry. Of course, it hadn't fixed anything with Harry, but she wouldn't change anything about that decision. She was devoted to her son, and he just had to be alive!

She found Russell walking slowly down the track toward the ranch, kicking rocks into the woods. She waved frantically at him, and he waved back. She jumped out of the saddle as soon as Blackjack stopped next to her boy.

"Oh thank god. Are you all right?" She tried to pull him into a hug, but Russell wasn't interested in hugging his mother and turned away.

"Yeah, ma. I'm fine."

"What happened?" Goldie saw a new tear in the shoulder of Russell's shirt. He saw her looking at it. He was bleeding under the tear, and another tear in the knee of his overalls showed broken skin and dried blood beneath it too.

"It wasn't my fault, ma. It was crazy Jess's dog. Jess tore outta his house, yellin' at me, and that dog was barkin' and Digger just took off. I fell off, ma."

Goldie sucked in her breath. Her boy could have been killed when he fell off his pony like that. Jess would pay for this.

Jess Geiger lived on the road to the old dump, and he was always chasing off people who still thought they could dump a load of trash near his house.

"Go on home, Russell. Mr. Cameron needs for you to go on up to where he's been felling trees and help him bring a load home. And stop at the house and clean up those cuts. Use plenty of water, and soap."

She waited for her son to saddle-up and ride away before she clicked softly at Blackjack, turning his head toward town.

Jess wasn't outside. "Jess, get on out here," she called loudly toward the house.

A paunchy man in worn overalls appeared at the door. "Whaddya want, Goldie?"

"I wanted to see what kind of scoundrel would scare a horse out from under a boy and then just let him walk home."

"I didn't have nothin' to do with it, Goldie. It was the dog—he yelled at the dog. It was his own fault."

Goldie could hardly see the man she was so angry. She cracked her whip next to the door frame. It was a muleskinner's trick that she'd learned while driving the sprinkler wagon—the noise was enough to scare anything to get moving. Jess jumped and knocked against the door frame.

"Now, Goldie, the kid's okay. He's not hurt or nothin'."

"How do you know? Did you even check on 'im?"

"I know." Jess took a few nervous steps toward her, hitching his thumbs in the pockets of his overalls. "He got up and walked away."

Goldie couldn't believe what she was hearing. She'd seen too many accidents that had resulted in torn ligaments, broken bones, and even death. No cowboy would watch someone fall from a horse and not help.

The whip sprang from her wrist and wrapped itself around Jess's neck. The man fell to his knees and unwrapped it. His neck was bleeding. As soon as he was disengaged from the whip he started running. Goldie cracked it again next to his ear. He ran faster.

"You stay away from my boy. If I ever hear that you're scarin' his pony again, I'll kill you."

Annie, Jess's wife, appeared at the door. When Goldie's whip cracked again, she screamed. "Leave him alone, Goldie. Leave him." The small, fragile-looking English woman had fire in her voice, and Goldie turned Blackjack toward the ranch. She was still shaking when they got out of sight of Jess's house, and Goldie slid off the big horse and walked alongside him until she calmed down. All she could think about was Russell. What if something had happened to him?

❧ THIRTY-ONE ❧

Code of the Range

"Hello, Lorena." For a moment Goldie thought Lorena would refuse to see her, but finally she said, "Hello, Goldie," and the guard unlocked the cell door and let Goldie inside.

"Oh my god, Lorena. How're you doin' in here?"

"How do you think?" the tiny cowgirl asked bitterly.

"Well, yeah. I just came—"

"Why did you come? To gloat?"

"What? No. No, I wouldn't—" Goldie paused. It was going to be hard for her to say what she'd come to tell Lorena. Maybe it would be best to just plunge into it, like she did with everything else in her life. "I wanted to tell you that I forgive you for walking out with Harry like that."

"Oh." Lorena sighed and sank onto the cot. "Well, thanks. I'm not sure I deserve it, though." She sighed again. "I wish I'da known that I actually had it good with Harry. Compared to Slim," her tone was rueful.

"You jus' never know, do you?" Goldie couldn't imagine how bad life with Slim Harris must have been for Lorena, if she thought life with Harry was 'good.'

"What are your chances, Lorena?"

"I didn't mean to do it, you know. It jus' happened. He was so drunk, and he was a mean sonofabitch when he was drunk. I didn't mean it—I loved him," Lorena wailed the last and blinked back tears.

Goldie sat down next to the tiny, dark-haired woman and put her arm around her shoulders.

"Well, let me tell you, I did mean it when I tried to kill Harry. I'm jus' so sorry I didn't do it right."

Lorena's smile was small, but it was enough. All seemed to be forgiven between the two women.

"We're a pair, aren't we?" Lorena blew her nose into her handkerchief. "I heard you married Doc Cameron. How'ya doin'? Ranchin', I heard?"

"That's right. At Nederland—in Colorado."

"That sounds nice. I wish I coulda found someone as easy-going as Doc."

"That shore wouldna been Harry."

Lorena snorted in agreement. "No, sir, I don't think anything about Harry was easy-goin'." They both grimaced at their own memories of Harry Sterling. And then, seeing the expression on each other's face, they laughed.

"I been readin' all the papers. You're in 'em all. Even the Denver paper had a big story."

"Really?" Lorena certainly wasn't the cowgirl Goldie remembered who had stomped out of her apartment with her husband. That Lorena was full of fire and wouldn't have let anything get in the way of what she wanted. This Lorena seemed defeated and confused about her life.

"You're gonna say it was self-defense, aren't you?"

"That's what my lawyer says I should do, but—"

"But what? It sounds like a good idea to me."

Lorena bit her lip and shook her head. "My lawyer says I'll have to tell everything in court."

"Yeah, what's wrong with that?"

"I loved him. I don't think I can."

"I see."

The other cowgirls who were in town for the trial had urged Goldie to go see Lorena. Goldie and Doc had come to Oregon, as had hundreds of other rodeo performers, to be there for Lorena during the trial which was scheduled to start November 7. The cowgirls were worried about their pal. She was getting paler every day she spent in the jail cell, and she'd been there since early September. There didn't seem to be much left of the courageous trick rider. The tough cowgirl was fading away in the jail cell.

"She's got to tell what Slim's been doin' to her. Goldie, you gotta go tell her. You been there." Goldie knew they were referring to her life with Harry and when she tried to kill him. "She needs you." Goldie finally agreed to do what she could.

But now that she was here she didn't seem to be convincing Lorena of anything. Finally she said, "I heard that the lawyer that Slim's family hired is sayin' that havin' all your trophies in the window of that jewelry store is prejudicin' the people in town in your favor."

It was a big display, and it included the prestigious McAlpin Trophies from 1920, 1921, and 1924 as champion all-around cowgirl at Cheyenne Frontier Days. Other gleaming trophies were from Lorena's bronc riding title at Chicago in 1925 and several championships at Pendleton, including the one from 1919 when she and Harry had gotten together, the year Russell was born. A few years ago, Goldie would have spat at it, but when she and Doc poked their boot toes into the dust that had blown into the bottom of the big window, she was awed by the trophies, by what they represented, and she felt sad for all that had happened to Lorena. She rubbed some of the fine, gray dust off the window with her shirt sleeve and wondered how much of Lorena's success could be attributed to Harry. Harry, she mused, might have been a liar and a disappearing act, but he was a damn good rider and had taught both of them plenty about horses and trick riding.

The deputy was at the cell door, beckoning to Goldie. Goldie hugged Lorena and whispered in her ear: "You gotta tell, Lorena. Don't let 'em lock you away in here forever. You gotta tell." This was one time when what people did in private didn't need to stay in private—after all, nothing else about Slim's death had been private—and it was time for Lorena to come clean.

The rodeo performers, who normally would have been drinking, dancing, and partying when so many of them were together, were a subdued lot as they waited for Lorena's trial to begin on Monday. Goldie and Doc barely made it inside the courtroom that first day, and the next few nights Goldie cut the stories from the newspaper.

Lorena Trickey, popular little rodeo star, went on trial today in Lake county circuit court on the charge of murdering J.P. (Smiling Slim) Harris, on the outskirts of Lakeview on the night of Sept. 2. At the time Harris was found dead, it was thought the cowgirl and Harris were married. Later she confessed she had not married Harris.

Her face was white and she did not talk to her attorney as members of the jury panel were questioned...

"God put the dagger there," Miss Trickey said after the slaying, in explanation of the crime. Her plea will be self-defense...

She is far different from the days when she made her wonderful rides at Cheyenne when she carried away a lifesize portrait of herself, the gift of the Denver Post, as the world's greatest cowgirl. The fight is gone from her eyes and the life from that active body.

A United Press Special Correspondent interviewed Lorena. *Just a trace of a teardrop coursed down the face of this hard-muscled little rider who has thrilled thousands by her daring tricks on the backs of wild mustangs.*

"Have you ever really loved a man?" she challenged. "If so, you will understand. I loved him, and he told me he was thru; that when

the Lakeview roundup was over he would put the horses in the barn
and ride over the hills.

"I couldn't let him leave me. I—I—"

She buried her face in her hands as if to hide the mental picture
of the night of Sept. 2, when, it is charged, she plunged a knife into
the heart of Smiling Slim. She did it, her attorneys contend, in self-
defense.

Many witnesses have been summoned to testify to abuse and
beatings which the happy-go-lucky Harris is alleged to have inflicted
upon her when he was intoxicated.

But Lorena, confessed slayer of her common-law husband,
subscribes to the code of the range—to take your medicine. She
indicated a willingness to sacrifice everything rather than to abuse
the memory of the man "who meant more to me than life itself."

Court adjourned Friday, November 11, in memory of the
signing of the armistice and resumed on Saturday. The United
Press reported: *Lorena Trickey, cowgirl and rodeo rider, has told her*
story of lawless love that led her to plunge a knife into the body of
curly-headed, hard-boiled Slim Harris…The sobbing tale of passion,
cruelty and fear told by the girl last night was admittedly the chief
hope of the defense to win her freedom. The newspaper story
recounted how two women fainted, others throughout the
courtroom were crying openly, and hard-boiled range riders
stared wide-eyed. The courtroom was filled beyond its capacity.
Men stood on top of the unlighted stove.

Fifty persons were milling about the door trying to catch a
glimpse of the dramatic episode within.

Outside, snow was falling.

Slowly, haltingly, for two hours the little cowgirl queen, who has
spent her life on the ranges since she ran away from high school to
join a wild west outfit, told of her love for Harris, their courtship,
her belief that Slim would marry her, and his drunken cruelty.

On the night of the fatal quarrel, she said, she found Slim drunk
at roundup headquarters and she was unable to get him to the car
until Pat McCarthy, a cowboy friend, urged him to go.

Along the edge of one of Goldie's scrapbook pages, she wrote about Lorena, "Though she stole my husband Hiram Sterling when my son Russell Sterling was 3 weeks old, she laughed in my face, I forgave and mate [met] her in her cell in Oregon. She was a great rider, one of the best. Goldie."

The Sterling family

During the ride Harris became so menacing and dangerous that she attempted to leap from the auto, but he knocked her to the floor of the machine.

Harris threatened to kill her, she testified. "I was terrified and I thought he would kill me. I reached in my pocket and got the knife I had bought earlier to mend a bridle. Finally getting it open, I hid it between my knees, defending myself as best I could against his blows. Twice I almost threw the knife out of the car.

"I was scared but I didn't want to hurt him. He kept beating me and I became desperate. Finally, I lunged out with the sharp knife, hoping I'd only wound him.

"The blade struck home. I leaped from the car and started running toward the rodeo barn. Slim started after me.

"I looked back. He was gaining on me. Then I glanced back again, he was sprawled in the dust.

"I said," she continued: " 'Slim, what's the matter?' He replied: 'God, Lorena, you've killed me.' It was the first time he had called me by that sweetheart name for years and, oh, how I wanted to die with him. It hurt so much and, God knows, I loved him, drunkenness and all.

"I kneeled in the dust of the road and held him in my lap, putting my head on his breast with a dread in my heart.

"Then I began to scream, but no one was near. It was lonesome there and I was so helpless. I knew a cowboy's hell in those few minutes."

By Sunday, Lorena was free. Her attorney's argument that she had killed her cowboy lover in self-defense was upheld by the jury. Lorena's elderly father had mortgaged his farm to help pay for her defense after she used up all her money. The United Press reported: *She was unworried by the fact that she had spent all her money on the trial. "I've been up against it before, and I've come out all right,"* she said.

Goldie had no doubt that her scrappy little friend would be all right. It seemed all the cowgirls were up against it all the time. Whether it was being flat broke, or flat on their backs in the hospital with an injury, or just flat-out fighting to be allowed to compete against the men at the rodeos for equal money, they were always up against it. But mostly they came out all right, and Goldie was proud to be cowgirl, thankful that her pal Lorena was free, and happy to be heading home with Mr. Cameron.

Part 3

✷ Town ✷

1928–1976

Goldie in her restaurant in 1952.

The Sterling family

❦ THIRTY-TWO ❦

No Longer Hitched

THE SILENCE BETWEEN THEM was a deep canyon. Goldie was too angry to cry. It had happened again. Her husband was in love with one of her girlfriends, and he was leaving.

They were living in Nederland, and like that other New Year's Day when they had moved to the ranch, Goldie was stuck inside, staring out the window at big snowflakes swarming in sideways circles. When one of the boys at the Tom Tucker camp turned them in for making moonshine in a still on the ranch last summer, they'd been forced to move. Doc found work as the town constable in spite of the business about the still, or maybe because of it. A lot of the townsfolk had benefited from that still, so now her Doc was Constable Tim Cameron. People in Nederland wanted a peace officer they could count on who would basically leave them alone, and everyone liked Doc. Goldie was more a housewife than ever, and Russell was doing okay in school—he liked living in town.

"I don't know why you're surprised," Doc said, and he laughed bitterly, his close-set eyes reflecting the late afternoon sun that slanted sideways through the front window. "Mebbe you been spendin' so much time with your boyfriend, you didn't notice how lonely I was."

He was wrong there. All show people played around a little—everyone knew that and expected it, and that's all it was between her and Alf. The thing between Doc and Mabel McDonald was so much more. How could Mabel do this to her? How could Doc think it was okay? He knew how hurt she'd been when Harry left her for Lorena. It just wasn't fair. Mabel was her friend. Goldie loved Doc, and she might have forgiven him, but her pride kept her in the house staring out the window. If he thought he had to leave her for Mabel...well, she'd just have to wish them a good life. She'd tried to be a good wife for him, but now that was over. Why were her men so fickle? Why couldn't they love her? It felt like her heart had flown out the door, chasing Doc, and she knew she'd never get it back. At least she had her women friends. Well, except for Mabel.

She'd have to start over again. She'd have to find a job in town. The things she'd been doing to help out—hauling tourists up to the glacier, renting out horses, and working with the horses on the ranch—that wouldn't be enough now. Whenever she was on top of the Continental Divide, telling her stories to the folks who had signed up to see Arapaho Glacier, she felt that she wasn't cut out to be a housewife, and this clinched it. With Doc out of her life, she'd have find some full-time work in town, but what to do? The only thing she knew how to do was to entertain people. Why, oh why, did this have to happen to her again? She sobbed into her handkerchief.

She would never, ever marry again—it was way too much trouble. Harry always thought his charms were irresistible, and for a while they were. She had been so young and trusting when she met him, and he used that against her. He thought he could make her love him and then do whatever he wanted with other women. Well, it didn't work—she'd finally gotten him out of her life. And now the same thing was happening with Doc. She yelled a string of words she'd learned from cowboys on the show

During the Depression everyone in Nederland hunted, including Goldie. She always had a dog, and was well known as a dog trainer. Doc is wearing the constable's star.

The Sterling family

circuit—words most people in Nederland had never heard—and she kicked a chair over. It clattered across the floor. One leg separated from the rest and almost skittered out the door. She started pacing, venting more anger with more invective. She felt a bit better.

She gulped at her cold coffee, dried her eyes and straightened her shoulders. She was almost forty years old, but she'd cast herself as a new person and come back from nothing before, and she could do it again. Once again, she would be starting with next to nothing. Doc told her he'd let her have their Nederland property, so that was a start. He bought the house for $300 four years ago, and since then they had added several lots that they bought for the back taxes owed on them. One of them had cost them $10.78, and another $8.95. She didn't know how much money she'd need to buy Doc out, but if it was too much, she'd talk him down. He owed her that much.

Goldie and Russell in Nederland. Goldie worked at a little bit of everything to make ends meet, including renting horses and taking tourists on rides.

The Sterling family

She needed to go down to the store and call her mother. Of course, that meant that everyone in town was going to find out about the divorce, but that was going to happen pretty soon anyway. Or at least as soon as Doc resigned as town marshal.

He was going to move to Denver to be close to Mabel. The job as town constable only paid a pittance anyway, but every little bit they cobbled together was a help these days. Dick Murdock had been after her to work for him in his restaurant, the Silver Dollar, so maybe she'd have to take him up on that, but it would have to be full time, not just some here and there arrangement. She didn't much like Dick, but she needed a job.

She rested her cheek against the cold glass of the window and stared again at the swirling snow. Russell would be home from school soon. With a start she realized she hadn't thought about Russell yet. He would be devastated. He liked Doc a lot. Well, he'd just have to get over it. It was just the two of them. Just like it was in the beginning. Just the two of them.

✎ THIRTY-THREE ✎

Out on Her Own

BETWEEN WILD WEST, CIRCUS, AND RODEO seasons, she'd
worked in restaurants—first in Chicago, then in Denver at the
stockyards when she was with Harry. There weren't many
choices for women who needed to work. Being a nurse or a
teacher paid better than waiting tables, but Goldie didn't have
the education for those jobs. She could have worked at a factory,
or as a retail or office clerk, but none of those jobs appealed to
her. Being a waitress paid as badly as a hotel maid, but at least
as a waitress she got to talk to people. When she and Doc were
first married and retired from show business, she worked in a
restaurant on Denver's downtown tramway loop with her good
pal Esther, who had introduced her to Alf Moore. After she and
Doc divorced, in March of 1932, Goldie drew on her experience
in restaurants to get a job working for Dick Murdock at the
Silver Dollar in Nederland.

Jovial-looking, balding Murdock was a bootlegger and a
shrewd business man. Almost every day he and Goldie argued
about how to run a business. Not only did he deal in liquor, he
hosted wild poker games at the Silver Dollar. Goldie never had

liked people who broke the law, even though she drank her share of moonshine during Prohibition and she'd helped Doc with the still on the ranch. She wasn't proud of what they'd done, but everyone needed money then, and it had gotten them through some hard times. They didn't flaunt what they were doing like the gangsters did, and like Dick Murdock.

In the town election on the first Tuesday in April, Dick Murdock received the fewest votes of anyone, validating Goldie's opinion of the man. He only got twenty-seven people to cast a ballot for him, and Goldie didn't doubt that he'd bought every one of those votes. She thought Dick was too slick for his own good and called him a crook, and he called her names, too. Their rows were loud and blue—neither one backing down. But Dick Murdock counted on Goldie. She was stronger than any of the men he had working for him, so it was her job to move the kegs of beer behind the bar. And her outgoing, fun-loving, rough-life nature was good for customer relations.

A few weeks later, the newspaper reported that Goldie was ill. Even though it was almost May, eight inches of snow blanketed the town, and Goldie stayed in bed. The divorce had been stressful enough, but she also was worried about how she'd make enough money and keep an eye on Russell—it was just too much.

She read about what had happened to Oscar from her bed. The sheriff of neighboring Gilpin County was indicted for conspiracy to violate the national prohibition law. Oscar and Doc had become friends when Doc was Nederland's constable, and Goldie liked Oscar. Now she wasn't so sure about him. He was charged with receiving $85 a week in protection money from Joseph Roma, a reputed Denver gang leader, in return for allowing Roma's associates to operate three whiskey stills in Gilpin County. Thank goodness Doc had moved to Denver, otherwise he might have been drawn into the scandal just because he was Nederland's constable.

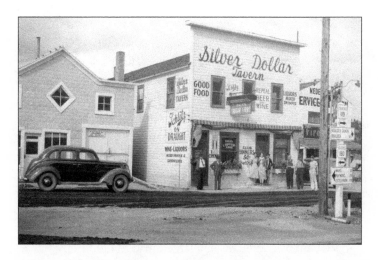

The Silver Dollar Tavern, where Goldie worked, and Dick's Liquor Store, about 1934. The Nederland Service Station is next door. The building on the left is now Nederland's Town Hall.

Carnegie Branch Library for Local History, Boulder, Colorado

In other news, the Lindberghs' baby, the twenty-month-old child of America's beloved famous aviator who had been kidnapped from his home in New Jersey, still hadn't been found. Goldie's heart ached thinking about the time Harry had tried to kidnap Russell and she almost lost her own son. She could feel the Lindberghs' agony vibrate through the big black headline, Lindbergh Baby Still Missing. *In a twisted way, their tragedy* made her feel better. As she stared at the newspaper, she realized she didn't have it so bad. At least she had her son, and she had a job. She got up to make a cup of coffee and smoke a cigarette, feeling much more like herself. If the Lindberghs could carry on, so could she.

The summer of 1932 was one of Nederland's busiest. In a special election, residents had voted overwhelmingly, 105 to 33, to allow the government to bring a state highway through town. Surveyors spent weeks figuring out where the road would go, and Goldie was afraid they meant to bring it right through her house.

A new tennis court was built west of the MacKenzie Hotel, and the Middlesworth Hotel was sold to a couple who changed the name to the Imperial Hotel and painted it a brilliant orange with black trim so it could be seen from the road to Boulder. In late June a massive flood in Bummer Gulch in Boulder Cañon injured 20 people, but by July there was no more rain and forest fires took over. There was a fire in a draw south and east of the Nederland lake dam, and Dewey Wright, the forest ranger, was summoned from Rollinsville. Boulder County Sheriff Robert Blum rushed five men to the fire, and Sam Downs from Public Service Company brought in a large squad to fight it. By July 6, about a hundred men were battling the five-acre blaze.

Goldie bought their house from Doc for $10, and, after they signed the papers, they motored to Estes Park for the day with Russell. She was still angry with Doc, but they all tried to make the day as pleasant as they could, and it did feel good to get out of town and out of the restaurant for a day. About a week later, Goldie's old waitressing pal Esther came up from Denver and spent a few days with Goldie and Russell. The women laughed and tried to out-tell each other with their stories. Esther had a beau, and they were thinking about marriage. Goldie was happy for her friend, but she was sad that she probably wouldn't see Esther as much after she was married. When Esther went back to Denver, Goldie went with her. Goldie stayed at her mother's apartment in Denver, and Allie came to Nederland to stay with Russell. It was a much-needed break for Goldie.

Fall brought with it more fires. Early in September a timber fire, the twenty-fourth fire of the summer, started near the town of Baltimore near Tolland. By the middle of the month it still wasn't out, and forty men were fighting it. Forest Ranger Wright telephoned the newspaper in Boulder saying seventy-five more men were needed to battle the blaze. The fire had

The MacKenzie Hotel, as it looked in the 1930s. The hotel featured an L-shaped floor plan and advertised its dining room on the hotel building and on a building across the street. The Nederland Lumber Supply Company building is in the background.

Denver Public Library, Western History Collection, Muriel Sibell Wolle, X-5559

burned its way over Tennessee Mountain and was threatening Nederland. The Boulder County Sheriff sent fifty-two men, and a hundred more came from Denver. By September 20, the fire, which had scorched nine hundred acres, was under control, but another fire had burst open on Jennie Creek, and the fire near Ward was still raging. A few days later, the Tolland fire was going again, even through a small snowstorm.

At the end of the month, the boys in the high school, including fourteen-year-old Russell, were called to help with the fire at Ward. At least part of the new road to the mining town north of Nederland had been finished, making the thirteen-mile trip less time-consuming than it had been just a few months ago, but Goldie still found plenty to worry about with her young son fighting a forest fire.

While Russell was in Ward, Alfred trailed his herd of one hundred and fifty-nine Herefords to the Denver market. Alfred was ranching on the DeLonde, close to where Doc and Goldie had been working their cattle with Alf's mother.

The day Russell left, Goldie was up at 4 a.m. She packed his things and tried to kiss him goodbye before his friends arrived to drive him to Denver. After he left, she drove to the turn-off for Coal Creek Cañon in the cold, still darkness before dawn to meet Alfred who had stopped there overnight after bringing the herd down from the high country. Their affair had been cooling off, mostly because Alf was hardly ever in Nederland, and, when he was, he was usually with his wife. So this was a rare opportunity for them to see each other in private. Goldie could barely remember the guilt she felt so long ago the first time she'd cheated on Harry after she'd found out about his cheating, but one thing being married to Harry had taught her was to take care of herself first. That had been a valuable lesson and one she'd learned well, and by the time Alf made advances after that fateful night at the theater, she no longer felt guilty about seeing men outside her marriage. Later, she rationalized that Doc was too easy-going, and that she would go stir-crazy if she didn't have a little excitement, a little drama, a little mystery and suspense in her life, and one way to do that was to sneak out to see other men. Harry had done it to her plenty of times, as had Doc. Seeing other men protected her from ever being hurt again as badly as she was when Harry walked out the door of their apartment with Lorena on his arm.

She pulled the automobile off the road and parked just as orange feathers fanned across the horizon, slowly burning light into the velvet black sky. When she first met Alf she assumed he was just a cowboy-crazy city man, but it turned out that he had grown up riding and ranching during the summers when he was going to school in Denver. She opened the automobile door and turned sideways in the seat so she could watch him. She lit a cigarette as Alf mounted his horse and reined him towards the automobile, stopping now and then to murmur something to one of the cows. She loved watching men on their horses. She had been privileged to watch, and ride with, some of the best horsemen and women in the world. That life

The DeLonde Homestead, where Alfred T. "Alf" Moore ranched in the late 1930s. In 1965, a second version of the movie *Stagecoach* with Alex Cord, Bing Crosby and Ann-Margaret was filmed in part on Caribou Ranch (formerly the Tucker Ranch). The ranch and homestead are now being preserved by Boulder County Open Space.

Kay Turnbaugh

seemed so long ago. She shivered and pulled her cardigan closer, tapping her foot against the running board with impatience. The horse's hooves set off showers of silvery dew. The silhouette of the tall man with a tall hat sitting gracefully on his horse moved closer to her as they trotted through the tall grass. She sighed with pleasure.

Goldie had always figured that the only reason Alf had taken up with her was because she was a cowgirl who had lived the life of his dreams. His wife thought Alf should get a job in Denver and give up his romantic ranching ways. Even though Alf had become a foreman or manager on most of the Colorado and Wyoming ranches he worked, he didn't make much money. Only the Hollywood stars like Tom Mix made a lot of money as cowboys these days. Goldie greatly admired Alf because he was determined to keep his dream alive.

She thought about her dreams as she stubbed out her cigarette. She'd lived her cowgirl dream, but sometimes it felt like she had shot herself when she'd tried to shoot Harry. She'd ripped open a hole of loneliness at the bottom of her heart that never closed. Even a good husband like Doc and a lover like Alf hadn't been enough to fill it. For her, it was best to just 'love 'em and leave 'em.' It was a good philosophy to always keep in mind, Goldie reminded herself, especially since Alf was going to take a job in Wyoming next season which meant she wouldn't be seeing him too much longer.

By then the silhouette was off his horse, holding out a hand to help her out of the automobile. They wasted no time—they both had work to do. Alf left first, urging his herd down the canyon road to Denver. Goldie spent some time smoking another cigarette. She sat with her eyes closed, listening to the sounds of the trees sighing and the squirrels scurrying. A breeze tickled her cheeks, and it brought with it the smell of faraway smoke. She couldn't tell for sure, but she thought it was smoke from the fire her son was fighting near Ward. The thought brought back all the worries that had been vanquished during her short time with Alf. She climbed back in the automobile and used the mirror in her compact to pin her hair back up and dust her cheeks with rouge. She was back in Nederland in time to open the restaurant for the first customers of the day.

At the end of that dry, windy season, thirty-two forest fires had raced through the hills near Nederland. The two biggest fires, north and south of Nederland, had cost $3,000 each to fight. The fire northwest of Ward had consumed 500 acres of timber, and the fire in Tolland swept over another 800 acres. Although the hills were brown and black, the Nederland men who fought the fires all summer were paid, and they spent much of their green money in town. In these tough times, it was a boon to the local economy.

⤙ THIRTY-FOUR ⤚

There's Gold in Those Stories

A FEW YEARS LATER, WHEN MURDOCK sold the Silver Dollar to Ralph Harlow, she was part of the deal, and she was paid $100 for a month to 'learn Ralph' how to mix drinks and tap beer kegs.

At the end of that month, she opened her own restaurant, The Last Roundup.

The country was still in the grip of the Great Depression, but people had to eat, and as long as the mines stayed open in Cardinal, she knew she'd have hungry customers. Besides, she was tired of working for someone else.

She installed her old show saddle on a wood stand in the restaurant and hung her whip and lariat on the wall. Goldie's clientele grew as word spread about her and her stories of life with the Wild Wests.

That first year running her own business was a wild one. One long summer weekend she couldn't close the restaurant. The Cardinal miners came to town for a dance, one thing led to another, and three days later, they finally stopped dancing. The dancing worked up appetites, and Goldie stayed open for three days and nights to feed them. If you wanted to drink and blow off some serious steam, you went to the dances in Nederland. If you wanted a tamer Saturday night, you went to the dances in Eldora, five miles up the road. Goldie felt right at home with Nederland's rougher crowd, and she never did have to do more than take her old bull whip off the wall to get customers who had become too rowdy to leave.

Everything that happened, good or bad, was good for Goldie's business at the restaurant. The Jack-O-Lantern dance hall was converted to a roller skating rink that was extremely popular with the young people in town, who worked up big appetites while they zipped around and around the wooden floor. Even when the Nederland baseball team lost to Central City or when Nederland lost again to the Eldora team, it was good for business because almost everyone who went to the games went out to get a Coca-Cola or a sandwich afterwards.

Goldie had a lot of regular customers, but Mrs. Tanner wasn't one of them. So it was curious when Mrs. Tanner walked into the restaurant one afternoon in October. The two women faced each other across the gleaming oak bar. Mrs. Tanner wore a lightweight gray wool suit with a white blouse that was a few years out of style, although it was still very white and neatly pressed. Her hair was pinned back from her long, impassive face. Goldie felt slightly out of place in her own restaurant. Her dress was older than Mrs. Tanner's blouse, and her apron was clean but stained. She wiped her hands on the apron and reached for the strands of hair that invariably escaped from her pins, whisking them back into place.

Mrs. Tanner announced that she was out gathering news for her column in the Boulder newspaper, which she always filled with tidbits about the clubs and who was coming and going. But once they had established that Goldie had no news for her column, Mrs. Tanner didn't leave. As if she'd just thought of it,

Many dances were held at the Nederland Lake Pavilion which extended over the water of Nederland Lake, now Barker Reservoir.

The Sterling family

she asked Goldie if she'd like to join the Friday Night Card Club, just for the one night, of course, as they were missing a member who was out of town for the weekend. Card clubs proliferated in Nederland, but Goldie preferred the standing poker game that was held in one of the restaurants after-hours.

"Nope, sorry, that's not me. You got the wrong gal for that. I'm not cut out for that kind of thing." Mrs. Tanner smiled deprecatingly at Goldie's continuing protests.

"Well, I didn't think it would hurt to ask." The way Mrs. Tanner said it, Goldie was sure Mrs. Tanner knew what Goldie's answer would be before she posed the question. Goldie turned, but Mrs. Tanner wasn't finished. "I hear you're real good at cards. Do you ever play anything other than poker?"

"Sure I do." Goldie looked at the other woman as if she were crazy. She figured she'd played just about every game that ever existed on all those long train and boat rides around this country and Canada.

"Oh. Well." Mrs. Tanner looked around the dining room making sure there were no other customers. She perched primly on a bar stool and accepted the glass of water Goldie offered. Goldie was washing glasses when Mrs. Tanner had walked in, and she went back to work. "I heard that you said you'd walk with the children to Lakewood on Saturday. That's real nice of you."

"It's nothin'. Russell wanted to go to the party, so I thought I might as well help out." One of the boys was celebrating his birthday with a hike to the town of Lakewood, three miles north of Nederland, where there would be a wienie roast and picnic supper, followed by games and singing.

Well, we all sure appreciate it. Thanks for the water." Mrs. Tanner handed Goldie the glass, brushed off her skirt, and got up from the bar stool.

"Oh, and I should warn you."

"Warn me?" At last, Goldie thought, we're getting down to why Mrs. Tanner came to the restaurant.

Mrs. Tanner cleared her throat and looked at the cash register over Goldie's shoulder. "Yes, warn you. I know you come from show stock," Goldie's eyebrow went up at the reference that likened her to cattle, "and you've always lived the loose life." Goldie squinted at Mrs. Tanner, thinking that the woman knew nothing about her life and wouldn't survive a single day living the way Goldie had to—she was too soft. If Mrs. Tanner didn't get to the point soon, Goldie would have to help her out the door.

Mrs. Tanner continued, still looking at the cash register, "Nederland isn't like that. We're respectable, and we have rules. We'd appreciate it if you would not use your foul language around our children any more. We appreciate what you're doing by taking the boys on walks, but please leave our men alone. That's all I came to say. I just thought you should know, before..." Mrs. Tanner didn't finish. She turned on her heel and walked out the door.

Before what? thought Goldie. *What are you going to do to me? All I do is flirt with your poor, hard-working husbands when they come in here for a meal. Nothin' illegal 'bout that.* Goldie's mischievous smile followed the good Mrs. Tanner as she strode across the street. *Nothin' wrong with a roll in the hay now and then, Mrs. Tanner, and it would do you a world of good. Now, if you had some liquor at your card games, and if I could smoke—if you had some fun—I'd think 'bout comin'. And wouldn't you get in a snit if I did?* When she finished fuming, Goldie realized she was staring blankly out the window at a deserted street. Mrs. Tanner didn't know what she was talking about, so the whole episode was meaningless and laughable. Goldie snorted. She spent all her time working and watching after her son, who was getting to be a teenage handful. Since things had cooled off with Alf, she hadn't found time for anyone else. And nothing that woman could ever say to her would change how she treated her customers in her restaurant.

She had learned that her stories about life in the Wild Wests and with Buffalo Bill were as good as gold in the restaurant business. Customers drove up the winding cañon roads from Boulder or Denver or Golden to stay at the autocamps and eat at the Roundup, hoping that she'd have time to come out of the kitchen and tell them a tale. She'd dust off her apron and pull up a chair or wriggle into the booth next to one of the men. She liked sitting close to those men, feeling the excitement in their twitching legs and quickened breath as she explained what it was like to ride a bucking bronco with Buffalo Bill. They could experience a part of the old West through her, and she was happy to help.

In many ways Nederland felt like the old West and set the stage perfectly for Goldie's tales—dusty streets, men chatting amiably in front of the stores, wooden sidewalks, false storefronts, and the kind of mountain scenery that made people think of Switzerland. The slow pace of life in Nederland and

Goldie shows off mining memorabilia to the Roose brothers in her restaurant. In the background are a teenage Helen Prime who worked as a waitress and Goldie's long-time cook Rosie.

Roberta Childers photo

the cooler mountain weather transported visitors to someplace so different it was like traveling to another country. The tourists who drove up Boulder Cañon eighteen miles to the top of the dam were rewarded with the view of the town set like a jewel between the sparkling lake and the soaring Indian Peaks. Inside the jewel, they found Goldie and her restaurant.

When Prohibition was erased from the law books in December, none of Nederland's restaurants seemed anxious to start serving alcohol. By spring, Goldie's friends had convinced her to apply for a liquor license, and before the summer season of 1934 she received Nederland's first post-Prohibition liquor license.

A few years later, she closed The Last Roundup and opened The Trail of the Yukon on the town's main street. When she had a chance to rent a building across the street, she took it and closed The Trail of the Yukon and opened Goldie's Corral. The Corral building had rooms that Goldie could rent out, and that meant a little more income. Her waitress Rosie, whom Goldie had rescued from an abusive relationship, moved to the new restaurant with her and took over the duties of cook. She also moved into Goldie's house. Sometimes Goldie couldn't afford to pay her, and at least this way she knew the girl had a roof over her head and food to eat.

By now Goldie had refined her business formula of providing good hamburgers and cold drinks at a good price along with some story-telling. Even though it was uncommon for a woman to own a business, Goldie reveled in being different and doing something she wasn't supposed to be able to do. If a man could run a restaurant, so could she. If you got right down to it, her restaurant was just another way of entertaining folks, what she'd been doing her whole life, and she never tired of telling stories from her wild past.

Cook Rosie points out some of the miners' hardhats in one of Goldie's Nederland restaurants.

Roberta Childers photo

Goldie cashed in on her
past when she opened her
own restaurants in Neder-
land. She kept her show
saddle on a stand and en-
tertained customers with
her stories.

The Sterling family

⟫⟫ THIRTY-FIVE ⟪⟪

Another Mouth to Feed

IN AUGUST GOLDIE TOOK ON ANOTHER GIRL from town. Earlier in the month she'd been taking a break with the girls who were working for her that summer. It had been a busy lunch, but at least for now, the restaurant was empty. Goldie always enjoyed talking with the girls, listening to them chatter about their lives and telling them lots about hers.

Goldie, Rosie, and their teenage waitresses Blanche and Dede were sitting at a table in the dining room, sipping iced teas. Blanche had run away from home when she was fourteen. She had fallen in love with George Giggey when her family was in Nederland the year before, but they wouldn't let her stay, so a few months later, she came back on her own. She didn't have any money when she arrived in town, and Goldie took the girl in and gave her a job washing dishes. Now she was a waitress. Before anyone else could say anything, she took a deep breath and looked imploringly at Goldie.

"Mrs. Cameron, you gotta help us."

"Hmmm?"

"You know Jean." When Goldie looked confused, Blanche expounded. "She used to come by here before she got pregnant and her parents sent her away."

"Did she have her baby?" Goldie asked. The teen girls in town were all close, and they visited each other at their jobs when they could, so Goldie knew most of Blanche's and Dede's friends. The girls' friendships reminded Goldie of the way the cowgirls had faced so many challenges together. She had even offered to give Jean the name of a doctor who could help her if she didn't want to have the baby, but the girl seemed horrified at the thought. Goldie thought she wasn't thinking things through clearly, although she certainly understood wanting to have a baby. It wasn't as easy as it used to be to find a doctor who would terminate a pregnancy. It used to be that you weren't really pregnant until the quickening, or until you could feel the baby move, so if you hadn't menstruated in a month or two, it really was a matter of restoring your body's normal order and having a doctor help you menstruate. That's what Dr. Alice Moore did. Alf had told Goldie lots of stories of how the law in Denver had tried to get to his mother, but they never could get anything on the 'baby' doctor. Maybe because in addition to terminating unwanted pregnancies, Dr. Moore had delivered babies who had grown up to be powerful politicians in Denver.

Goldie remembered how distraught she'd been with Harry when he asked her to abort that pregnancy before his trial in Texas. Now she was glad she hadn't had that child. Just as she was glad she had raised a son. Children were a blessing and a curse. You were blessed to have them and cursed when they grew up and left home. She had fiercely protected her son Russell and tried to keep him close, but she knew the time was coming soon when she would have to let him go.

"Yes, it's a little boy." With a start Goldie returned to the present where she was sitting at a table in her restaurant with two distressed young girls. "He's not much of a looker. No hair. Ugh."

Rosie and Goldie pose for a photograph in front of one of Goldie's restaurants in Nederland.

The Sterling family

"That's great. A boy. When did she get home? Did she get married?"

"No. That's the terrible thing. She just got home, and Mrs. Cameron, she doesn't have anywhere to go. You've got to help us."

"Whaddya mean, she doesn't have anywhere?"

"Her parents kicked her out. She has until the end of the week to find some place, and she doesn't have any money. She can't work, not now, now she's got the baby."

"Oh my." Goldie clucked sympathetically. She knew she had a reputation for helping folks who couldn't afford a meal, especially when the Depression hit so hard in Nederland. She wasn't the only one in Nederland who made sure nobody ever went hungry. If a family ran out of food, a package of meat would appear on their doorstep. Lots of people hunted, and they were fortunate they didn't have to go far to find game. Doc had taught Goldie how to hunt elk and deer while they were on the ranch, and now Goldie hunted when she could, and her aim had improved considerably since that day she'd tried to shoot Harry. But leaving packages of meat, or fronting someone a meal in the restaurant, or letting some of the war refugees live for free above the Corral, or setting aside a can of milk from Williams Dairy in Tungsten every week for the big Wise family that needed it with all those kids—all those things were easy, and Goldie did them gladly. Taking in a young girl and her baby—that was something else.

"What do you think, Mrs. Cameron, can we help her?" Goldie looked from Blanche's stricken face to Rosie's thoughtful one to Dede's tearful one.

"Of course we can. Tell her to bring her things to my house. She can come live with us."

Russell wasn't happy about having someone else move into the house, but Rosie understood. She moved out of her room for Jean and the baby. The house was getting crowded with Russell, his grandmother Allie, Rosie, and now Jean and her baby, but Goldie figured they'd get by as long as people wanted to hear her stories and came to eat at the restaurant.

✎ THIRTY-SIX ✎

Ring the Bells of Heaven

THE BELLS SHOULD BE RINGING. That was all she could think about at first. She had tried to put the news out of her head the moment she heard, but she could no longer escape what had happened. Dear Alfred was dead.

He was still riding full time, at the age of 59. This summer he was the manager of the Canyon Ranch near Encampment, Wyoming. He and his wife had left in the early spring, before the bluebirds had returned, before anyone had planted their potatoes, before the snow had melted, before Nederland's lake had filled and become "a rippling, silvery sheet, spreading almost to Main street," as Mrs. Guy Tanner had written in her column in the Boulder newspaper. Goldie bet that Mrs. Tanner wouldn't put anything in her column about Alfred's death. Mrs. Tanner regularly ignored both Alf and his mother. Occasionally she put an item about Goldie in, but it was almost always at the very end where it could easily be cut off if there wasn't enough space to print everything.

Alf would have liked to know that fifty of the men who were working at the CCC camp in Peaceful Valley were to be transferred to Brainard Lake to work on the circle drive. He had worked hard over the years to get people up to his precious mountains, bringing them on horseback in groups or singly like he did with Goldie. He'd even been involved in the campaign to build an automobile road over Arapaho Pass. It seemed like that would never happen now, not after the long Depression. Alf had wanted everyone to love the country around Nederland as much as he did. He thought it was the most beautiful place in the world.

Goldie had always thought that neither Alfred nor his mother had ever gotten the recognition they deserved in Nederland. His mother was the town's first doctor, and her son Alfred was born in Nederland. Alf was still as "cowboy crazy" as he'd appeared to Goldie when they first met at the theater in Denver. He'd ranched all his life—when he died, the newspapers in Denver called him "a pioneer Colorado and Wyoming livestock man."

He was killed in a riding accident on that ranch in Wyoming. He'd only been gone a few months, but while he was up there, life had gone on in Nederland—the MacKenzie Hotel and the Silver Dollar Tavern were remodeled, the autocamps had opened, summer cottages had been opened and occupied, the town's summer activities were planned, and the weather had changed from cool days and cold nights to warm days and cool nights. Alf had promised her that they would go for long rides in the high country when he finished the season in Wyoming. They would have ridden through the decaying aspen leaves and the first fast snowstorms. They would have talked about his season in Wyoming. They would have stretched out on warm rocks to watch the clouds while their horses browsed in a meadow. But Alf had taken his last ride without her, and it was time to say good-bye, even if Nederland didn't ring the bells for him.

At least the bells had rung for Doc when he had his accident, and Goldie took some comfort in that memory. When the Depression deepened after their divorce, Doc couldn't make it in Denver, so he'd moved back to Nederland where he could scrape together a little work and hunt for food. Nederland was a place where everyone took care of each other, and Doc felt at home in the small mountain town. He'd been working in one of the few mines that was struggling to stay open, and the day of his accident every bell in town was ringing. Everyone immediately dropped what they were doing and said a prayer for the hurt miner. Goldie was in the restaurant kitchen, smoking a cigarette. It wasn't the bells she heard first, it was the quiet. For the first time that day, she wasn't hearing the rock-grinding stamp, stamp, stamp of the mill as it crushed ore just a few blocks away.

She followed everyone else out to the street. Dogs were wandering in circles, chasing each other in little clouds of dust and howling or barking in concert with the bells. It had been one of the hottest summers ever. Thousands of people in the Midwest had died from the heat, up to 113 degrees in Minnesota. Nederland escaped the worst of the heat wave because of its high altitude at 8,200 feet, and it had actually been good for business. Anyone who could afford to flee the high temperatures of the flatland cities of Denver and Boulder drove to the mountains for a day. Even on that day, a weekday at the end of August, the restaurant had been pretty full. After a few minutes, the bells stopped ringing, but their pealing was replaced with the sound of someone running towards them. No one moved. Goldie squinted into the afternoon sun, starting its plunge into the peaks, trying to see who it was.

Her son's friend Barney slid to a stop in front of Goldie. She clutched her heart, fearing the worst, not wanting to hear, but anxious to know. "Come quick. It's Mr. Cameron. They gonna take 'im to Boulder." Goldie didn't bother untying her flowered apron. She tossed her cigarette down in the street and followed as fast as she could. Both Doc and Russell were working for the Wolftongue Mining Company, and Barney had had enough sense to tell her that it was Doc, not Russell, who was injured.

Doc, who was known now as Tim, had broken up with Mabel and come back to Nederland the year before to live with his sister and her husband, who also was a miner. He'd asked before he moved back, and Goldie told him it would all right with her. They were divorced, and she wasn't mad at him any more. They were pals, and they always would be. Doc had been a huge part of both her and Russell's lives, and he was a steadying influence on both of them. Living in the same small town wasn't too hard with such an easy-going ex-husband, and it had been good for Russell, who was a difficult thirteen years old when Doc moved to Denver. Russell was heart-broken, and he'd blamed the divorce on Goldie. He'd started drinking, but she didn't think it would hurt him. He needed to get the anger out. She knew he also blamed her for never letting him see his father Harry, but she hoped he'd understand someday.

That summer, when the mines were hiring again, Barney, Russell, and Doc all got jobs. The country still needed tungsten, and although many of the mines that had opened during the Great War were still closed, others were continuing to operate, and it meant steady work for many of the men in town.

They had brought Doc to the mill office. He was lying on the couch, his head wrapped in bloody bandages. A group of men was hovering nearby, murmuring softly. Goldie charged into the room, and they all turned to her. Someone grabbed her arm, trying to turn her away, but she'd seen plenty of head injuries in her day, and she'd judge for herself how bad this one was.

"Hey, Doc, how'ya doin?" she cooed at the still figure. His eyelashes fluttered, and she knew that was a good sign. She knelt beside him and took his hand. "Hang in there, Doc. We have to get you to Boulder to the hospital. You gonna be all right—jus' lie still there, okay?"

She felt a presence behind her, and Alberta, Doc's sister, clutched her shoulder. "Oh my god, do you think—?" Goldie shook her head.

Two men entered the office carrying a stretcher. They held it next to the couch, and Goldie helped them move Doc's limp body onto it. Russell held the door, and they carried Doc to the waiting automobile. Goldie realized it belonged to the mine's manager, William Loach. She offered to hold Doc's head in her lap and comfort him on the long ride ahead, but the men turned first to Alberta. She shook her head. "I'll go get Lewis, and we'll follow you in our machine." Goldie hopped into back seat of the automobile and cradled Doc's blood-soaked head on her lap, holding it carefully between her hands, just as she had years ago with her cowgirl pal. Maggie had died like that, with her head in Goldie's lap. She closed her eyes and said a short prayer. *Please don't let him die, please.* She wiped the tears off her glasses and nodded, and William Loach himself climbed behind the wheel. Russell gently wrapped a blanket around Doc and took the other front seat, and they were off. Even though it didn't appear he could hear her, she talked to Doc non-stop through the hours it took to get to the hospital, telling him to fight, to be strong, to live.

Doc's accident had a profound effect on Russell. After his lengthy stay in the hospital in Boulder, Doc returned to Denver, where his sister and her husband had moved after the accident. Goldie and Russell knew that Doc would probably never return to Nederland, and now that was one more reason Russell wanted to leave. He was arguing with her more and more about the future, telling her, "You know this is what I've always wanted to do, Ma. You can't stop me." When did her son become a man? It seemed like it happened overnight. She wondered if he'd inherited his wanderlust from her. Or was it that he disliked being underground that much? She couldn't remember exactly how it felt to want to be somewhere, anywhere but here, but she knew she'd felt it too, and she knew she couldn't hold onto him much longer. Doc's return to Nederland had stopped the demands to let him go, but after Doc's accident and long recovery, eighteen-year-old Russell was more determined than ever to leave his small town behind.

Some of the other boys had enlisted in the Merchant Marines, and that's what Russell did. With Russell gone, Alf dead, and Doc living in Denver, Goldie felt bereft. Except, of course, for her mother, and all her friends, and her customers. She felt blessed to have them, but they couldn't fill the hole left by all those lost and absent men-folk.

ᗛ THIRTY-SEVEN ᗛ

The Home Front

ABOVE THE CLATTER OF THE MACHINES, the women traded gossip and news. Goldie worked on the old Sears and Roebuck sewing machine that was a wedding gift from the other cowgirls in the Buffalo Bill show when she and Harry were married in Madison Square Garden in 1913. She had used the trusty machine to make all her Wild West outfits and her clothes in the last thirty years. Brownlee Guyer, the long-legged prankster who was their new Fish and Game Warden, made a wood stand for it and converted it to run on electricity in his shop on Second Street.

The other women usually left their machines at her restaurant, the Trap Door, and when they weren't in use, Goldie stored them back of the bar. The flannelette pneumonia jackets they were making to keep wounded soldiers warm and insulated from the drafts that often floated through the hospital wards hung everywhere. Reflections of the black sewing machines and the half-sewn jackets in the bar's wall-size mirror became such an integral part of the restaurant that neither Goldie nor most of her customers noticed them anymore.

Most everyone was pitching in doing whatever they could during the war, the second World War, and women everywhere, including Nederland, sewed. Russell's boyhood wish had come true; he was serving in the Merchant Marines on a ship in the Pacific.

Her little boy was married now. He'd taken up with Maxine Cline when they both were in high school. Her father owned a mine in Tungsten. Just before Russell shipped out for the Pacific, they married. It was a day Goldie would never forget. She was so proud to have raised a son who was married to a girl Goldie loved like a daughter. Goldie cried and hugged both of them over and over, wondering how the years could have passed so quickly. It was hard to believe that some day soon her child could be having children. She wanted to gather Maxine under her wing and made sure the young woman knew she would always be welcome to live in Goldie's home while Russell was away at war.

As the weeks passed, the news from the war in the Pacific got worse and worse, and Goldie's worry was ever present. Russell just had to come back from the war if he was going to have a family and if she was going to be a grandmother. The grandmother thought made her check her reflection in the mirror and pull at some of the gray hair that was curling around her face, but she soon realized there was too much of it to bother.

Goldie worried about her son's safety every day, especially with all the talk about possible sabotage by people of Japanese descent who were now living in the U.S., even if they were American citizens.

Colorado's governor refused to put the state's Japanese-American citizens in relocation camps, and the decision had done nothing to dissipate the fear everyone felt about the Japanese. Word had spread to California that Colorado was friendly toward Japanese-American citizens, and many of them

Goldie sent a hand-tinted print of this photograph taken in October 1947 to her son Russell, whose picture sits on the counter.

The Sterling family

fled their homes in California for Colorado. The news reports of hundreds of Japanese-Americans flowing across the state's borders everyday panicked most Coloradans who were as afraid of possible fifth column spying activities by people of Japanese descent as were Californians. But Colorado Governor Carr called California's wholesale roundup of Japanese people a travesty. "They are American citizens," he told the residents of his state. The Governor believed that alien Japanese, the ones who might be involved in espionage and sabotage, should be jailed, but he said he was "not going to put any United States citizen in jail."

Pretty much everyone else in the United States disagreed with Colorado's governor. Success against the Japanese forces in the Pacific looked bleak, and tales of humiliating treatment by the Japanese of captured U.S. soldiers created frustration and anger in citizens everywhere. U.S. Attorney General Francis Biddle warned that "no false sense of security" should be derived from the fact that no large-scale act of sabotage had yet been committed in America, and camps in the Western states were quickly built to house thousands of American citizens of Japanese descent. The government thought it was safer to send them inland, away from the coast of California where the results of spy activities could be catastrophic. But the citizens of the states slated to receive those American citizens of Japanese descent, including Colorado, didn't want them—even if they were incarcerated in fenced camps with twenty-four-hour guards.

Many of the Japanese families that were evacuated from California were brought to Camp Granada in Colorado, in one of the bleakest spots on the eastern plains. Evacuees arrived at Granada as American casualties continued to mount on Guadalcanal. The Japanese landed forces in the Soloman Islands, and the Red Cross announced that Japan would not allow ships or vehicles carrying supplies for American prisoners of war to have access to them. Mistrust and fear of the camp detainees continued to rise.

Fear had turned to hate in many people, and it became dangerous for an American of Japanese descent to walk the streets in most of Colorado's cities. Many, if not most, of Colorado's businesses refused to serve them. Only a handful of people agreed with Colorado's governor that Japanese-American citizens deserved the same protections under the Constitution as any other citizen. For the vast majority, fear dictated agreement that the concentration camps for the Japanese-American citizens were necessary.

Goldie's fears were exacerbated by worry about her only son, serving in the Merchant Marines in the Pacific. She expressed her worry the only way she could think of: she painted a sign on a four-foot-by-ten-foot board and propped it up outside her restaurant. It said "No Japs" in huge letters.

Brownlee Guyer came in about a week after she put up the sign to tell her that he'd caught a Japanese man without a fishing license at the lake. He said the man was fishing because he was hungry, and asked if he could bring him into the Trap Door for a meal. If she would help out, Governor Carr would be proud of her. Goldie blinked, and stared at Brownlee. She couldn't believe what she was hearing. Her head roared with anger. She was so angry she forgot that Brownlee loved to play practical jokes. She called Brownlee every dastardly name she'd learned from years on the road and threatened his manhood if he didn't get out and stay out. Her son was in the Pacific theater bringing supplies to American forces that were fighting the Japanese, and she didn't care what anyone else, especially Governor Ralph Carr, thought, no Jap was coming in her restaurant, hungry or not. Brownlee chuckled and said he didn't understand why she would be so kind to the displaced Germans who had landed in Nederland, but not the Japanese. Didn't the Japanese-Americans share much the same situation as her Sioux friends? Weren't they all Americans? Including her friends from the circus, like the Pin Heads and the Four-Legged Girl? Brownlee's booming baritone bounced off the restaurant's walls. He didn't relent; he kept pushing her. They were all different, but they were all Americans, just like Governor Carr was saying. Was she just going to let this poor Japanese guy go hungry? By this time Goldie was so furious she couldn't see straight. She moved by instinct toward her bull whip that hung on the wall behind the bar, and Brownlee backed quickly out the door. He apologized a week later, and she understood that the whole affair was one of his practical jokes. They were speaking again, but she wouldn't ever forget what he'd done.

Today was Wednesday, and every Wednesday six or eight women from the community came to Goldie's restaurant to sew the pneumonia jackets. Goldie closed the restaurant so they could use the tables and counters for cutting out the sleeveless jackets and sewing them up. The wind had cranked up after

Looking east down First Street in Nederland on a snowy day in January 1948. Goldie's friends, the Childers, owned the Piggly Wiggly, on the corner of First Street and Bridge Street, now the corner of First Street and the combined Colo. 119 and 72 highways.

The Sterling family

lunch, blowing frigid air from the Continental Divide straight down First Street, and it had the town's tattered flags snapping and dust from the street swirling. Inside, the restaurant felt cozy and safe from the wind, in part because no one could see out the front windows that were frosted from years of sand-blasting by Nederland's wind. It used to be that people complained about not being able to see out the windows, but since the United States had entered the war, no one said a word. Materials for maintenance or building were practically non-existent, and those kinds of projects had to wait.

Today was the first day the high school girls would come in after school to help with the sewing. Goldie was expecting as many as six or eight girls. The bus driver said he could drop them off right on First Street. With the girls' help, the women were hoping to deliver their pile of pneumonia jackets in two weeks to the Collection Center in Boulder.

"What do you hear from Russell?" every woman asked as they arrived one by one after their household chores were finished. Since walking to do errands or get groceries was encouraged by the government, those who could, walked to Goldie's for the sewing afternoons. Those who lived so far they couldn't walk would either ride together or only come when they had enough gasoline left over at the end of the month.

"Nothin'. I never hear nothin'. But I think that's good news—not to hear," was Goldie's standard reply. Or she'd make a joke about getting a new gray hair every day she didn't hear. "How's Maxine holding up?" was the next question, and Goldie could tell them that her daughter-in-law was well. After Goldie and Maxine had written to each other a few times, Goldie invited Maxine to come live at her boarding house in Nederland for as long as Russell was serving in the war. Goldie was glad for the company. Usually Maxine worked with them on the sewing projects, but today she was down the canyon in Boulder, volunteering at the Red Cross with some of the other younger Nederland women. Work on the canyon road was halted because of the war effort, but at least the first part of the project, the road up the hill from Tungsten to the top of the dam, had been finished.

Goldie had coffee brewing, a treat during that time of ration books. The room was bubbling with news as the women took out their sewing machines and settled into their seats.

"Did you hear that John Birkeman got a little drunk and took their car out for a spin? Grace was so mad, she'd been saving that gasoline for a trip to Boulder."

"I hope she beaned 'im good," Goldie commented. Everyone tut-tutted, but Goldie meant it. Everyone had to do without, and John Birkeman was no exception. If he was going to get drunk, and she didn't see how he'd managed that unless he'd bought something on the black market, that was one thing, but to deprive Grace of her monthly trip to Boulder was mean, to say nothing of the rubber he'd used. Goldie made a mental note to ask Grace if she wanted to come next time Goldie could afford a trip to Boulder.

"He shouldn't have used that much rubber—that's the reason we're not supposed to drive over 35—ever since the Japs seized those rubber plantations—everyone should know how scarce it is." Goldie was just warming up to a full tirade. Her friends Esther and Sadie laughed, but the other women looked annoyed.

"Let's not go into that again, shall we?" Annie said softly. Goldie harrumphed and sat down, pointedly lighting a cigarette. After a few puffs, she stubbed it out, jumped up and noisily set a dozen coffee mugs on the bar.

"Does everyone know about the clothing exchange?" Flossie raised her voice over Goldie's commotion so everyone could hear. "It's next week, Tuesday night, at the school. Everyone is welcome." About every six months, the women in town gathered for a clothing exchange, since new clothes and shoes also were rationed. The exchange was good for their morale, although it was always a little weird to see someone else in town wearing your old dress. Some of their kids were wearing shoes that had been part of the exchange three or four times, but no one ever complained.

After Goldie handed out mugs and poured every drop out of the coffee pot, she sat in the back corner of the dining room with her friends Sadie and Esther. Sadie's husband Harvey was a miner in Central City before they moved to Nederland. After a few years, Harvey quit mining and got a job working on the county roads. Sadie's piano took up most of the front room of their little house, but Sadie couldn't live without it, and Harvey—and her friends—loved to hear her play. Sadie was careful about her looks and wouldn't go out of the house without a lot of makeup. She kept her hair blond even though it had turned gray a long time ago. Most of the women in Nederland wore very little or no makeup, but Sadie's lips were red and her eyebrows carefully arched. She always looked out of place in the old mining town.

Everyone in town called Esther "the Swede" even though her married name was Pedro. Goldie first met her when they were both working tables in Denver restaurants, and she was

Esther Olsen. The two young women found they had a similar view of life and what one could make of it. Now Esther was a round, middle-aged blond, with almost transparent fair skin and merry blue eyes. She lost her husband early in the war and decided to move to Nederland to be close to her old friend Goldie. She got a quit claim on a little house on Third Street, and Goldie assured her she would never be poor in the generous little town.

The three of them worked efficiently even though they talked non-stop, thanks in part to the coffee and in part to the fact they hadn't seen each other in a few days. Sadie, constantly humming to herself, cut the fabric, and Esther and Goldie sewed the seams and hems. Every week the women who could brought Goldie small amounts of sugar so she could make oat-meal-raisin cookies for their sewing day. Some of the women savored their cookie while they sewed or chatted; others care-fully wrapped their cookie to take home to their children.

They all sewed until their backs ached and they had to go home to fix supper. Then the high school girls arrived, and Goldie served French fries and Coca-Colas, treats that no one asked how she managed to supply. The girls giggled and horsed around, but they worked hard on the jackets, and Goldie wondered if they could also sew slippers for the men who were injured and stuck in hospitals overseas when they finished the jackets.

After the girls left to walk home for supper, Esther and Goldie stayed at the Trap Door. Once in a while, Sadie would join them, but usually she went home to make supper for her husband. Goldie and Esther made macaroni and cheese—you could get two of the blue boxes for one coupon—and drank some beers. Having dinner together had become a tradition since they started working on the pneumonia jackets and the Trap Door was closed for the day. Sometimes, a few men would wander in after supper for some poker. Marguerite used to play

Like everyone else, Goldie, second from the left sitting, did what she could to aid the war effort during WWII.

The Sterling family

with them before she joined the WAACs, the Women's Army Auxiliary Corps. Sometimes, they would drift over to Sadie's little house across the street from Brownlee's shop, and Goldie would sing and dance as Marguerite and Sadie took turns thumping out tunes on the piano. Sometimes, with a few more beers, the women talked Marguerite into bringing her piano-accordion or her banjo. For Goldie, relaxing with her friends was a great stress relief in a worrisome time.

She often wished she could do more to help the war effort. If she could have, she would have signed up to serve in the WAACs with Marguerite, who, since she'd been the postmaster in Nederland, was made postmaster at Camp White, Oregon. Not at all what Marguerite wanted to do—she'd wanted to be in the motor division because she loved tinkering—but she was actively serving her country. Goldie had decided against the

WAACs because she had bills to pay, a daughter-in-law and a mother to take care of, and as long as she had customers she would keep the restaurant running. Plus, she was a bit older than Marguerite.

A lot of her customers in the restaurant were miners who stopped by for a hot meal after a long shift at the Wolftongue Mill or the Conger. With the war, tungsten was in demand again, and many of the tungsten mines near Nederland that had closed down after the First World War were de-watered and re-timbered. Nederland's tungsten mines and mills supplied much of the precious metal that was needed in the production of the country's armaments. The old mining town was back in business, and it seemed that any able-bodied man who hadn't signed up to fight for whatever reason was a miner.

Goldie was proud that her son Russell had tried his hand at mining before he signed up for the Merchant Marines and left Nederland for good. He said it was only to do his part in the war, but Goldie knew he was gone for good. Russell had never taken to Nederland the way she had. She truly had come to love the quiet of small town life, and Nederland had become her home—the home she'd never had during all those years on the road—even if some people still didn't accept her. She may have traveled hundreds of thousands of miles more than anyone else in town and seen ten times more of the country than they had, but she could tell that some people didn't think much of her former life. One thing that had horrified many of the "society" ladies of Nederland was the night she couldn't wait to use the outhouse at the billiard hall. She and Doc had brought Russell down from the ranch and let him go to the picture show at Fatty Mills' by himself. They went to get a couple of drinks. She had to pee so bad, she just did what she'd done for years on the road with the rodeos and Wild Wests. She found a spot behind the outhouse. It took her a few years to discover what she'd done wrong. Now, despite her rocky start with town life and the people who still didn't like her, she felt that she had become an

Goldie in front of her restaurant.

The Sterling family

integral part of the community, a business owner, someone people counted on.

All her friends were here, except, of course, for her old cowgirl pals. She kept in touch with them as best she could, and she'd discovered some other people in Nederland who had been in show business who could reminisce with her about the old times. One of them was Marian, who had married Bob Childers, who owned one of the grocery stores. Marian and her twin sister had toured the country as the Mann Sisters. Now, Marian taught rope tricks to youngsters in town. Once in a while, she and Goldie got together to muse over their days in show business. Or, if Marian wasn't around and Goldie wanted to recall those days, she would pull out her scrapbooks or the box full of fan mail she still received.

One of the saddest letters was the one she got in March of 1939 with the news that Prairie Rose Henderson had died in Wyoming. The news of Rose's death was first reported in the newspapers in 1933. She was referred to as one of the country's most beloved cowgirls, and Goldie cut the stories out and pasted them in her scrapbook, even though they didn't really capture the spirit of her old pal. Rose told her she got her nickname when Charlie Irwin, one of the original rodeo promoters, put her on a hobbled bucker and told her it just takes a weak mind and a strong back, "so you just sit on up there." As she flew by, blond curls bouncing, he said, "There goes my Prairie Rose." In 1924 Rose and cowgirls Mabel Strickland, Fox Hastings, and Lorena Trickey asked to compete in the same contests as the cowboys so they could be in the running for the all-around cowboy prize—and money—at the Pendleton Roundup. The Pendleton Roundup Association denied their request, even though cowgirl Bertha Blancett and others had regularly challenged the men for the all-around title in previous years. Rose laughed about the incident, but she called it the beginning of the end of the good old days of rodeoing.

All of Rose's handmade outfits were outrageous even in the cowgirl world where outfits were made to stand out for a crowd that was far removed from the arena where the cowgirl was performing. No one did it better than Prairie Rose. Her most outrageous outfit might have been that short skirt of ostrich feathers that Goldie remembered so well from the Albany Hotel after Buffalo Bill died. Rose made the skirt and a matching bolero jacket out of colorful ribbons and sequins and, of course, the ostrich feathers. She would trim her blouses with chiffon and sequins and marabou feathers. Her generous grin under her tall, wide-brimmed hat was infectious and men loved her. Rose had married at least five times that Goldie knew of.

In the winter of 1932 the authorities came to the Wyoming ranch where Rose was living with her last husband, a cattle rustler. They arrested him and took him off to jail. When he got out and came back to the ranch several weeks later, his wife was missing. It wasn't until 1939 that a sheepherder found her body. All along, during those seven years when no one knew for sure what had happened to Rose, Goldie harbored secret hopes that her pal was still alive somewhere, that she had just run out on her husband and would appear one day at a rodeo or at her doorstep. But it turned out Rose was trying to catch a horse and froze to death in a snowstorm. She was fifty-eight when she died. Rose would have added some flair and fun to the flannel jackets—Goldie figured they would have been trimmed with ostrich feathers and some swinging beads. What Goldie missed most about her friend was the way Rose's face lit up with her wide, gap-toothed smile. Rose was a woman who managed to make every twist and turn in her life into an opportunity to have some more fun. That would have been difficult the way things were now, Goldie thought, and she was thankful her friend had missed this damn war.

After she pasted Prairie Rose's obituary in her scrapbook, Goldie wrote a note next to it: *At this clipping, I stop to pay tribute to a great rider, woman and pal. The happiest days of my life were spent being her pal. We came from Chicago together to be cowgirls. She was given the name of Prairie Rose by Charley Irwin in Cheyenne, Wyo. When she mounted her first bronco he said there goes my Prairie Rose. The name she kept until she died. She was a good sport weather [sic] she won or lost she allways [sic] had a smile. I made many rodeos with her, and it was allways [sic] first and second money we won. May her soul rest in peace across the Range. Allways [sic] her Pal. Goldie*

THIRTY-EIGHT

Tricks and Training

"KING, COME," GOLDIE CALLED. She hated to pull the German Shepherd away from the back room where dog and boy were sprawled on a rug in front of the television. When her granddaughter Linda got polio, Goldie offered to bring her older brother Mike to live in Nederland for as long as necessary. The six-year-old would be no problem at all, Goldie told his worried and harried parents. She even went out and got one of the new televisions to entertain him. The picture didn't come in very well in Nederland, but she figured the boy wouldn't know the difference.

After she sold the Trap Door, she opened Goldie's Corral, a restaurant and a boardinghouse with four rooms up and four rooms down. The boardinghouse was full that summer, mostly with hard-luck cases Goldie was supporting. Even when Nick the barber, who cut hair in a partitioned room in the front of the restaurant, could pay his rent, it was still hard to make a go of it. At the back of the restaurant was a room closed off with accordion doors that Goldie used to accommodate overflow diners. It became Mike's room, and she installed a television to keep him occupied while she worked.

Goldie, her mother Allie, her son Russell, and her first grandson, Mike, pose for a picture in back of Goldie's Corral, her restaurant and boarding house in Nederland.

The Sterling family

During the day she let him wander town if he wanted, but he had to take King with him. The only thing she allowed him to do by himself was to fetch the mail. The post office was in the drug store on the corner across from the Corral, and Goldie told her grandson he could charge a piece of candy when he went to retrieve the mail from her box.

When Goldie had to go somewhere, like today when she took soup to her friend Esther who was sick in bed, she entrusted her cook Rosie with the boy's welfare. When she returned, she found Rosie anxiously waiting for her. No, there wasn't any trouble in the restaurant, Rosie told her.

"Then, what? Why are you smirking like that?"

"When Mike went..."

"Oh my god, is he okay?"

Rosie nodded. "He's fine. Do you want to hear the story, or not? If you do, be quiet a minute."

"All right, jus' get on with it."

"Okay." Rosie was smiling now. "What happened is this. You always let him go get the mail, so I said it would be okay. But he came back in just a few minutes, and he wasn't just crying, he was wailin'. Said he'd seen a monster."

"A monster? What in the world?"

"Yep, a monster. I finally got him calmed down and got him to tell me what the monster looked like. You'll never guess." Rosie paused dramatically. Finally, Goldie shrugged her shoulders, "Jus' tell me."

"He saw Jess Geiger. I guess he bumped into 'im, and ol' Jess growled—you know how he can do that. Anyway, little Mike looked up, and all he saw was the big ol' scar you gave Jess. Scared the little guy to death." Now an old man, Jess still had a nasty, multi-layered scar that wrapped around his neck from the time Goldie had chased him with the bull whip after her son Russell had fallen off his pony.

"A monster, huh? I cain't believe ol' Jess is still scarin' little boys."

"Whaddya expect? With those scars you gave 'im, he looks like a monster, at least to Mike." Goldie shrugged again. Jess's problems weren't her concern. "I told Mike that maybe he should take King everywhere with him for a while. That seemed to calm him down some."

"Thanks, Rosie. Where are they now?" Rosie flicked her thumb toward Mike's room, and now that Rosie's story was told and Goldie's anxiety relieved, she could hear the television. When she opened the door, Mike ran into her arms, eager to tell her his story. King stood up, stretched, and watched grandmother and grandson intently, nudging his shoulder under the boy's arm so boy and dog seemed to be one, as if to put himself between Mike and any future monsters.

Although King was devoted to little Mike, when Goldie called him into the restaurant, he obeyed instantly. If Goldie needed to summon a boarder, she sent King. Or if someone came into the bar looking for one of her boarders, she would tell the dog the room number. King opened the door to the boarding house, dutifully went to the room, and scratched at the door. If he got no answer, he returned to the bar, closing the door behind him, and barked twice. If the boarder was in, King barked only once.

Goldie had inherited Allie's aptitude for training dogs, and the two women were well known across the state for their ability. Goldie especially enjoyed working with the intelligent King. She also appreciated his loyalty—on at least one occasion he had sprung to her defense when a customer in the bar who was in a fight had made the mistake of attacking her. King had the man on the ground with his jaw clamped around the man's throat in an instant. Fortunately, she was able to call the dog off before he killed the customer. The man complained afterwards to Marshal Jimmy Griffith, who ran him out of town.

King had learned to attack if provoked in the war. Goldie had donated him to the Dogs for Defense effort when she read about the need for trained war dogs. She knew her King would be perfect. The ad in the newspaper had specified the height, length, and weight of the dog, and that it couldn't have any white in its coat. King's intelligence and aggressiveness were enough to get him in the program for sentry dogs. Goldie never knew exactly where King had served, but she suspected it was in the Pacific Basin.

The Quartermaster Corps established war dog platoons in March 1944. Dogs donated by a patriotic public for Dogs for Defense were used by the Coast Guard and by the Army in its K-9 Corps. Actually, only a small percentage of the animals donated met the final specifications and were accepted into the program. In its three years of operation, Dogs for Defense obtained approximately 18,000 dogs through donations. Only 10,000 finished the training for work as sentries, delivering messages on the front lines, and finding land mines. Goldie had even served as a volunteer civilian trainer for some of the dogs. After "basic training" for eight to twelve weeks, the dogs were accustomed to muzzles, gas masks, riding in military vehicles, and to gunfire. At that point, King went through more training to be a sentry. He was taught to accompany a guard on patrol, give warning if a stranger was in the area, and to attack if necessary.

After the war, King was sent to a reprocessing section for rehabilitation for civilian life. There, dogs were trained that every human was friendly and tested around lots of human activity and noise before being returned to their owners. King came home at the end of 1946. He still had his military identification number tattooed inside his ear.

The restaurant was full that afternoon, and Goldie gave silent thanks for King. She wouldn't have been able to take care of both her business and Mike without him. As soon as Mike and King curled into each other on the pillow in front of the television, she headed back to the kitchen, just as the door to the restaurant opened. It was Brownlee Guyer, the game warden.

"Here're your doughnuts, Goldie," he called out in his booming voice. He pulled a dirty old coal sack behind him through the restaurant and into the kitchen. Goldie was horrified. When Brownlee offered to pick up some doughnuts for her while he was in Boulder, she'd been pleased. How thoughtful, she thought. Brownlee's offer meant Goldie didn't have to spend money, which was always tight, on gas for a trip to Boulder, but she should have known he'd be up to something. He'd made a big show of pulling that sack through the restaurant, and Goldie could hear the exclamations of dismay from customers who were ready to leave their food untouched just thinking about the doughnuts that would come out of that disgusting, sooty coal sack.

"Get out of here, you sonofabitch," Goldie roared at him. She picked up the coal sack and was going to throw it at him but then thought better of it. Instead she grabbed a fry pan and waved it in his face. The tall, skinny man was laughing, as always. Goldie could still hear the buzzing of worried voices in

Brownlee and Lois Guyer visited the Buffalo Bill Museum in their later years.

Guyer family

the dining room. Rosie had followed Brownlee into the kitchen, and she looked from him to Goldie and back again, trying not to giggle.

Brownlee was incorrigible, and most people eventually laughed when they realized what he'd done to them. Even King wouldn't come to her defense against Brownlee. The German Shepherd and the lanky game warden were good friends. Goldie didn't feel like laughing this time—it was hard enough to make ends meet without having a freeloader like Brownlee play a trick like this. At least once a week, just to make her mad, he would come into her restaurant with his lunch in a brown paper bag. His tiny wife Lois always packed a good lunch for him before he left the house in the morning, and Goldie couldn't understand why he didn't eat it somewhere else. He'd walk in the door, greeting everyone he knew with a joke or a story, and then he'd fold those long legs around a chair and carefully unpack his lunch and spread it out on the table. He'd ask for a glass of water. He never bought anything, although he made a show of eating her condiments. He was a storyteller, and his thunderous voice usually drowned her out as she was regaling her customers with her tales of riding with Buffalo Bill. And, if he wasn't telling one of his own stories, he'd bring up Buffalo Bill's burial spot. Goldie's story about the trip she and the other cowgirls made to the top of Mount Lookout with Buffalo Bill just before he went broke in Denver was cited as a major reason to bury him in Colorado. Sometimes she had the feeling that Brownlee would say that Buffalo Bill should have been buried in Cody, Wyoming, just to get her goat.

"Well, now, you be careful with that pan, Goldie. Some of your customers out there might be wantin' one of these here doughnuts, and you wouldn't want me to step on 'em tryin' to get out of your way, now, would you?"

"I could kill you for this. Get out!" Losing customers was no laughing matter for Goldie. She worked hard to keep folks coming back to her restaurant, and she couldn't have them thinking that their doughnuts were delivered in a dirty old coal sack.

Brownlee backed carefully out of Goldie's kitchen, and he didn't come back to the restaurant for a couple of weeks. This was worse than the trick he'd played on her during the war. She heard through the grapevine that he knew he'd gone too far this time, and he freely admitted to anyone who wanted to listen to the story of the doughnuts that she had every reason to be angry.

People always seemed to enjoy playing jokes on her. At first it was the other cowgirls the night before her wedding. They hid the wedding outfit that she had labored on so long. Her friends, the wives of Two Lance and Good Lance, Sioux Indians with the Buffalo Bill show, had beaded the steer's heads that decorated the red leather show dress for her wedding, and they had presented her with a beaded belt, like the ones they made to sell to the audiences who wandered around their tipi village before the show. When Goldie couldn't find the dress or the belt, she had exploded. Maybe it was that quick-fuse temper of hers that made her an attractive target for practical jokes.

Was it a practical joke when Buffalo Bill picked out her wedding song? "It's my favorite song," the aging showman had told her, and she hadn't resisted, although she was horrified. Now that she was older, she could laugh at the gloomy choice: Camping on the Old Campground. She sang a few lines to herself as she carefully lifted the bag of doughnuts, which Brownlee had thoughtfully stapled shut, out of the filthy coal sack.

> *Many are the hearts that are weary tonight,*
> *Wishing for the war to cease;*
> *Many are the hearts looking for the light,*
> *To see the dawn of peace.*
> *Dying tonight, dying tonight,*
> *Dying on the old camp-ground.*

The song was a favorite during the Civil War, but it was hardly a good choice for a wedding. In spite of the allusion to dying, every time Goldie heard the song she felt her horse under her as she galloped into the arena on her wedding day. Thankfully, the memories of how painful it was to ride a galloping horse just a couple of days after she'd been tossed into the grandstands had dimmed. Mostly, she recalled the crowds cheering in the grandstands and her friends whooping and shooting blanks in the air as they rode crazily around her. God, she missed Buffalo Bill and her friends from those days.

ᴡᴡᴡ THIRTY-NINE ᴡᴡᴡ

Willie's Clothes

"WILL YOU LOOK AT THIS?"

"What?" Goldie's friend Marguerite was wandering past the grave markers ahead of her.

"This. Look," Goldie demanded. The tall woman with close-cropped hair limped back to where Goldie was pointing at a sunken site with a dilapidated wooden marker.

"It says this is Tom Horn," Goldie said in astonishment.

"That's right. I believe he was involved in those killings for the ranchmen in Wyoming."

"Oh my gosh. What's he doin' here?"

"I think his brother may have brought his body here after they hanged him."

What a shame, Goldie thought, looking at the marker whose letters were about to be lost to the wind and sun. Charlie Irwin used to talk for hours on end about Tom Horn, one of the West's most famous hired guns, who also had been a lawman, a scout, a soldier, a detective, an outlaw, and finally an assassin. Goldie and her first husband, Harry, were working for Irwin at Frontier Days in Cheyenne in 1915, and whenever

Charlie got a chance, he'd tell them stories about Horn. How he was a scout for the Army, then an operative for Pinkerton's and a deputy sheriff. As a cattle detective, Horn was sent to where cattle barons were having trouble with rustlers. Supposedly, he was paid five dollars for each man he killed. Where Horn went, the trouble disappeared. But then he started drinking and bragging about the men he'd killed, and they finally hanged him in Cheyenne.

Charlie Irwin claimed that they always knew when a man was killed by Horn because he left a rock under the corpse's head, positioned in a certain way. It was like his signature.

The last person Horn supposedly killed was a boy, fourteen-year-old Willie Nickell, at the gate to his family's ranch in the Iron Mountain country of southeast Wyoming. Horn happened to be in the area where the boy, the son of a sheepherding rancher, was murdered. Horn was arrested for the murder although he insisted that if he had committed the murder, he would have said so if asked, but he did not. Two years later, in 1903, Horn was convicted and hanged at the Laramie County jail. Irwin said Horn sprang the trap door himself. Every time Charlie told the story, Goldie shivered when he got to that part. That's what could have happened to Harry in Texas.

Goldie had seen what remained of young Willie's clothes. When she and Harry were working for Irwin's Wild West in Cheyenne, Harry's brother, Buddy, who also was working for Irwin, got into a fight and landed in jail. The next day Harry said to her, "You better go down there and see if he needs anything."

After visiting with Buddy, Goldie stopped to talk to the sheriff who was helping to move everything out so the new courthouse could be built. He was carrying a bundle of clothes tied with a string.

"See this, Goldie? This here's the last remains of the last man Tom Horn killed."

"You mean that boy?"

"Yep."

Having heard all the stories about Tom Horn from Charlie Irwin, Goldie was fascinated by the forlorn bundle.

"You know, Goldie, you're so full of stories, I never know if you're full of shit," Marguerite taunted. The two friends argued as often as they got along. Every few years they both ran for seats on the Nederland town council, and usually they didn't speak during their campaigns unless the issues were hot ones, in which case they yelled profanities at each other. A month after the election, they were friends again. Marguerite won a seat several times, but Goldie never was elected to the town board. Goldie had found lots to complain about who was elected to office last year, 1952, and she was thinking she might run again, but it was still too early to think much about next year's election.

Marguerite and Goldie were friends for now, and they had come to Boulder to enjoy the warmer weather of the lower altitude spring, and to celebrate Marguerite's health. Marguerite had been sick and unable to get out of bed for several weeks—she couldn't even feed her dog. When Goldie heard how bad off her friend was, she picked up Marguerite's dog and kept him at the restaurant. Now that Marguerite felt better, they had brought their dogs with them to Boulder to walk in the warm sun. The dogs ran in circles around the women as they wandered through the historic headstones, occasionally reading the inscriptions out loud. Marguerite's limp had become more pronounced through the years, and now she walked with a cane. She was in a car accident while serving with the WAACs in Oregon during World War II. She was discharged and put on a disability pension, and she came back to Nederland in 1945, the same year her father died. She and her mother worked at Gates Rubber Factory doing tire trimming for a couple of years, and, when they returned to Nederland, Marguerite became the postmaster and the police magistrate, a job Goldie had always admired and wished she'd had. Marguerite worked both jobs out of the front room of her house until she retired the year

Goldie's long-time friend Marguerite Shellhaas posed for a photographer in the front room of her house in Nederland from which she dispensed hunting and fishing violations as Nederland's Police Magistrate. She also served as Nederland's postmaster and Justice of the Peace.

Nederland Area Historical Society, Nederland, Colorado

before. Goldie was surprised that her friend, the police magistrate, didn't know the story about Tom Horn.

"Marguerite, you mark my words. It's true. I saw those clothes, and I know what Charlie Irwin told us. He may have been a sonofabitch to work for, but Charlie knew a lot about Tom Horn."

"Wasn't Irwin the one who took half your earnings?"

"Yep, he's the one. He'd pay us outright to work on his show in Cheyenne, but when we went on the road, which we had to do to 'cause he didn't pay us enough to live on, he'd take half our winnings. Harry's the only one who ever beat Charlie's son at Irwin's own show. It almost killed ol' Charlie when that son was killed in a roping accident." Goldie felt a tear at the corner of her eye and wiped it away. Talking about Charlie's son dying in the arena made her think about Alf. Riding was a dangerous profession—even for sonofabitchs like Harry and Charlie Irwin. Marguerite was waiting for the rest of her story. "He always was a big man, that Charlie Irwin. It took six pallbearers to carry him when he died. Oh lord, I'd guess he was four hundred pounds. Good ol' Charlie Irwin. They don't make 'em like that any more. Or like Tom Horn."

Goldie walked around the pathetic-looking grave.

"This is such a shame. Somebody should take care of this."

"You're right, Goldie, somebody should."

"I'm not sayin' you or me."

"Sure, I know."

"Well, I'm not."

The old friends squared off over the grave. Marguerite's eyes carried the weight of the world. Her short hair barely showed under her practical hat, and she wore slacks and a man's shirt over her lean frame. Goldie was shorter, fuller, and she would never even consider wearing pants, although her shoes were as practical as Marguerite's boots for walking in the mountains, and her hat was big enough to protect her face from the sun.

"You know you can't tell me what to do and get away with it." Marguerite's fierce look didn't need answering, but Goldie couldn't help herself.

"I'm just tellin' you what oughta be done."

"All right. You done that."

They both wanted the last word, but Goldie didn't want to get in a yelling match in the old graveyard. She bit her lip so she wouldn't say anything else, and they walked side by side through the headstones towards Marguerite's car, which was parked on Ninth Street. Marguerite's attention was sidetracked by a marker she wanted to read more closely, and she swerved towards it. Goldie stubbornly remained where she was, waiting impatiently for her friend to return. When she thought Marguerite was taking too long, she went after her.

ADVISES "ANNIE" — Goldie Cameron of Nederland, former trick rider with Buffalo Bill Wild West Show, is shown giving Joan Van Ark some pointers for her role of Annie Oakle in "Annie Get Your Gun," playing in Folsom Stadium July 12 and 13.

In July of 1961, Goldie worked with actress Joan Van Ark as she prepared for her role in "Annie Get Your Gun." This was one of the last clippings Goldie pasted in her scrapbook.

The Sterling family

"Look at this, would ya? I remember him—I busted him once for not having a fishing license." Marguerite waved her cane at the headstone.

"I think you busted just about everybody, including me." Both women had to laugh at Goldie's droll observation, and the tension was broken.

"I just hate to see these graves like this."

"Are you thinking you want to take on another cemetery?" Goldie spent many hours working in Nederland's cemetery, and, no, she told Marguerite, she didn't want to take on anything else. Running a restaurant, taking care of her current boarders and her mother, and worrying about Russell were enough to keep her busy.

As if she'd read Goldie's mind, Marguerite asked, "What have you heard from Russell?"

"Nothin'. And that's what's bad. When I don't hear it's 'cause he's doin' somethin' dangerous, you know." Russell had served in the Merchant Marines in World War II, and now he was involved in the Korean War.

"My sweet grandkids are good, though. My daughter-in-law is such a peach. I think it's hard on her when Russell isn't around." Goldie was proud of her grandchildren, Mike, Linda and Rick, and never missed a chance to tell her friends about them. Although Mike, the oldest, from her son's first marriage, had shown some interest in horses when he'd come to live with her when his sister got polio, Goldie had finally come to accept the fact that neither her son nor his children loved horses the way she did.

"Linda will be here in a few weeks. She's gonna stay with me agin' this summer."

"Is she going to help in the restaurant?"

"She sure is. And she's a hard worker, you know." At least the grandkids seemed interested in her stories about her life with the Wild Wests, although Rick was still too small to really comprehend what she was telling him. Linda would be a willing audience this summer. Goldie smiled. She had lots more stories to tell.

After Goldie and Marguerite left the cemetery, they went for a cup of coffee and a piece of pie. They needed to talk about the new restaurant Marguerite and her mother and their friend Frank were building for Goldie. She was going to move out of the Trap Door in the fall and into the new restaurant building that would be next to Marguerite's house, and they needed to make plans.

Rosie, right, and one of Goldie's young waitresses outside the Trap Door Grill.

The Sterling family

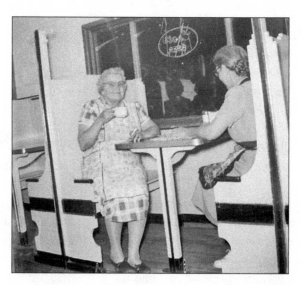

Goldie in one of her restaurants.

The Sterling family

FORTY

One Last Parade

HER FEARS THAT THEY WOULD MOVE her two houses to make way for the new highway came true. Where she used to live was now a two-lane state highway, a much faster, and probably safer, way to get to Boulder without all the bridges and with a new tunnel that cut off one of the worst blind curves. Instead of driving into Nederland and turning to follow the western shore of the lake, the new highway was straighter, and it bypassed the main street businesses. After they picked up her houses and planted them a block away on Third Street, she decided to rent out the bigger one which had landed on the corner facing the new highway. It was now a drive-in restaurant. She didn't have all those people living with her any more, so she'd moved everything into the little green house and added an indoor bathroom. It was just the right size for one person.

The year before—1965—the town council members who knocked on her door wanted her to ride in the parade for the new celebration they were planning, and they wanted her to ask the Colorado State Historical Society if she could borrow her

Goldie's house in Nederland before it was moved to its new location.

The Sterling family

House-moving day to make way for the new road to Boulder. This is probably Goldie's second house, which later became a drive-in restaurant.

The Sterling family

outfit back from them. She'd just donated it a few years before. She tried to explain, "I jus' don't think it's right. You don't give somethin' to someone and then go ask for it back." Goldie couldn't believe these men on the town council didn't understand this principle.

"All right, if that's how you feel. We'll ask for you."

"No, you won't ask for me. If you do any askin', you'll ask for yourselves. Not for me."

They had asked, and the Historical Society had allowed it, but she never felt right about it, although she certainly did enjoy herself riding in that parade.

This year, the committee hoped to exceed last year's attendance because of the filming at the Caribou Ranch, where she and Doc had ranched when they first arrived in Nederland. Hollywood was coming to Nederland to re-make Stagecoach, one of the country's most beloved Westerns, and the committee hoped the stars, including Slim Pickens, Bing Crosby, Ann-Margret, Van Heflen, and Robert Cummings, would come to their Jamboree and thrill this year's crowds.

The Jamboree was just the latest in a long string of Nederland celebrations. When they first moved to Nederland, Goldie and Doc laughed at the stories about the town's 1925 rodeo that was produced by Diamond Jack, the Denver gangster who absconded with all the proceeds. After that, the town held a rodeo almost every year, keeping the proceeds in town, and eventually they built a rodeo arena in the mid-1930s. Now, they combined mining contests with a little bit of rodeoing—just barrel racing—for the Jamboree. Goldie missed seeing a real rodeo—but what could you do?

This new celebration had started because the Lion's Club bought the old Hodgson grocery store building and wanted to turn it into a community center. To help with funding, the club came up with the idea for a Jamboree. Goldie helped with the horse rides, and she gave the kids who were going to give the shooting exhibitions on the 'old West' streets a few tips about how to make their scenes dramatic and believable. Fish were donated for the kids' fishing pond, booths were erected, a chuck wagon dinner was held, hand rock drilling exhibitions and horse show exhibitions were given, and then, of course, there were the dances. Nederland always was a dancing town. The old dancing pavilion that extended over the lake was gone now, and instead a band played for an hour and half for a street dance, and then after that, at 11 p.m., Elmer Claycomb took over and called for square dancing. Just like the old days, when folks came to a dance with a covered dish for a potluck and danced their hearts out until late at night, when most of the children were asleep on the benches surrounding the dance floor. At midnight, the fiddler, the piano player, and the caller took a break and everyone ate, fortifying themselves for another hour or two of dancing.

And there was the Jamboree's parade down the highway. Last year's crowd was about five thousand people, and the men on this year's committee told Goldie they expected even more this time. Could she ride again?

"Of course." At least they weren't asking her to wear her old outfit again. Even though she'd been in many thousands of parades—at least one every few days when she was traveling with a Wild West or promoting a rodeo—she still loved them.

Unfortunately, the volatile high-country weather decided not to cooperate with the folks planning the Jamboree. A few weeks later, most of the events were cancelled because of the constant rain. Filming at Caribou Ranch had become difficult at best, and finally, when it seemed there would be no end to the daily downpours, the filmmakers retreated to California where the weather was more reliable. Goldie couldn't help noticing the irony. She had left California and the movie business to go on the road, and she ended up here, in Nederland, where the movie-making business had managed to catch up with her, but, once again, it was just a brief encounter. After the film crews and the

A square dance on Nederland's Main Street in the 1950s. The Super-Market is in the building that was the Piggly Wiggly.

The Sterling family

stars made their exit, life settled back into its normal small-town rhythm. And the sun returned.

The year before, the weather was exemplary for the parade during that first Jamboree celebration in Nederland. Goldie's friend Mabel came up from Denver to ride with her in the parade. The two women had become friends when Mabel rode into Overland Park to see what she could do to help the performers stranded in Denver when the sheriff seized Buffalo Bill's show in 1913, the year Goldie married Harry. Goldie figured they'd been friends, off and on, for about fifty years.

Goldie started talking as soon as she heard Mabel's knock on the screen door. "Oh Mabel, did I tell you that my darling little peck-in-e-see died?" she called out as her friend let herself in. Mabel wore a leather riding skirt and a silk blouse that had gone out of style in 1930. Goldie had squeezed into the red, now a faded maroon color, leather wedding outfit that the town council had borrowed back from the museum. She wasn't as tall as when she was the robust young woman who rode bucking broncos, and the skirt hung almost to the ground. She'd pinned her thinning, gray hair back so it would stay out of her face under the big-brimmed hat that was sitting on the kitchen table. Mabel also wore a big hat, and she tossed it on the table next to Goldie's.

"No, you didn't. I'm sorry to hear."

"She was such a lovely little thing. You know she would fetch anything I threw into the other room. That's how she got her exercise after we ate dinner." Goldie had given up on cooking, after all those years in the restaurant business, and now she enjoyed sitting down to a TV dinner every night. She bought one for herself and one for the dog. Goldie continued without even taking a breath, "She was fifteen when she died, that's over a hundred years in dog time."

"Is that right?"

"Yes, I had two vets come up and look at her, but there was nothin' they could do. I'll miss her." She would have to get another dog now.

"I bet—"

"I wasn't sure you were going to come up to ride in the parade this year."

"I wouldn't miss—"

"The doctor said I could ride again, finally. I'm sure I could have ridden last year too, but he said my heart couldn't take it. You still ride every day?"

"I do. You know—"

A knock on the door interrupted them.

A couple of kids had brought horses for the women to ride in the parade. Goldie had kept a couple of ponies at her house in town until her grandchildren had outgrown coming to stay with her. She'd given up the last two, Ginger and Spitfire, who had been named by her grandkids, a few years ago. Goldie invited the boys inside for Cokes. They accepted and walked wide-eyed around the tiny living room, admiring Goldie's old saddle that had taken the place of honor in the room after she donated the fancy one with the long tapaderos to the state historical society. It sat on the stand that used to be in her restaurant. Goldie had painted the wall behind it red. She'd had a red wall in her house even in the '30s, when few people dared to paint such vibrant colors inside their houses. When Goldie saw the boys' interest in the old saddle, she opened her scrapbook and told them the story of her wedding.

"What's this?" asked the smaller, younger one, jabbing his finger at a receipt. Goldie had written on it in pencil: "My best invested dollar. –G.W." Mabel bent over to get a better look. The receipt from the District Court, Criminal Division, dated May 3, 1916, was for payment of sheriff's costs, listed as "Bond," in the amount of one dollar. G.W. was Goldie Walters, of course. When Mabel looked up, she winked at Goldie.

"That's just a little somethin' that we're not gonna talk about today because we got ourselves a parade to get to," Mabel told the boys, indicating the door. The boys looked at each other and excused themselves, saying they would wait outside for the two aging cowgirls.

"I never was sorry about trying to kill that sonofabitch, you know. That really was the best dollar I ever spent."

"I know."

"Good ol' Harry," Goldie remarked dryly, slapping the scrapbook shut.

"Are you ever gonna tell Russell where's he's at?"

"Never. I spent all those years keepin' Russell from 'im. I'm not tellin' now."

"How's Russell doin'?"

"He's good now that he's back from Vietnam. I was so worried the whole time he was gone. You know, he sent me a letter, and he put 'North Korea' on the top. He'd never put where he

When Goldie put the court receipt from her arrest for attempting to kill her husband Harry in her scrapbook, she wrote on it: *My Best Invested Dollar. G.W.*

The Sterling family

was sending a letter from on it like that before, so it made me worry. Now that he's back, I find out he really was in Vietnam. He's gonna come visit soon, and he'll take care of that television set he bought for me. You know it's never worked right, even with the antenna I put up on the roof." Goldie had wired a number of metal spindles together for her antenna. They had been left over from her restaurant days and used to hold the piles of receipts and orders. Unfortunately, the antenna didn't seem to help much with her reception. Now that Russell had a good job with Standard Oil, Goldie was happy that she no longer had to worry about him, and he was able to come to Nederland once in a while and help her with the chores and maintenance that she was getting too old to do. He had survived service in three wars: World War II, the Korean War, and Vietnam.

"Does he call you often?"

"Not as much as I'd like. He never did. I guess he got that from his father."

"He out in California?"

"Yep. And so's Harry. They live pretty close by each other, but they don't know it."

"If you miss 'im so much, why'n't ya go on out to see 'im?"

"I couldn't ever drive that far. And I'm done with trains. They jus' don't keep up the schedules like they used to."

"You could fly."

"No, I absolutely re-fuse to get on an airplane," Goldie shook her head vehemently. She'd just have to be patient and wait for Russell and her grandchildren to visit her. "No, I'll take mine on the ground if I'm going to get smeared all over."

The boys were waiting for them when the women stepped outside, and, despite their age, the old cowgirls swung into their saddles with enough of their former ease to make it look effortless. Their job done, the boys lost interest in them and turned their horses toward the dam where the parade started, and the women's horses followed.

Goldie had finally retired, after twenty-seven years in business on Nederland's main street. The building that Marguerite, her mother, and Frank had built for her was awfully small, especially on summer days like this when so many of her customers who had come to hear her stories for the last fifteen or twenty years arrived in town. She had been trying to make the best of it, but finally she'd decided to retire. The doctor told her it would be best for her heart if she laid off, and she'd decided to take his advice.

Although they were on a side street and away from the main parade route, heads turned when people saw the women in their Wild West outfits. Goldie was seventy-six and Mabel was eighty.

"I lost fifty-five pounds," Goldie bragged to Mabel. "The doctor said I should, so I did. I lost it in ninety days. I weigh one-hundred-and-twenty-four-and-a-half pounds now."

Mabel nodded appreciatively. "When you put your mind to somethin', Goldie, you're jus' like a dog gnawin' at a bone—you don't let go."

"I think we're all like that, you know, Mabel. 'Cept now we're all old dogs. Used to be our bone was to stick up for ourselves, don't you think? We sure had to stick up for ourselves or there wouldn'da been no cowgirls, would there?"

They made a striking pair, sitting tall and erect in their saddles, chatting amiably, although it seemed to onlookers that Goldie was doing most of the chatting. Beads and fringe on her old outfit swung to the rhythm of the horses' leisurely walk, and sunlight glinted off the conchos on the ponies' breast straps.

"You know, Goldie, if you'da killed Harry, you might not be here now—"

"Oh, don't I know it. Do you know, they set my bail at $2,000. Can you believe it? Where was I gonna get that kind of money, I ask you? But, still, I'm not sorry I tried. And, of course, you know, Mabel, I never would'a found out what he was up to if it wasn't for my mother. She was awfully nosy—"

"Mine too," Mabel agreed. They had led such similar lives they didn't have to say anything else. They both rode with Buffalo Bill, specializing in the bucking broncos, but also doing trick riding and riding 'high school' horses. They both settled in Denver after the Wild West shows. They met that day Mabel had ridden into Overland Park and ended up showing Goldie how to run the sprinkler wagon after she got the job bringing water to the show's stock. Mabel married a Denver policeman about fifteen years her senior who she'd met when she was exercising horses for the department, a job she still did occasionally, not for the police department, but for people who couldn't find the time to ride their horses as much as they should. Goldie's first husband, Harry, was ten years her senior, about the same age as her second husband, Doc, or Tim as he came to known in Nederland. Goldie divorced both of her husbands, and Mabel was widowed. Mabel had lived with and taken care of her mother, who was a nurse, until she died. When Mabel gave up horse trading, she became the receiving clerk at Denver General Hospital. Goldie's mother died in 1963, after living with Goldie for many years in Denver and Nederland. Goldie and Mabel had lived with dominating mothers long after most other young people their age had entered middle age. And, of course, they had both loved the same cowboy, Doc Cameron. That had dissolved their friendship for a few years, but they became friends again after Doc's death in 1952.

"Everything has changed so much, have you noticed, Mabel? Everyone around here is building, building, building. They yank out the trees by the roots and put in filling stations, they move buildings when they don't like where they are, and they even put buildings on the mill pond."

"It's not right."

"No, it's not. And then some of the stores don't want any of these young people that have the long hair to come inside. We don't mind them, do we, Mabel?"

"No, how could we?" Mabel chuckled, and then they both laughed, remembering their days with Buffalo Bill, and how vain he was about his long hair.

The leather in Goldie's outfit had faded to a dull weatherbeaten maroon, but it was still soft after all those years of sweat and sun in the arenas. Occasionally, a bead popped off the fringe with a ping. Although the museum called it her wedding dress, she hadn't worn it for the famous photo she had shown the two boys at the house.

That morning she had laid the old outfit out on the bed. She sat next to it and let the colorful, misshaped old beads fall through her fingers. Her stomach was queasy—it felt just like it had back at Madison Square Garden in 1913. She had lots of guests in the arena, and eight-thousand spectators filled the stands. The schooner act had just ended behind them as the reverend asked her if she would take Harry for her husband in sickness and in health. Well, life had a way of changing all that, didn't it? She'd not seen Harry since that parade for the Fort Collins show after their divorce, when her friends, fearful of more gunplay, had to call on some of the cowboys to separate them. She would never forgive him for what he'd done to her, or for trying to steal her son.

Goldie posed in her wedding outfit, with her black hat, beaded gauntlets, and her saddle, next to her house on Second Street in Nederland before riding in the parade, below.

Buffalo Bill Museum and Grave, Lookout Mountain, Golden, Colorado

She'd learned long ago that it was safer to just love her men and leave them, or let them leave her. She didn't fight for them. No, she didn't fight for them, she mused. She'd never been able to count on the men in her life, but, no matter what, her girl-friends were always her friends, even though it had been other women who had broken up both of her marriages. She and Lorena had finally become friends that day Goldie had visited her in the jail cell, and she'd made up with Mabel after all that had happened between them over Doc.

Mabel waved at a little girl who was looking up at them in awe. Pete Smythe, Denver's first disc jockey and the emcee of today's parade which would be broadcast on his show, had mentioned Mabel on his radio show yesterday, and Goldie knew he would talk about her, too, when they stopped in front of the judging stand. This parade would be a proud moment for her, a time when folks learned more about her. Early in her career as a professional cowgirl, riding in parades helped attract people to the shows. Now, it just felt good to dress in a fancy outfit and ride for a crowd.

As if she could read her thoughts, Mabel asked, "How's it feel, not to be in business any more?"

"I'm not yet used to not working. I always worked, no matter what, since I was just a little bitty thing travelin' with my parents." She missed it all, even the nights when she couldn't sleep because she couldn't find a comfortable position for her aching body, even the days when she had blood in her pee from riding a particularly ornery bronc, even the heartaches she endured from her cowboy husbands and boyfriends. But what she treasured most she still had: good friends and an adoring audience.

They didn't have to wait long before their names were called, and they urged their ponies along the parade route toward the judges. When they stopped at the judging stand, Pete Smythe did tell some colorful stories about both of them, and, as always, they turned and waved at the cheering throngs that waited alongside the dirt road to see the former Wild West stars.

Goldie blew a kiss at a handsome young man who was watching the parade with his girlfriend. He blew a kiss back at her.

"Goldie, you're bad. Such a flirt."

"If you can't be a flirt at our age, Mabel, what can you do? Anyway, you know I'm no angel, don't give me no wings."

"And after all the good things Pete Smythe just said about you!" The women laughed again and turned their ponies to the other side of the street, treating the crowd to their big smiles under their big hats.

"You know, Goldie, I think we're gonna ride until the day we die."

"I think yo're right, Mabel." Goldie turned toward her friend and tipped her hat. The crowd thought she'd tipped her hat to them, and everyone started clapping. Goldie raised her gauntleted and gloved hand high in the air, the beads on the fringe swaying and clinking. She smiled and waved at her fans.

###

⤙ EPILOGUE ⤚

NEDERLAND CURRENTLY has about 1,500 residents, far fewer than the 5,000 people who lived here during its tungsten boom years. During World War I, Nederland provided twenty-five percent of the world's tungsten, and the Conger Mine was known as the greatest tungsten mine in the world. Not only was Nederland a thriving, bustling community, so was Lakewood—now no more than a few foundations—and Tungsten—now a couple of houses below the dam—and Caribou—now just a ghost town. The residences that are still standing in New Cardinal, which was still an active mining community when Goldie lived on the nearby ranch, are being restored privately, and the old mill has been purchased by Boulder County Open Space. If you ever visit Nederland, Colorado, we pronounce it 'Nedderland.' (There is a Nederland, Texas, which is pronounced 'Neederland.')

In 1936, Lynn W. Van Vleet purchased the Tucker Ranch and established the first Arabian horse breeding operation in Colorado. The Van Vleet Flying VV Ranch hosted the filming of two movies: *Arabians of the Rockies* and *Sons of Courage*. In

1971 the ranch was bought by music producer Jim Guercio and renamed Caribou Ranch. He opened a world-famous recording studio, hosting artists such as Elton John, Rod Stewart, Chicago, the Beach Boys, Carole King, Waylon Jennings, Billy Joel, U2, and Frank Zappa. The recording studio burned down in 1985. In 1996, Boulder County and the city of Boulder purchased most of the ranch as Caribou Ranch Open Space. Today, it is still home to hawks and an elk herd and hay meadows that once were ranched by Alfred Moore. The old DeLonde ranch house and barn have been restored and may someday be open for visitors.

In the 1930s, Charley Mulhall worked as arena director for a number of small rodeos, and he employed his sister Lucille to star in a few special acts. Towards the end of the decade he sponsored some rodeos, but none of them were ever the extravagant affairs of his and Lucille's heyday. On December 21, 1940, Lucille was killed in an automobile accident. The driver also was killed when the car was hit by a truck on a curve in the highway about a mile north of the Mulhall ranch in Oklahoma. Charley and his wife Esther were in the car and hospitalized, but not seriously injured. Lucille, who had never learned to drive a car, was fifty-five. It is widely accepted that the word 'cowgirl' was coined by President Theodore Roosevelt to describe Lucille Mulhall.

In 1941, Charley started working as a security guard at the Cimarron Flying School near Oklahoma City after losing the ranch to unpaid taxes. He and his wife moved near the airfield. Charley's sister, Mildred Mulhall, managed to buy the ranch at a sheriff's sale. She sold the ranch in 1946. Charley died in 1958.

Charley, Mildred and Lucille's father Zack died peacefully at the ranch in 1931.

Gordon W. "Pawnee Bill" Lillie returned to live at his buffalo ranch in Pawnee, Oklahoma. An ardent conservationist and activist in the buffalo-preservation movement, Lillie and his wife May, the former Champion Girl Horseback Shot of the

Sunday, November 29, 1970   Boulder, Colorado   Daily Camera's FOCUS

Goldie Cameron

Goldie was interviewed by the Boulder Daily Camera in 1970.

The Sterling family

West, featured yearly rodeos on their ranch. They celebrated their fiftieth wedding anniversary in 1936, and that same year, while driving home to the ranch, Pawnee Bill lost control of the vehicle, and May died as a result of her injuries. Lillie never fully recovered. He died in his sleep in 1942.

After her acquittal, Lorena Trickey met Magnus "Pete" Peterson, a rugged, humorous Norwegian, and they opened a racing stable. Lorena became a jockey, and Pete took part in small rodeos and horse shows. After a train wreck killed several of their racing horses and maimed many of the others, they turned to prospecting around Tonopah, Nevada, in 1929. A few years later she and Pete enrolled at the Tonopah School of Mining and Engineering. Lorena studied mineralogy, and Pete studied geology. Lorena was good at finding minerals, including gold and titanium, in unlikely spots. She also took to taming wild horses, breaking her favorite, Rusty, to ride when he was three years old and she was sixty-seven. She died in 1961 and is buried in Tonopah.

Diamond Jack didn't get to produce a lot of rodeos. He shot two men at the Denver Hotel and was convicted of assault with attempt to commit mayhem. He was ordered to leave Colorado by the court and was killed gangland-style in Chicago in 1935.

Allie, Goldie's mother, lived with her daughter in Nederland until she had to go to a nursing home. She died at the age of ninety on November 29, 1963, in Pueblo. She shares a headstone with her daughter in Green Mountain Cemetery in Boulder.

Goldie's son, Russell, died October 22, 1999, at his home in Weed, California. He served in the Merchant Marines in World War II, the Korean War, and in Vietnam. He worked for Standard Oil for 20 years and retired in 1982. He was survived by his two sons, a daughter, and five grandchildren.

Hiram (Harry) Sterling (Walters, Smith) finally settled in California where he married again. He died of heart disease on September 22, 1961, in Bonita, California. His younger brother, Walter (Buddy), died in 1972.

Doc Cameron's real name was Tyra Evira Campbell. Also known as T.E. and as Tim, Doc moved to Denver and owned an apartment house. He died at the age of 59 on March 21, 1952. He never re-married.

The only records I could find of Goldie's friends Esther and Sadie were listings in the county directories, the deeds for their houses in Nederland, and Goldie's and Brownlee Guyer's stories about them. Brownlee said he convinced Goldie's two friends to help him jack up the pinball machine in her restaurant one night so you could constantly win and keep playing. The three of them played and played until Goldie exploded with anger about the noise and commotion. One day when Goldie went to visit her friend Sadie, she found her dead beside the coal shed.

Mabel McDonald continued to ride horses as long as possible. After she died in 1972 at the age of eighty-seven, she was cremated and buried in the 'pauper's block' at Fairmount Cemetery in Denver.

Soon after cowgirl Bonnie McCarroll, who was riding her horse hobbled and got tangled in the stirrups, was thrown and fatally trampled at the Pendleton Roundup in a bronc riding accident in 1929, rodeo promoters stopped hosting many of the contests that had previously been open to women. The Pendleton Roundup dropped cowgirl bronc riding from their programs. The fledgling Rodeo Association of America (RAA) officially opposed women's contests, and gradually women's bronc riding became obsolete. As the years passed, only cowgirl relay racing was kept on rodeo programs. Now, women compete only in barrel racing. Since the formation of the Women's Professional Rodeo Association (WPRA) in 1967, barrel racers have a chance to win big money.

The cowgirls of Goldie's generation "demonstrated that outstanding female athletes could earn favorable headlines and several hundred thousand dollars through sport without having to be exceptionally beautiful or deemed 'sex symbols' by the press…they helped to change the public image of women…" writes Mary Lou LeCompte in *Cowgirls of the Rodeo*. The era of the Wild Wests "offered great opportunities for cowgirls, who could and did compete directly against men in steer roping, trick roping, trick riding, and Roman racing. Rodeo was the first, and perhaps the only, sport in which men and women truly competed as equals. …Those cowgirls who competed before the war had few peers in sport. In the 1870s and 1880s, women and men had competed in professional pedestrian races, but the contests died out before the cowgirls rode into the picture. The only other female professional athletes during the late nineteenth and early twentieth centuries were a few sharpshooters and professional weight lifters. Like the cowgirls they longed for genuine compeition in which to prove their prowess, but found limited opportunities other than specially arranged challenge matches. Also like the cowgirls, they found it necessary to

Goldie and a friend pose near her house in Nederland.

The Sterling family

Despite Goldie's reluctance to let Harry back into her life, he was in Nederland during the Great Depression. Russell Cameron and Harry Walters are two of the men on the scaffolding during the construction of Nederland's stone garage which is now the Mining Museum and home to the bar from Goldie's restaurant.

Carnegie Branch Library for Local History, Boulder, Colorado

perform in circuses or vaudeville in order to earn a living from their sports."

In the 1920s, the Hollywood studios melted many of their old films for the silver content, including the Westerns that Goldie made.

The bar from Goldie's restaurant is now in the Nederland Mining Museum. A woman visiting the museum one summer told me that she would never forget Goldie. Her mother suffered from mental illness and often would lock her daughter out of the house. Goldie always took her in, sometimes for weeks at a time.

Goldie Griffith Sterling Cameron (Walters, Smith, Campbell) lived in her house in Nederland as long as she could. The Nederland community organized to bring her the chicken TV dinners she loved—one for her and one for her dog—but, finally, she had to leave Nederland. She died at the Mesa Vista Sanatorium at the age of eighty-three in 1976. Her last formal honor was to be named the Queen of the Golden Years by the Colorado Nursing Care Association. She was presented with a crown by the governor's wife. She was still telling stories when a newspaper photographer snapped her picture after the presentation.

ACKNOWLEDGEMENTS

MY FIRST EPIPHANY was when I discovered how many different names Goldie and her husbands used. Suddenly, the scope of my research expanded exponentially. The second revelation came when I visited with her grandson Mike and he gave me copies of some of her scrapbook pages, including the stories about her attempt to kill Harry. There was a lot more to Goldie Cameron than I had thought. She was more than one of the first professional female athletes. She was more than her fearlessness, her abilities as a horsewoman, her tales of life with some of our country's legends. She was a complex person who had her ups and downs with life, but somehow, she always came out on top. She had to start over several times, but she never let that stop her, she just rolled up her sleeves and got to work.

Many, many thanks go to all the people who helped with this book.

My sincere gratitude goes to my husband, who read my numerous drafts and listened to my chatter about Goldie and her life, and to my friends, readers and dauntless supporters, fellow Walkie Talkies book club members Lee Tillotson, Kate Readio, Cynda Arsenault, Paula Palmer, Ellen Moore, Bonnie

Carol, and Anne Guilfoile. And readers Hughes Moir, Susan Gerhart, and Dawn Dennison helped immensely with their insights.

The Buffalo Bill Museum, located near Buffalo Bill's grave, received many of Goldie's photographs and news clippings. The stories of Buffalo Bill and the many performers in his show, like Goldie Griffith, are illustrated in exhibits at the Museum. Steve Friesen, Betsy Martinson and the staff at the museum on Lookout Mountain spent many hours working with me and helping me find photographs, and I will be forever indebted to them.

Glenna Carline and Dale Porter of the Nederland Historical Society graciously allowed me access to their archives. Librarians at the Western History Department of the Denver Public Library, the Colorado State Historical Society Library, the Oklahoma University library, Carnegie Library and Boulder Public Library in Boulder, Suzi Taylor and the staff at the Wyoming State Archives, and, of course, Gretchen Beatty and her staff at my hometown library, the Nederland Community Library, all were tremendous help. Thanks also go to Pat Maynard, Alice Hansen, Skeeter Numelin, Roberta Childers, Sheila Ranegar, Jack Snyder, and Shirley Green for granting me interviews and answering endless questions. My sister, Kristin Miller, who helped me with research in Los Angeles, was a godsend for someone with limited means for traveling.

Bea and George Campbell gave me great details about the Campbell (Cameron) family history. Mike Sterling provided priceless insights into Goldie's life and family, and I can't thank him and his family enough for all the stories, photos, and scrap-books they let me use in my research.

But most of all, I thank Goldie for all her stories and for a fun four years.

A studio portrait of Goldie Griffith.

⤙ BIBLIOGRAPHY ⤚

Adams, Ramon F. *Cowboy Lingo*. New York: Houghton Mifflin Company, 1936, renewed 1964.

Armitage, Sue; James Balogh; Rebecca Hensley; Riley Kyle; Roseanna Sneed; Carolyn Stefanco-Schill; Lana Waldron; and Faith Williams. *Boulder County Women: Some Oral Histories*. University of Colorado at Boulder: Women's Studies Program, 1978.

Becker, Isabel M. Nederland, *A Trip to Cloudland*. Denver: Scott Becker Press, 1989.

Cameron, Goldie. *Oral History, Goldie Griffith Reminiscences, oral history by Harry E. Chrisman, 1967 and 1969*. The Denver Public Library, Western History/Genealogy Department.

Cameron, Goldie. Oral History interview with Eleanor Kingery, High Kingery, Nancy Dean, and Ellen Valentine. *Goldie Cameron, Mabel McDonald, Vivian Pedigo* for Colorado Historical Society. April 4, 1967.

Campbell, Bea and George. Telephone interviews with author. 2007.

Cary, Diana Serra. *The Hollywood Posse: The Story of a Gallant Band of Horsemen Who Made Movie History*. University of Oklahoma Press, 1975, 1996.

Carter, Robert A. *Buffalo Bill Cody: The Man Behind the Legend*. New York: John Wiley & Sons, Inc., 2000.

Childers, Roberta. Personal interview with author. Boulder, 2007.

Cobb, Harrison S. *Prospecting Our Past: Gold, Silver and Tungsten Mills of Boulder County.* Longmont, Colorado: The Book Lode, 1999.

Collings, Ellsworth, in collaboration with Alma Miller England. *The 101 Ranch.* Norman, Oklahoma: University of Oklahoma Press, 1937, 1971.

Dallas, Sandra. *Yesterday's Denver.* Miami: E.A. Seemann Publishing, 1974.

Dean, Frank E. *Trick and Fancy Riding.* Caldwell, Idaho: The Caxton Printers, Ltd., 1975.

Derry, Kathryn. *Corsets and Broncs, the Wild West Show Cowgirl, 1890–1920.* Colorado Historical Society: Colorado Heritage, Summer 1992.

Evans, Lee S. *From Happy Valley to the Mountaintop*, An Autobiography. Boulder, Colorado: Daniel Publishing Group, 2002.

Flood, Elizabeth Clair, and William Manns. *Cowgirls, Women of the Wild West.* Santa Fe: Zon International Publishing Company, 2000.

Guyer, Brownlee. Oral History interview with Glenna Carline for Nederland Historical Society, 1995.

Hansen, Alice. Telephone interview with author, 2007.

Jones, William C. and Forrest, Kenton. *Denver: A Pictorial History from Frontier Camp to Queen City of the Plains.* Boulder, Colorado: Pruett Publishing Co., 1973.

Jordan, Teresa. *Cowgirls, Women of the American West.* Lincoln and London: University of Nebraska, 1982, 1992.

Kasson, Joy S. *Buffalo Bill's Wild West, Celebrity, Memory and Popular History.* New York: Hill and Wang, 2000.

Le Compte, Mary Lou. *Cowgirls of the Rodeo, Pioneer Professional Athletes.* Urbana and Chicago: University of Illinois Press, Illini Books Edition, 2000.

Lemish, Michael G. *War Dogs, Canines in Combat.* Washington and London: Brassey's, 1996.

Maynard, Pat. Personal interview with author. Nederland, May 11, 2005.

Meyring, Geneva. *Nederland, Then and Now.* Out of print, 1941.

Nummelin, Skeeter. Personal interview with author. Nederland, Sept. 13, 2005.

Ranegar, Sheila. Telephone interview with author. Nederland, 2008.

Reddin, Paul. *Wild West Shows*. Urbana and Chicago: University of Illinois Press, 1999.

Riley, Glenda and Richard W Etulain. *Wild Women of the Old West*. Golden, Colorado: Fulcrum Publishing, 2003.

Savage, Candace. *Born To Be A Cowgirl: A Spirited Ride Through The Old West*. Berkeley, California: Tricycle Press, 2001.

Savage, Candace. *Cowgirls*. Berkeley: Ten Speed Press, 1996.

Schrager, Adam. *The Principled Politician: The Ralph Carr Story*. Golden, Colorado: Fulcrum Publishing, 2008.

Seagraves, Anne. *Daughters of the West*. Post Falls, Idaho: Wesanne Publications, 1996.

Seider, O.J.; Stan Zaminski, historical editor. *Buffalo Bill—His Life & Legend, Museum Edition*. Denver: Stonehenge Books, 1981.

Stansbury, Kathryn B. *Lucille Mulhall: Her Family, Her Life, Her Times*. Mulhall, Oklahoma: Homestead Heirlooms Publishing Co., 1985, 1992.

Sterling, Mike. Personal interview with author. June 15, 2005.

Wallis, Michael. *The Real Wild West, The 101 Ranch and the Creation of the American West*. New York: St. Martin's Press, 1999.

Yost, Nellie Snyder. *Buffalo Bill, His Family, Friends, Fame, Failures, and Fortunes*. Chicago: Sage Books, Swallow Press, 1979.

Historic newspapers: *The New York Times, The Chicago Daily Tribune, Boulder Daily Camera, Rocky Mountain News, The Denver Post, Nederland Bugle*.

About the Author

 Long-time Nederland, Colorado, resident Kay Turnbaugh owned the local newspaper for 27 years. During that time she wrote several articles about Goldie Cameron, never guessing that when she sold the paper she would devote four years of her life to researching the fascinating life of one of our country's first professional female athletes who worked as a cowgirl, bronco buster, and local entrepreneur.

The Last of the Wild West Cowgirls: A True Story was a finalist for a Willa Literary Award in Creative Non-Fiction for 2010. Turnbaugh also has written books about local history, a kids' book about the mountain pine beetle, and co-authored a hiking guidebook. Find her at www.kayturnbaugh.com.

Other books by the author:

Rocky Mountain National Park Dining Room Girl: The Summer of 1926 at the Horseshoe Inn (with Lee Tillotson)

Images of America: Around Nederland

The Mountain Pine Beetle—Tiny but Mighty

Afoot & Afield: Denver, Boulder, Fort Collins and Rocky Mountain National Park (with Alan Apt)

CPSIA information can be obtained
at www.ICGtesting.com
Printed in the USA
JSHW010829010819
1011JS00001B/6